"To make a difference in a kid's life, we must ▮▮▮▮ ▮lt
Mueller does a great job of researching what ▮ ▮n
and tells us how to best relate to them. I learr

D0462162

JIM BURNS, PH.D., PRESIDENT, HOMEWORD

"The Chronicler describes the tribe of Issachar as 'men who understood the times and knew what Israel should do.' Walt Mueller's wisdom, compassion and courage in *Engaging the Soul of Youth Culture* mark him as a twenty-first-century man of Issachar. If I had to recommend one book to adults seeking a contemporary understanding of youth culture in order to make an eternal difference in students' lives, this book would be my choice."

RICK DUNN, LEAD PASTOR, FELLOWSHIP CHURCH, KNOXVILLE, TENNESSEE; AUTHOR OF *SHAPING THE SPIRITUAL LIFE OF STUDENTS* AND COEDITOR OF *REACHING A GENERATION FOR CHRIST*

"Walt Mueller has emerged as a prominent voice, gracious yet powerful, concerning popular culture and its impact on adolescent thinking, behavior and worldviews. Walt takes seriously Paul's example of missional engagement in Athens in order to communicate a message that isn't easily dismissed as a blanket attack against culture. You may not agree with everything that Walt has to say, but it will make you think and help you navigate through the Mars Hill environments you find yourself in. In this book you will discover why so many of us working with young people look to Walt Mueller as a crucial resource for youth ministry."

MIKE KING, PRESIDENT, YOUTHFRONT

"Walt Mueller's years of experience from 'walking around' youth culture (see Acts 17:23), and his careful biblical observations, have made him one of the most respected voices in youth ministry today. With his stated intent of falling into neither trap of unrealistic optimism or unhopeful pessimism, Walt has given us a sobering, compassionate, informed and hopeful survey of adolescent culture that will be a real help for youth workers, parents, educators and anybody else who cares about teenagers. What I most appreciate about this book is not the thorough research—although it is supported by meticulous research. Nor is it the broad range of resources—although Walt's lively discussion invites comments from voices as diverse as Hans Rookmaaker (art critic), John Stott (theologian), Dave Matthews (rock musician), Christian Smith (sociologist), and the hundreds of teenagers whose hopes, haunts and hurts he has over the years carefully heard. No, what I most appreciate about this book is that this is not just a call to observe, to educate, to lament or to reimagine orthodox Christianity. It's a call to 'engage the soul' of youth culture with the historic gospel of Jesus Christ, and it's a call Walt Mueller fleshes out in full, thoughtful, vivid, articulate detail."

DUFFY ROBBINS, PROFESSOR OF YOUTH MINISTRY, EASTERN UNIVERSITY

"We all agree that life is changing all around us, and changing fast. For those of us committed to introducing Jesus Christ to future generations, we have to stay on top of their thinking, their worldview and their very souls. To share the good news to a hurt and cynical community of students, we need to be trained in how to 'walk in their Athens' and connect with their stories. *Engaging the Soul of Youth Culture* is a valuable tool for just that. Walt Mueller not only encourages adults to be proactive in our care for the young, he equips us to come alongside of them with compassion.   I recommend this book to all who seek to walk with kids in their Athens."

CHAP CLARK, ASSOCIATE PROFESSOR OF YOUTH, FAMILY, AND CULTURE, FULLER THEOLOGICAL SEMINARY

"Walt Mueller offers a valuable tool to help us understand youth and youth ministry in today's world. Walt writes the same way he talks to those of us who know him—plainspeakng, reasonable, humble, understanding and insightful. Reading this book is like having an engaging conversation with a wise friend. I highly recommend it to you."

PAUL FLEISCHMANN, PRESIDENT, NATIONAL NETWORK OF YOUTH MINISTRIES, AND CHAIRMAN, WEA GLOBAL YOUTH COMMISSION

Walt Mueller

ENGAGING THE SOUL
OF YOUTH CULTURE

Bridging Teen Worldviews and Christian Truth

IVP Books

An imprint of InterVarsity Press
Downers Grove, Illinois

InterVarsity Press
P.O. Box 1400, Downers Grove, IL 60515-1426
World Wide Web: www.ivpress.com
E-mail: mail@ivpress.com

InterVarsity Press® is the book-publishing division of InterVarsity Christian Fellowship/USA®, a student movement active on campus at hundreds of universities, colleges and schools of nursing in the United States of America, and a member movement of the International Fellowship of Evangelical Students. For information about local and regional activities, write Public Relations Dept., InterVarsity Christian Fellowship/USA, 6400 Schroeder Rd., P.O. Box 7895, Madison, WI 53707-7895, or visit the IVCF website at <www.intervarsity.org>.

Design: Cindy Kiple

Images: Michael Llewellyn/Getty Images

ISBN-10: 0-8308-3337-4
ISBN-13: 978-0-8308-3337-5

Printed in the United States of America ∞

Library of Congress Cataloging-in-Publication Data

Mueller, Walt, 1956-
Engaging the soul of youth culture: bridging teen worldviews and
Christian truth / Walt Mueller.
p. cm.
Includes bibliographical references and index.
1. Christian teenagers—Religious life. 2. Popular
culture—Religious aspects—Christianity. 3. Parent and
teenager—Religious aspects—Christianity. I. Title.
BV4531.3.M84 2006
2259'.23—dc22

2005028721

P	17	16	15	14	13	12	11	10	9	8	7	6		
Y	19	18	17	16	15	14	13	12	11	10	09	08	07	

To the glory of God with thanks to him

for the gift of my earthly father,

Dr. Walter Mueller Jr.,

a man who has modeled a deep faith,

unwavering conviction, bold commitment

and—in recent days—tremendous courage

CONTENTS

ACKNOWLEDGMENTS

THIS BOOK IS THE RESULT OF AN ongoing process of study, reflection, ministry with teenagers and families, and interaction with an expanding list of institutions and people who have been used by God to shape my thinking on matters of faith and culture. It is my prayer that the convictions reflected here reveal an ongoing personal movement toward conformity to God's way and will.

Where this book reflects thinking and practice that bring honor and glory to God, I recognize that is the case purely by the grace of God. As a person in process, I am fully aware that there may be errors or shortcomings contained in these pages. Where that is the case, I take full responsibility and pray that God will continue to graciously shape my thinking more clearly.

That said, I would like to thank several people who have been especially helpful during the process of writing. I would like to thank my wife and friend, Lisa, for her encouragement to embark on this intense journey and her ongoing support during the entire process. She—along with my children, Caitlin, Josh, Bethany and Nathaniel—have contributed to this project immensely. I am deeply grateful to them.

I would like to thank the board of directors of the Center for Parent/ Youth Understanding for granting me the time and resources to satisfy my desire to pursue and address these important issues facing the church. At several points during this process I have hit major "bumps in the road." I am grateful for the support and encouragement the board has been to me and to my family. I trust that the fruit of this endeavor will greatly expand the mission and ministry of CPYU as we seek to serve Christ and his kingdom.

I would like to thank Dr. Gary Parrett for his sustained input into my life, and my colleagues in the Ministry to Postmodern Generations doctoral track at Gordon-Conwell Theological Seminary. Each of you has touched me deeply, and I count you all as friends for life. I miss our annual gatherings intensely.

I am deeply indebted to the CPYU staff for their help, encouragement and support during this process. God has gifted me by allowing me to be surrounded with wonderful and dedicated coworkers who make me look a lot better than I am!

Dr. Timothy Tennent served as my secondary reader. I am grateful to him for his observations and suggestions that have served to clarify my thinking. In addition, I need to thank Derek Melleby, Cliff Frick, Ken Mueller, Doug West and Chris Wagner for taking the time to read and critique my writing as it was in process.

I am grateful for the gift and wisdom of numerous individuals and institutions which God has used to shape my faith and life. I will always be indebted to Geneva College, the Coalition for Christian Outreach and Gordon-Conwell Theological Seminary for providing me with the best education imaginable. I owe a huge debt of gratitude to my parents, Walt and Janet Mueller, for their consistent model of biblical faithfulness and what it means to love and serve Jesus Christ. And I'm thankful to people like John Stott, Francis Schaeffer, Abraham Kuyper, Charles Colson, Hans Rookmaaker, David Wells and others far too numerous to mention here whose thinking has deeply influenced my life.

Finally, I'd like to thank Dave Zimmerman, Cindy Bunch, Drew Blankman and others at InterVarsity Press whose feedback, suggestions and assistance yielded a finished book that's much better than what I could have ever done on my own.

INTRODUCTION

IT MAY SEEM ODD TO QUOTE longtime rocker Tom Petty as the source of a timely prayer for our young in his recent song "Lost Children." Even though he's a man who's never made claims to be a follower of Christ, he's concerned enough about children and the myriad of problems they face to intercede on their behalf. When he asks the Lord to shine "light on these lost children far away from home" and to "lead them all home again" he captures the essence of what the twenty-first-century church should be praying for the emerging generations.

In a world where the lost long to be found, Jesus still commands his followers to "go and make disciples of all nations."

This is a book about obedience to the Great Commission in a rapidly changing culture. I want to help you think seriously about our responsibility to go to the unique "nation" of young people living in our current postmodern culture, as well as subsequent cultures sure to emerge.

Whether we admit it or not, we've become increasingly ineffective at the task. We haven't kept up in our ability to listen to and understand our world and its cries for redemption. We need to take a fresh look at what it means to live and proclaim God's will and way as we cross cultures into the mission field of youth.

Having attended ministry conferences for years, I've walked through numerous exhibit halls resembling Middle-Eastern bazaars and heard promising pitches on hundreds of sure-fire ministry methods and tools. "Buy this and your ministry success is guaranteed!" While there are surely some helpful things we can glean from many of these, we don't need any new ministry inventions. Rather, we need to prayerfully reexamine the Scriptures to see how Jesus and his apostles did ministry. If we would only recover the distinctives of who they were and how they did ministry as they loved God and their neighbors, we'd be surprised at how God would use us as we engage the emerging generations with the gospel.

Because our particular historical situation and spiritual climate is strikingly similar to what Paul encountered in Athens, we will examine how Paul's ministry there can serve as a model for us. I've become increasingly convinced of the validity of his Mars Hill ministry as an approach that opens doors for significant discussions with young people about life in the kingdom of God. None of this material is new, earthshattering or original. It's been here for two thousand years. Somehow, though, we've forgotten it.

This Book's for You

I've written this book for those who wish to (1) obediently live out the Great Commission in our particular time in history, and (2) love and minister to young people.

Though this isn't a book on parenting, I've written with *parents* in mind. This book will help parents understand their children and the postmodern culture they inhabit. While the postmodern worldview has been discussed by many ministry practitioners in the years surrounding the turn of the millennium, it remains largely unknown or misunderstood by parents and many others. Consequently, I've endeavored to offer an introductory overview to this emerging mindset.

Youth workers will also find this book helpful in supporting parents as they raise their children. Many young people, though, receive no positive spiritual guidance from their parents. In those cases, I pray

God would use this book to help youth workers point young people to the cross and new life in the kingdom.

Many young people in church feel a disconnect with the person in the pulpit. Therefore I believe that *pastors* must listen to, understand and reach out to youth. This book should help them renew their ministry to young people.

Finally, *Christian educators,* who are in daily contact with students in public and private schools, will discover that the information and principles in this book will foster deep and significant connections with the emerging generations.

Remember Four Truths

This book will challenge your thinking. You may find yourself struggling with a concept, a definition or even a perceived tone in my writing. For this reason I'd like you to remember four things as you read.

First, I've striven to be faithful to the written and incarnate Word. I don't believe either needs to be reinvented or reimagined as some have said. I believe that the Word continues to speak to today's world. I've endeavored at every turn to look at our world through the corrective lenses of a biblical worldview.

Second, I've tried to avoid the traps of *false optimism* and *habitual pessimism.* False optimism looks at the world and with a shrug of the shoulders says, "No need to worry. Everything is going to be all right." Truth is, the collective lot of children and teens hasn't gotten any better. False optimism leads to forfeited influence because there's nothing anyone *needs* to do. Habitual pessimism looks at the world and says, "It's so bad and so far gone that there's nothing anyone can do about it." Not only does this view belittle God, but it too forfeits influence because there's nothing anyone *can* do.

In recent years Christians and cultural analysts have traveled down both of these roads as they've looked at the emerging generations— particularly Generation X and the Millennials. I've sought to avoid both of these extremes by taking an approach that I trust is *biblically realistic.* Through this approach, I believe we can accurately understand our mission field and plan our mission approach.

Third, at times I am critical of the "faith" we're calling young people to. For too long youth ministry has been about getting young people "saved." I struggle with our definition of what it means to be saved and the methods we employ to get young people saved. Gordon Smith says that the church is guilty of thinking of conversion in "minimalist terms: What is the very least that a person needs to do in order to be freed from the horrors of hell and assured of the glories of heaven?"[1]

We have failed to understand that conversion is not just about belief, repentance, forgiveness and eternal life. Something else has to happen after someone accepts Christ as Savior. Salvation makes a person free from sin *and* a slave to righteousness—integrating the Christian faith and kingdom of God into all of life. When we call young people to faith, we are not calling them out of the world and into heaven. Rather, we're calling them to live God's will and way in the world. Theologian David Wells describes it this way:

> True conversion is not an isolated experience but one that is related to a life of discipleship. . . . Discipleship belongs to and should follow from conversion the way that natural life belongs to and should follow from live birth. . . . And just as there is no discipleship without conversion, so there is no conversion without an ensuing life of discipleship that involves growth in moral maturity, a deepening faith, and loving service.[2]

The goal of our missionary efforts is to call the emerging generations to a compelling faith that transforms every area of life and every nook and cranny of God's creation.

Fourth, this book does not teach a method of evangelism. Rather, it calls us to a lifestyle of listening to and understanding our mission field long before we speak. It's a lifestyle that's always looking for ways to communicate the unchanging Word to a rapidly changing world.

---

[1]Gordon T. Smith, *Beginning Well: Christian Conversion and Authentic Transformation* (Downers Grove, Ill.: InterVarsity Press, 2001), p. 135.
[2]David F. Wells, *Turning to God* (Carlisle, U.K.: World Evangelical Fellowship, 1989), p. 25.

Overview

This book is divided into three sections. Section one analyzes the mission field of the emerging generations. Here we'll examine the world of youth and the influence of the postmodern worldview.

In section two we'll lay out the steps of our missionary journey into the culture and world of the emerging generations. First, we will consider the phenomenon of culture. Then we will look at how followers of Christ are called to approach culture. This may be the most difficult section for many, because the church has traditionally avoided rubbing shoulders with the world.

Section three lays out the strategy for engaging the postmodern generations. First we will look at the marks that must be evident in our lives as we fulfill our calling as messengers. Then we will examine Paul's first-century missionary journey into Athens and how to use his Mars Hill ministry as a model for ministry today.

While some might pessimistically label the emerging postmodern generations as hopelessly lost or something to put up with, in reality things are, as the Beatles might say, "getting better all the time." The emerging generations are self-consciously spiritual, and their interest in discussing and examining spirituality continues to rise. If church history remembers our particular time and place in God's world as one marked by our indifference, retreat or isolation, we will not only have been disobedient to our Master who tells us to "go," but we will have missed an amazing ministry opportunity.

1

REALITY BYTES

Snapshots of a Crying and Dying Culture

HE SITS THERE FOR HOURS. His parents wonder why he isn't outside expending the energy they had when they were his age. He's satisfied to stay in his chair, fingers flying across the keyboard as his eyes focus on the monitor. Like millions of other young people, fourteen-year-old Derrick "lives" for several hours a day in an online world.[1] He sends and receives e-mails, posts comments on blogs, surfs the Web, and IMs his online friends in real time.

When his parents ask him about his obsession, he can't explain it. But visitors to his blog can read about Derrick's feelings of loneliness and confusion, and his inability to connect with adults—even the adults who live under his roof.

Derrick, like all teens, is trying to find his place in this world. When he's most honest and transparent, he admits he feels overwhelmed and lost. Even though he's never personally met most of his online friends, they offer acceptance, understanding, community, meaning and guidance that he doesn't get from anywhere else. Most of them feel just like Derrick.

---

[1]The stories in this book are true. At times, I have combined stories to offer a broader picture of contemporary adolescent reality. Names have been changed to protect identity.

To Derrick, the hours spent in front of his computer afford him the best place to be open and honest. Sadly, the best that Derrick has experienced isn't very good. One look at the thoughts he's posted on his blog reveal his disturbing reality.

> i miss brooke. . . . she never talks to me anymore. ever. i get this feeling, whenever i look at her picture, the one she sent of her and me before she left . . . a feeling like the coolest person was torn away from me. . . . i miss myself . . . f—ing depressed f—ing depressed f—ing depressed. . . . ya know what the sad thing is? i typed that all out. so confused. . . . no clue what im gonna do about anything or everything. . . . i wanna just disappear, but ive got such anxiety that i cant sleep in 10 minutes past my alarm during the school week without my heart pounding out of my chest. . . . why am i so ugly? . . . i look in the mirror and i wanna claw my body to shreds. . . . so imperfect. . . . i think i might stop typing now . . . but thatd require . . . stopping doing the one thing i have to do. . . . im sorry im sorry im sorry and i lie and i lie and i lie and im not worth it and im not good enough and all i want is someone to hold me. . . . and for some reason everything is crashing down. . . . i should be happy now but im not

As horrible as Derrick's words sound, the adults in his life don't have a clue about what lies beneath the surface of his seemingly "normal" teenage life.

Is Anybody Listening?

Derrick's experience is not unusual or even surprising. His generation, known as the Millennial Generation or Generation Y, is the second to grow up in a world driven by the emerging postmodern worldview. For them the world is filled with questions, but very few answers. The cries rising out of their deep hunger and thirst are loud, very loud. If we listen, we'll hear it in their music, books and films. We observe it in their choices and behaviors. They long to be "meaningfully con-

nected to life."[2] But the complexities of their world have made it difficult for them to hear the good news—at least in the way the church
is now "spreading" it—in a timely and understandable manner.

As hope-filled ambassadors of Jesus Christ, we should be listening
and responding with urgent compassion. Instead, those of us who
have been given the task of leading the young to the soul-satisfying
"bread of life" (Jn 6:35) and "streams of living water" (Jn 7:38) may
have unknowingly locked the bread box and shut off the water valve
through our inability or unwillingness to hear the nuances of their
unique worldview and experience *before* attempting to answer their
cries. If we try to talk to our young people *before* listening to their reality, we will, as Francis Schaeffer said, "only beat the air."[3]

Teenagers are by nature hopeful and idealistic. But for many, their
wonderfully refreshing and youthful idealism has no solid foundation
and will eventually yield to the presumption that life just isn't satisfy-
ing. Ironically, instead of finding eternal life, their earthly lives are suck-
ing the very life out of them. For the sake of their future and the advance of God's kingdom, the church must start listening.

Several years ago I traveled to the Midwest to speak in a church in
a small community about the changing world of Derrick and his
peers. Shortly after my return I received a thank you note from a
mother who had attended my seminars. In it she described her frustrating efforts to care for her fourteen-and-a-half-year-old daughter
Erin. Their relationship had been fine until Erin turned twelve. Almost
overnight, it all began to unravel. The aching mother directed me to
Erin's handwritten poem penned as a message from daughter to
mother, summed up in the potent phrase "Somehow I lost my
mouth. / Somehow you lost your ears." Erin's poem is more than a
message to mom. It's a message to God's people today. Erin communicates a surprising and startling reality—we aren't listening, and we
don't even know it!

---

[2]Steven Garber, *The Fabric of Faithfulness* (Downers Grove, Ill.: InterVarsity Press, 1996), p. 106.
[3]Francis A. Schaeffer, *The God Who Is There*, in *The Complete Works of Francis Schaeffer*, 2nd
   ed. (Wheaton, Ill.: Crossway, 1985), p. 9.

Fighting for Meaning

Over the years I've talked to hundreds of young people who have spent their adolescent years feeling and living like Derrick and Erin. When they're children, life typically seems easy. But when they reach their teenage years, more and more young people feel and experience something markedly different. They can't always put it into words, but they know something's wrong. Change confronts them from every direction as they grow. Simultaneously they face the challenges, choices, expectations and pressures of a rapidly changing world. Even those who are able to maintain their spirit of youthful idealism become "idealists" who have "not been able to find an ideal."[4]

While all teens struggle at some level, teens who lack a distinctively biblical foundation and the security of a strong home face greater difficulty. Our world is populated by increasing numbers who bear the ugly marks of relational breakdown. By the time they move into young adulthood, far too many continue to wander on a painful and confusing path with the aching awareness that something is terribly wrong. Many unknowingly fall into a nihilistic way of life that sees everything as meaningless and chaotic. In the 1999 cult film *Fight Club,* Tyler Durden speaks on their behalf; if they don't come to faith, the emerging generation of Millennials will soon find themselves echoing his words: "Our great war is a spiritual war. Our great depression is our lives. We've all been raised on television to believe that one day we'd be millionaires, and movie gods, and rock stars. But we won't. We're slowly learning that fact. And we're very, very pissed off."[5]

For over twenty years Steve Garber has been working with university students. He consistently asks them, "Why do you get up in the morning?" because

it gets at the relationship between what one believes about the world and how one lives in the world, particularly as that dynamic interaction is being formed as young people move out of

---

[4]Ibid., p. 37.
[5]*Fight Club,* dir. David Fincher, Twentieth Century Fox, 1999.

their parents' worlds and worldviews and tape up their own convictions as frameworks within which to live and move and have
their being.

Among other things, he's discovered that young people "are finding it increasingly difficult to make sense of the world and their
place in it."[6]

Some generational analysts believe these problems are unique to
the postboomer generation known as Generation X. But without a
solid and firm biblical foundation and view of life that helps them
make sense of God's world and their place in it, the same is certain to
be true for the Millennial generation as they enter into young adulthood. If nothing changes, we can be sure the post-Millennial generation will be marked by the same confusion.

The end result can be heard in the music of Dave Matthews, an artist embraced by a faithful legion of young listeners. A series of family
tragedies shaped his music and view of life. In his 1994 song "Rhyme
& Reason," a first-person testimony of human sadness, hopelessness
and pain written after the murder of his sister Anne, he sings: "My
head aches—warped and tied up / I need to kill this pain / My head
won't leave my head alone / And I don't believe it will / 'Til I'm dead
and gone / My head won't leave my head alone / And I don't believe
it will / 'Til I'm six feet under ground. . . . Well I know these voices must
be my soul / I've had enough / I've had enough / Of being alone / I've
got no place to go."

Unmet Needs

All human beings need to be heard and understood. Those needs are
amplified during the critical change-filled years where teenagers are
moving from the dependence of childhood to the independence of
adulthood. However, they aren't always expressed in ways that are
easily understood or that make us feel comfortable. When they can
put their pain into words, the emerging generations are usually critical

---

[6]Garber, *Fabric of Faithfulness,* p. 106.

of the institutions that have let them down: family, church, school or maybe adult society in general. When they can't put the pain and feelings into words, they put them into actions—sometimes acts of violence inflicted on themselves or others.[7]

Multiplatinum recording artist Christina Aguilera sings about the gnawing emptiness of her generation. When Christina turned six, her mother left Christina's violent and abusive father and moved with Christina and her sister to Pittsburgh. Christina's emotional pain and emptiness increased as she spent her elementary and junior-high school years being rejected by her peers. Even after winning a 1999 Best New Artist Grammy and achieving fame and financial fortune, she was spurned by her high school classmates. Her 2003 Grammy-winning single, "Beautiful," sums up the relational pain and spiritual yearnings of so many in our culture. Each new morning brings her the hope and promise of fulfillment, but as the day wears on, reality takes hold and "suddenly it's hard to breathe," she feels insecure and ashamed. She emotionally addresses her listeners as they too try "to fill the emptiness." In her yearning she asks, "Is that the way it is?"[8]

Adults often fail to see such expressions as cries resulting from teens' unmet hunger and thirst for God. Theologian Alister McGrath articulates this need that is so elusive to adolescents:

> If there is something that has the power to fulfill truly and deeply, then for many it is something unknown, hidden in mystery and secrecy. We move from one thing and place to another, lingering only long enough to discover that it is not what we were hoping for before renewing our quest for fulfillment. The great certainty of our time seems to be that satisfaction is nowhere to be found. We roam around, searching without finding, yearning without being satisfied. The pursuit of happiness is often said to be one of the most fundamental human rights. Yet this happiness proves

---

[7]For information on the growing problem of cutting and other forms of self-abuse, visit the Center for Parent/Youth Understanding website. Especially helpful is the article "Crying Through Their Cuts: The Stark Reality of Self-Abuse" <www.cpyu.org/Page.aspx?id=76714>.

[8]Walt Mueller, "Christina & Justin: Innocence Lost or Truth Be Told?" *youthculture@today*, spring 2003, pp. 3-11.

astonishingly elusive. So often, those who actively pursue happiness find that it slips through their fingers. It is an ideal which is easily put into words, yet seems to remain beyond our reach. We have long become used to the fact that the richest people in this world are often the most miserable, yet fail to see the irony of this. Perhaps this is just one of the sad paradoxes of being human. Maybe we will have to get used to the fact that we are always going to fail in our search for happiness. Part of the cruel irony of human existence seems to be that the things we thought would make us happy fail to do so.[9]

Blaise Pascal epitomized Aguilera's quest from a Christian perspective. McGrath describes Pascal's model as "a God-shaped emptiness within us, which only God can fill. We may try to fill it in other ways and with other things. Yet one of the few certainties of life is that nothing in this world satisfies our longing for something that is ultimately beyond this world."[10] As it has been for all people since the Fall of humanity and expulsion from Eden, this is the great need of young people today. They are crying out to have their God-shaped emptiness filled.

Who Will Be There for Me?

God spoke through Moses to the people of Israel regarding their responsibility to the young among them:

Hear, O Israel: The LORD our God, the LORD is one. Love the LORD your God with all your heart and with all your soul and with all your strength. These commandments that I give you today are to be upon your hearts. Impress them on your children. Talk about them when you sit at home and when you walk along the road, when you lie down and when you get up. Tie them as symbols on your hands and bind them on your foreheads. Write them on

---

[9]Alister McGrath, *The Unknown God* (Grand Rapids: Eerdmans, 1999), pp. 8-9.
[10]McGrath, *Unknown God*, p. 120.

the doorframes of your houses and on your gates. (Deut 6:4-9)

God's design is to use families and the larger body of Christ to point young people to their divine purpose. But teenage life in today's culture leaves us wondering if we've heeded God's command. Families, even those in the church, are falling apart and malfunctioning. While many in the church have not intentionally turned their backs on the young, they are only "beating the air" and as a result, our youth are leaving the church in droves. In some cases, the family and church are present but unaccounted for. In other words, we're there but we aren't paying attention. Even though members of the emerging generations try to connect, it seems to them that nobody's home. At times, we're occupied with other things—some important, some not. At other times, our children's inability or unwillingness to live up to our expectations and behavioral standards leads to an angry retort or disingenuous lecture on our part. Sometimes they scare us. Or maybe we don't think they have any interest in what we have to offer. More than likely, the real problem is we haven't been listening. Veteran youth worker and cultural analyst Dean Borgman issues a timely warning to the church: "When young people cry out in pain, we cannot respond with a shaking of our heads, detachment, and silence."[11]

The fact of the matter is that young people have very little experience in how to effectively communicate what's on their mind, but they are painfully aware when we fail to hear what they have to say. Erin's words are powerful—she felt her parents "lost" their ears. As a result, she "lost" her mouth and the cycle of communication breakdown moved full speed ahead. In the end, her parents weren't worth listening to anymore.

This sad progression of relational collapse has been repeated in too many families. Unfortunately, it's happening in the church as well— to Christian parents charged by God with the spiritual nurture of their children, to pastors called to preach the Word to the full spectrum of the people in the pews, to youth pastors who work with students during their adolescent years, and to those involved in educational

---

[11]Dean Borgman, *Hear My Story* (Peabody, Mass.: Hendrickson, 2003), p. 9.

ministry. If the church doesn't listen, the church can't understand. When young people realize they aren't understood, church becomes a place where they don't belong. Then, as they try other places in their efforts to satisfy the spiritual hunger, the unmet groans for redemption (Rom 8:22) grow louder and more intense with the passing of time. As part of the creation subjected to "frustration" because of sin, the lost and unredeemed suffer "emptiness, futility, purposelessness, and transitoriness."[12]

The cost of losing *our* ears is great. Whoever takes interest and listens with both ears will be given the privilege of influence. God's people are typically surprised not only to learn that our young are not listening to us but who they *are* listening to.

Guess Who's All Ears?

In the early 1980s a series of eighteen studies compared the changing influence of various institutions on the values and behaviors of thirteen- to nineteen-year-olds. In 1960 the family exercised the greatest influence on teen values and behavior, followed in order by school, friends and peers, and the church.[13] While 1960 was by no means a perfect time, families in general were still active in the lives of their children. In addition, schools and churches were for the most part reinforcing the basic values taught in the home. There was a more unified voice influencing teens. The young were generally more settled and had a place to belong.

Fast-forward to 1980, by which point friends and peers had taken the number one spot as influencer of teen values and behavior. The family dropped to number two and the media[14] jumped onto the list

---

[12]John R. W. Stott, *The Message of Romans* (Downers Grove, Ill.: InterVarsity Press, 1994), pp. 238-39.

[13]Joe Francomano, Wayne Lavitt and Darryl Lavitt, *Junior Achievement: A History* (Colorado Springs, Col.: Junior Achievement Inc., 1988), pp. 93-95, cited in Walt Mueller, *Understanding Today's Youth Culture* (Wheaton, Ill.: Tyndale House, 1999), p. 68.

[14]"Media," as used in this book, refers to all popular entertainment outlets targeted and marketed to children and teens. This includes but is not limited to television, film, music, radio, video games, magazines, books, advertising and websites. "Popular culture" in today's world is created, driven and dispensed by the media.

at number three. School dropped two notches to number four, and the church dropped out of the top four list altogether.[15] Not only had the influences changed, but the messages sent to young people were less consistent as those institutions disagree on basic values.

What would this list look like today? The global pervasiveness of MTV and the Internet boost the media's influence to the top of the list. Friends and peers—a group targeted by an aggressive marketing machine looking to make money and generate lifelong brand loyalty— would drop to number two. The family—for numerous reasons, including breakdown and parental indifference—continues to drop to number three,[16] and the school stays at number four.[17]

Consider the conclusion of media analyst Quentin Schultze and his colleagues in their book *Dancing in the Dark,* a compelling study of the role electronic media play in the lives of our young people:

Youth and the electronic media today are dependent upon each other. The media need the youth market, as it is called, for their own economic survival. Youth, in turn, need the media for guid-

---

[15]Mueller, *Understanding Today's Youth Culture,* p. 68.

[16]It is my belief that while the semantics of this study's results point to the fact that the institutions of influence on teen values, attitudes and behaviors are shifting in balance of degree of influence, parents *are always* the single most significant socializing force in the lives of the emerging generations. God ordained the institution of the family at creation and established the family as the arena in which spiritual nurture is to take place (Deut 6:1-9). In the economy of today's culture, the failure of the family to function according to God's design and intent fosters a situation where the tasks of nurture and socialization are handed by default to other institutions or cultural forces. In other words, the family is always the greatest influencer of teen values, attitudes and behaviors *for better or for worse* depending on the role the family is or is not playing in the life of the young person.

Consequently, it is possible to affirm the results of the cited study along with the research conclusions of The National Study of Youth and Religion, and researcher Christian Smith in his book *Soul Searching:* "Contrary to popular misguided cultural stereotypes and frequent parental misperceptions, we believe that the evidence clearly shows that the single most important social influence on the religious and spiritual lives of adolescents is their parents. Grandparents and other relatives, mentors, and youth workers can be very influential as well, but normally, parents are most important in forming their children's religious and spiritual lives. . . . The best social predictor, although not a guarantee, of what the religious and spiritual lives of youth will look like is what the religious and spiritual lives of their parents *do* look like. Parents and other adults, as we have suggested, most likely 'will get what they are.'" Christian Smith with Melinda Lundquist Denton, *Soul Searching: The Religious and Spiritual Lives of American Teenagers* (New York: Oxford University Press, 2005), p. 261.

[17]While this list is speculative, my own experience, anecdotal evidence, youth research and ongoing discussions with other culture watchers support these conclusions.

ance and nurture in a society where other social institutions, such as the family and the school, do not shape the youth culture as powerfully as they once did.[18]

The authors suggest that the media provides the emerging generations with "maps of reality" to guide them into adulthood. Because teens see the media as understanding them and their place in life, it is "extremely well-suited to provide information relevant to many of the questions adolescents face."[19] It serves to define the meaning of life, values, attitudes, behavioral norms and social and gender roles, which then translate into behaviors.[20] Media speaks back to young people, giving them "equipment for living" their day to day lives in the world.[21]

Dean Borgman has spent years studying the power of media in the lives of young people. He recognizes that media's function is multifaceted. For young people, especially those who don't already have a place to belong, media can serve as an escape from the cares, concerns and pains of life. The media gives them a voice that frees them from social neglect and the resulting silence. It can serve as a form of lament, much like the biblical psalms. At times it serves as a form of protest against victimization and oppression. For some it can actually become an addiction. And, of greatest importance to our discussion, media can serve as religion, especially where the church seems to have little or nothing to say.[22]

As a directive force, the media is uniquely suited to fill instructional voids left by families and churches. Young people want "to be certain about how to live and to understand why things happen as they do—and the popular arts help them navigate through life."[23] In effect, popular culture gives them purpose. Because it has listened to them, the young are returning the favor.

Sociologist Donna Gaines says that "to those who've grown up feeling abject, strangers to themselves and the world around them, rock &

---

[18]Quentin J. Schultze et al., *Dancing in the Dark* (Grand Rapids: Eerdmans, 1991), pp. 12-13.
[19]Peter G. Christenson and Donald F. Roberts, *It's Not Only Rock & Roll* (Cresskill, N.J.: Hampton Press, 1988), p. 29.
[20]Schultze et al., *Dancing in the Dark*, p. 99.
[21]Christenson and Roberts, *It's Not Only Rock & Roll*, pp. 31-71.
[22]Dean Borgman, *When Kumbaya Is Not Enough* (Peabody, Mass.: Hendrickson, 1997), p. 128.
[23]William D. Romanowski, *Eyes Wide Open* (Grand Rapids: Brazos, 2001), p. 28.

roll has meant much more than just the music; it offers salvation, a new lease on life." As a result, "youth culture remains a powerful, meaningful force in kids' lives. Many need it to live. Sometimes it's the only thing left to hold on to."[24] Gaines's experience as a lost teen looking for answers led her to study the role pop culture plays in the lives of children and teens. In A Misfit's Manifesto, Gaines's memoir of her life as a rock and roll fan, she refers to pop culture as her "unholy redeemer," explaining that "for many, the music has the potential to obliterate pain, transform experience, reinvent meaning, alter feeling states. It can change personal identity and cultural history."[25]

Still, she admits that in her experience ultimate redemption never came. "Strung out, hunting down redemption, I felt like s— for most of my life," she writes. "Joy was ephemeral, like holy water rolling off my fingertips, quickly disappearing. And then I had to start all over again. Running on empty, looking for a fix and a kiss, I did what I had to do, filling the hole, filling the hole."[26] From a biblical perspective we know that unless media (or any other institution) points to redemption in Christ, it's only taking people on a rabbit chase. But young people would rather chase rabbits than wait for someone to hear and understand their cries. It's easy to justify life on the wide and well-traveled road that leads to destruction if nobody takes the time to effectively show the way to the narrow road that leads to life (Mt 7:13-14).

Opening Our Ears

Can we regain our ears and give them back their mouths? If our goal is to shape an appropriate biblical response, where can we go to hear what they have to say?

In my work with students over the last three decades, I have learned that the most powerful conduit to understanding young people is to hear their words. Through one-on-one conversations, reading their poetry, digesting their journals or tapping into other creative outlets, we

---

[24]Donna Gaines, A Misfit's Manifesto (New York: Villard, 2003), pp. xvi, xvii.
[25]Ibid., p. xiii.
[26]Ibid., p. xiv.

discover their joys, concerns, questions, frustrations and ideas. We must let them speak for themselves as we listen with undivided attention.

But a second way sometimes speaks louder and with greater clarity than young people themselves. Popular culture speaks through a variety of media outlets, including music, television, advertising, books and film. It can speak *for* them *to* us.

Hans Rookmaaker, art critic and Christian scholar, "listened" to art in order to hear what the culture was saying about itself. Rookmaaker's comments in his book *Modern Art and the Death of a Culture,* while written in specific reference to modern art, apply equally well to contemporary popular culture and its youthful audience:

> This art is the work of your neighbors, your contemporaries, [your children,] human beings who are crying out in despair for the loss of their humanity, their values, their lost absolutes, groping in the dark for answers. It is already late, if not too late, but if we want to help our generation we must hear their cry. We must listen to them as they cry out from their prison, the prison of a universe which is aimless, meaningless, and absurd.[27]

Gen X theologian Thomas Beaudoin says that popular culture must be heard because for the young it's "a major meaning-making system." In addition, the young express their "religious interests, dreams, fears, hopes, and desires through popular culture."[28] Listening opens our eyes to the reality and depth of the needs of young people. And once we know the reality, we can communicate the gospel in ways that can be heard and understood.

Listening to Tracy's Generation Speak

Jean-Luc Godard says that "a film is the world in an hour and a half."[29]

---

[27]H. R. Rookmaaker, *Modern Art and the Death of a Culture* (Wheaton, Ill.: Crossway, 1994), p. 136. Parenthetical remarks mine.
[28]Thomas Beaudoin, *Virtual Faith* (San Francisco: Jossey-Bass, 1998), p. xiv.
[29]Jean-Luc Godard, quoted in Craig Detweiler and Barry Taylor, *A Matrix of Meanings* (Grand Rapids: Baker, 2003), p. 162.

The ninety-nine-minute film *Thirteen* serves as a mouthpiece for the young and an effective example of how pop culture can open our eyes and ears to a troubling reality.[30] If this is indeed the world of young people, we'd better start paying attention.

A 2003 film about thirteen-year-olds written by thirteen-year-old Nikki Reed with help from writer/director Catherine Hardwicke, *Thirteen* autobiographically chronicles the desperate confusion of teenagers and their search for significance, purpose and belonging. In an interview with Oprah Winfrey, Reed said her own personal coming-of-age struggles and confusion were rooted in the fact that "I felt like I wasn't understood and like no one was listening to me."[31]

At the outset of the film Tracy Frieland enters adolescence and morphs from a cute and perky straight-A student into a confused and rebellious teenager. Tracy turns her back on her girlfriends in favor of a connection with the charismatic yet painfully broken Evie Zamora (played by the film's writer), the most popular girl in the seventh grade. Tracy experiences a variety of situations not uncommon among today's teens. As Tracy and her generation speak to the church, what do we hear them say?

"We're changing, confused, and vulnerable." On the first day of seventh grade Tracy gleefully walks the outside corridors of the middle school campus with her lifelong neighborhood girlfriends. As they stop to interact with Tracy's older brother Mason and a group of his friends, they notice the boys' attention shift to Evie Zamora, who has changed from a girl to a woman over the summer. Evie's voluptuous body and seductive dress grab the attention of all. As the boys lustily comment on Evie, the girls realize that they fall far short. While little or nothing is said, Tracy's expression communicates that she sees herself as the little girl left behind.

Tracy resolves to move into adulthood as quickly as possible. She gets home from school and angrily throws her cherished stuffed animals and little girl toys—and other things representative of her child-

---

[30] *Thirteen*, dir. Catherine Hardwicke, Twentieth Century Fox, 2003.
[31] Televised interview with Oprah Winfrey, *The Oprah Winfrey Show*, original air date, October 2, 2004.

hood—into the trash. She then "trashes" her friends so she can pursue a friendship with Evie. The door of childhood is closing on Tracy's life. The doorway into adolescence is opening wide, and she's not sure what she sees or where to go.

For Tracy and many of her friends, the teenage years are all about surviving and finding their way. They are vulnerable, facing not only the normal developmental changes associated with the adolescent years (physical, social, emotional, intellectual, moral) but a culture where social pressures are on the rise, and many of the social supports that should guide young people through these years have collapsed or disappeared altogether.

In his book *Age of Opportunity* Paul Tripp finds in the first seven chapters of Proverbs a biblical perspective on the struggles facing Tracy's generation. First, adolescents have "no hunger for wisdom or correction." Tripp explains, "Most teenagers . . . think they are much wiser than they actually are, and they mistakenly believe that their parents have little practical insight to offer." Second, they have "a tendency towards legalism." In other words, "they tend to emphasize the letter of the law rather than the spirit. Teenagers tend to push at the fences while telling you that they are still in the yard." Third, they have "a tendency to be unwise in their choice of companions." Tripp recognizes that friendship is important to teens and that "it is impossible to be uninfluenced by one's friends."[32]

Fourth, life for an adolescent is marked by "a susceptibility to sexual temptation." Because the teenage years are a time where God's design for the body is realized by the body's new ability to reproduce itself, our teens experience a variety of sexual feelings. Fifth, adolescents manifest "an absence of eschatological perspective." In other words, "they don't tend to live with eternity in view. They don't think in terms of delayed gratification. Teenagers are shockingly present-focused." Finally, teenagers evidence "a lack of heart awareness."[33] They don't always know that they are hungering and thirsting for

---

[32] Paul David Tripp, *Age of Opportunity* (Phillipsburg, N.J.: Presbyterian & Reformed, 1997), pp. 76, 81-83.
[33] Ibid., pp. 85, 87, 89.

God. As the emerging generations cry out to the church, they are asking us to understand them better than they understand themselves. For the most part, we aren't.

"Our support systems aren't working and it's stressing us out." Many 1980s era "coming of age" films featured the conspicuous absence of healthy adults. Parents were frequently portrayed as self-absorbed, marginally involved in their children's lives and easily manipulated by teenagers. School administrators are portrayed in a similarly negative light in films such as *Ferris Bueller's Day Off* and *The Breakfast Club*.

While popular culture was a significant factor in the youth of baby boomers, Thomas Beaudoin notes that Generation Xers "found it at an earlier, more critical age and without the familial supervision of previous generations."[34] They're now old enough to see how the absence of healthy, involved adults during the developmental years produces long-term fallout. Consequently, today's thoughtful coming-of-age films reflect that reality.

In Tracy's case the foundational institution of the family has been broken by divorce. Dad is conspicuously absent. When he does appear, Tracy's longings for a connection with her father are shattered. Their planned weekend visit is cancelled because he has business responsibilities, and their short face-to-face conversation is interrupted by his ringing cell phone. Tracy lives with her mom, Mel, a recovering alcoholic struggling to make ends meet for her family. Mel attempts to meet her own relational needs by opening her home and bed to an on-again, off-again boyfriend, a recovering cocaine addict. While Mel's attempts to provide for and guide her two children are valiant, her efforts are frustrated by the reality of a family terribly broken by past choices and present circumstances. Tracy has no support.

Like so many other teens from broken homes, the vulnerable young Tracy seeks support from a peer. Sadly, Evie's situation is markedly worse. Her father and mother are totally out of the picture. Abuse is

---

[34]Beaudoin, *Virtual Faith,* p. 5.

part of her past. Currently, she lives with a guardian whose own life is a train wreck. Thus a confused child is led by an even more confused child in a difficult and confusing adult world. The reality of living in today's society has made Tracy and her peers more vulnerable to stress while exposing them to stresses and situations almost unknown to previous generations.

Developmental expert David Elkind believes that adults have forced children out of childhood—the time they need to grow—and into a premature adulthood.

In today's society we seem unable to accept the fact of adolescence, that there are young people in transition from childhood to adulthood who need adult guidance and direction. Rather, we assume the teenager is a kind of adult. Whether we confer premature adulthood upon teenagers because we are too caught up in our own lives to give them the time and attention they require or because we feel helpless to provide them with the safe world they need, the end result is the same: teenagers have no place in society.[35]

This imposition of premature adulthood robs teenagers of that all-important period of life when they are able to define who they are. "By impairing his or her ability to construct a secure personal identity, today's society leaves the teenager more vulnerable and less competent to meet the challenges that are inevitable in life." With too many freedoms, loss of security and "the frustration of trying to prepare for their life's work in school settings that hinder rather than facilitate this goal," teenagers "are subject to more stress than were teenagers in previous generations."[36]

As a result of his ongoing study of what is happening in the developmental stage known as midadolescence (roughly ages fourteen to eighteen), Chap Clark discovered that "a far wider relational and social chasm exists between adults and adolescents than I had previously

---

[35]David Elkind, *All Grown Up & No Place to Go* (Reading, Mass.: Addison-Wesley, 1984), p. 4.
[36]Ibid., pp. 5-6.

considered."[37] Clark says that "the way midadolescents have been forced to design their own world and separate social system has created perhaps the most serious and yet understudied social crisis of our time,"[38] a crisis he labels as a crisis of systemic abandonment of our teenagers. This "systemic abandonment by institutions and adults who are in positions originally designed to care for adolescents has created a culture of isolation"[39] that has left many members of the emerging generation—who by all appearances seem to thrive and have it all together—"one step away from the abyss of isolation and despair."[40]

Conspicuously absent from *Thirteen* are the church and its ambassadors. The only positive adult presence is a teacher who challenges Tracy on the sudden decline in the quality of her schoolwork. The film winds up being a story of the blind leading the blind. Who is to blame? The young teenagers who have been deprived of support and who struggle to find their way? Or the support systems that have miserably failed due to their weaknesses, lack of understanding or absence?

"We need a place to belong." Tracy initiates a "chance" encounter with Evie and dances with ecstatic joy when Evie invites her to go shopping later that day. Suddenly, feelings of significance surge through her being, but her newfound place of belonging is actually the start of a downward spiral that takes Tracy to the brink of self-destruction.

In the adolescent mind the risk of self-destruction is a small price to pay for acceptance. Teenagers desire to fit in and belong. If they don't, they see themselves as abnormal. "Consequently, pursuing and adopting the image of those who are accepted, desirable, and interesting can become a consuming passion dictating appearance and behavior."[41] Researcher Marcel Danesi observed adolescent behavior for years and came to the conclusion that kids are either "cool" or "losers." He writes, "*Coolness* has become a synonym for social attractive-

---

[37]Chap Clark, *Hurt: Inside the World of Today's Teenagers* (Grand Rapids: Baker Academic, 2004), p. 43.
[38]Ibid.
[39]Ibid., p. 55.
[40]Ibid.
[41]Mueller, *Understanding Today's Youth Culture,* p. 216.

ness, and its opposite, *loserness,* has become a synonym for ugliness and alienation."[42] Nobody wants to be a loser.

Peer pressure is incredibly difficult for a child growing up in an intact and healthy functioning home. It's that much more intense where the family is failing. When the places they were made to belong fail to meet their most basic emotional and spiritual needs, teenagers will seek other options.

Just as a street gang serves as a "family" for the disenfranchised urban kid on the streets, Tracy's new circle of friends becomes a family that provides her with a place, a set of rules and some significance. She is being socialized by a confused peer group instead of her parents. In no time at all Tracy engages in theft, shoplifting, drug abuse, sexual activity and a variety of other distressing behaviors. Her mom continually looks at her with a helpless expression that begs an explanation for the sudden change in her little girl.

Dean Borgman recognizes that a child "grows up as part of, and is shaped by, various social systems. It is God's plan that these systems lead children to maturity and fullness of life. Disorder in these systems can produce disorder in the life of the emerging adult."[43] Tracy was suffering both the consequences of her choices and the fallout from her lack of belonging.

"We're hurting, and hurting deeply." Tracy and countless of her peers are hurting deeply. One estimate is that at least one out of every four teenagers in the United States is currently "at serious risk of not achieving productive adulthood. According to one study, about 21 percent of U.S. children ages nine to 17 have a diagnosable mental or addictive disorder associated with at least minimum impairment."[44] Dean Borgman sees relational brokenness as the root cause of the pain that young people like Tracy exhibit: "In one dramatic way after another, adult society has shoved young people into silent margins;

---

[42]Marcel Danesi, *Cool: The Signs and Meanings of Adolescence* (Toronto: University of Toronto Press, 1994), p. 41.
[43]Borgman, *Hear My Story,* p. 50.
[44]*Hardwired to Connect: The New Scientific Case for Authoritative Communities* (New York: Institute for American Values, YMCA of the USA, and Dartmouth Medical School, 2003), p. 8.

there they must tell their stories—if not in words, in silent, self-destructive acts or bold outbursts of violence. This is the simplest explanation of self-injury or self-immolation, of gangsta rap, school shootings and perhaps bullying and rape."[45]

Tracy's obsession with body image leads to eating issues, an epidemic in today's youth culture. She engages in a range of risky and immoral sexual behaviors, including an attempt to seduce an older male neighbor. She experiments with drugs and alcohol. At one point she and Evie—both giddy and high from huffing—willingly exchange face punches so severe that they are left bloodied. On three occasions during the film, she slices her arms in an effort to release her emotional burdens. Tracy and Evie have become in Borgman's words, "troubled youth"—that is, "young people in imminent danger of inflicting serious injury on themselves or others."[46] Tracy and her peers are hurting, and hurting deeply.

"Will you be here for us?" As *Thirteen* comes to a close three scenes send a clear message to our adult culture and to the church. In the first scene, Tracy's mother, desperate to do something to help her daughter, pulls her in close and squeezes her in a way that says, "I am here and I will not let you go." For a moment Tracy resists, but eventually her resistance stops and she collapses into her mother's arms while both weep.

Next, the camera focuses on the two as they lie together sleeping in Tracy's bed. Tracy is backed into her mother's body. Lost in her mother's embrace, Tracy feels a safety and peace she has not experienced for quite some time. Her mother is there for her.

In the final scene the camera captures Tracy's face as she spins on a piece of playground apparatus. The picture of youthful innocence is shattered as the little thirteen-year-old girl lets out a blood-curdling scream. Just like that, the film ends.

The scenes combine to summarize Tracey's journey. She is young. She is vulnerable. She has been through great pain. And finally, she wants and needs someone to be there for her.

---

[45]Borgman, *Hear My Story,* p. 13.
[46]Ibid., p. 23.

What Will We Do?

Thirteen testifies to the universal longing of fallen humanity—especially the emerging generations—for spiritual wholeness and restoration. Sadly, some in the church disapprove of films like *Thirteen* and the world it reflects, retreating back from its messy reality into the safety of a cloistered existence. After all, if we don't look at the ugliness, it won't be able to do anything to us and we won't have to do anything about it.

Jesus challenged this sinful attitude. One time, some Jewish leaders presented to Jesus a woman who had been caught in adultery. They wondered whether they should follow the law of Moses and put her to death by stoning. Jesus invited anyone who was without sin to begin the stoning. Those who *thought* they had understanding were silenced by his words. One by one they walked away, until Jesus and the woman were the only two remaining. He told her that he would not condemn her, but that she should "go now and leave your life of sin" (Jn 8:1-11). In compassion he reached out to the woman and loved her. He filled the hole in her soul.

There's not one person who is unredeemable. Even the traditionally cautious and spiritually gun-shy world of social science is recognizing a yearning among young people. A recent report from the Institute for American Values indicates that there is an abundance of "scientific evidence—largely from the field of neuroscience, which concerns our basic biology and how our brains develop—showing that the human child is 'hardwired to connect.' " The two primary connections all humanity needs in order to function and flourish are other people and "moral meaning and openness to the transcendent."[47] The desire for connections—human and divine—is undeniably present.

The church faces a moment of unprecedented opportunity. The youth culture is calling. If we fail to listen and faithfully respond, we're effectively telling them we don't care or we have nothing to say. We hold back the good news from those who so desperately need to hear.

---

[47]*Hardwired to Connect*, p. 6.

38 N G A G I N G   T H E   S O U L   O F   Y O U T H   C U L T U R E

Perhaps saddest of all is that we don't even know when we're doing it.
John Stott challenges us to look at the incarnation of our Lord as a
model of cultural identification.

> For the Son of God did not stay in the safe immunity of his
> heaven, remote from human sin and tragedy. He actually entered
> our world. He emptied himself of his glory and humbled himself
> to serve. He took our nature, lived our life, endured our sorrows,
> felt our hurts, bore our sins and died our death. He penetrated
> deeply into our humanness. He never stayed aloof from the peo-
> ple he might have been expected to avoid. He made friends with
> the dropouts of society. He even touched the untouchables. He
> could not have become more one with us than he did. It was the
> total identification of love.[48]

Before we speak for Jesus, we must live among our young people—
like Jesus. We must participate in their lives—like Jesus. And we must
listen—like Jesus. Let's begin our journey to communicate to the
emerging generations by listening—listening to generations that need
to hear, understand and respond to the good news. It's a generation
Jesus invites to "come" (Mt 11:28-29). It's a generation to which Jesus
commands us to "go" (Mt 28:19-20).

---

[48]John Stott, *The Contemporary Christian* (Downers Grove, Ill.: InterVarsity Press, 1992), p. 357.

2

Communication lenses, worldview chpt.

THERE'S SOMETHING HAPPENIN' HERE

THE PHONE CALL LEFT ME FLATTERED, somewhat fearful and at a loss for words. Jenna was calling as a representative of the senior class from our local high school. I was flattered because Jenna had enthusiastically asked me if I would be willing to be the speaker at the class's upcoming baccalaureate service. "Why are you asking me?" I queried. "We all want you to do this, Walt. We know that you know kids, and we think you'd be a great speaker." I was honored, especially since my own son, Josh, would be graduating in this class.

You might think I shouldn't be scared. After all, I've spent over thirty years working with young people. But that's the very reason why I was a bit frightened. They've grown up in a world that's very different from the world I knew as a teen. The pressures and expectations they face in today's postmodern world are confusing and complex. And the changes are taking place at warp speed. How could I speak to them in a way that would connect and have meaning for them?

Jenna's phone call prompted a quick trip down Memory Lane. When Josh was in second grade I would go into his classroom to help with reading time. I remember looking at the twenty-five children and praying, "Lord, what will the lives of these little children be like when they graduate in ten years?" Who among them would grow up to be spiritually and emotionally healthy? I wondered about the heartache they might face, the choices they would make and how those things would affect their lives. Even those who had healthy support systems were going to grow up in a difficult and confusing world. Who would they listen to? Would they respect authority? How would they know the difference between right and wrong? The questions kept coming.

Ten years had passed and they were ready to graduate. I had witnessed lots of ups and downs. They had grown up, developed and achieved much. I had studied their postmodern culture and seen the powerful influence it had on their lives. I had listened to the way they talk. I knew their music. I had observed the decisions they made. Some had been in and out of drug rehab. Some had dropped out. Some were already parents. Others could have been, but a "quiet" medical procedure had taken care of that "interruption." I had watched Josh drive off to funerals for classmates who, because of their decisions, wouldn't be sitting at graduation with the rest of their class. I had sat with many of their bewildered parents as they wondered why their child was thinking or doing this or that. At times, I was a bewildered parent myself. But all these behaviors, troubling as they were, were only symptomatic of deeper issues. Something was happening beneath the surface that was driving these kids to increasingly make choices detrimental to their physical, emotional and spiritual health.

I accepted the invitation with apprehension. My fear wasn't about being in front of three hundred graduating seniors, their families and their friends. Neither was it about *what* I should say. Instead, the source of my apprehension was rooted in *how* to tell the truth in a simple and straightforward manner that would engage their minds and touch their hearts. Now I had to pray, think and plan how to clearly communicate timeless truths. This was a great opportunity.

It's a New World

Cultural analyst Gerard Kelly likens our call to minister to today's youth to driving through Spaghetti Junction. This complex intersection in his native Britain brings together eighteen different route options on six different levels of roadway. Getting to the right destination requires advance planning and great concentration. Ministering to the world of Josh, Jenna and their young peers is likewise complex, threatening and confusing.

As a new century is born, movements of significant change are surfacing in unconnected areas of our lives, like multilane highways converging around us. Gathering pace and complexity, disparate changes compound one another to add up to a corporate "change of life," an interchange in the traffic of society. Changes are not happening one after the other on a single level but simultaneously on many levels. Diverse fields of inquiry are finding unexpected connections and spinning off in radical new directions. Like drivers in the approach to Spaghetti Junction, we see the signs of change flash by with increasing frequency—we are aware of options offered, of choices demanded, of life-changing decisions ahead. Choose your route, or the road will choose it for you. We are caught up in the knots of a culture junction.[1]

Kelly recognizes that as you approach a major, unfamiliar interchange, freeway driving can get a bit stressful. He believes that "likewise, the culture junction offers us a speeding blur of choices, demanding that we make them fast." Drivers can be uncertain, apprehensive and even stricken by panic. However, "change can be approached in two ways—primarily as threat or primarily as opportunity."[2]

Opportunity Knocks: *Recognizing the Mission Field Under Our Noses*

Even though I was a big Beatles fan in the 1960s, I soured on John Lennon when he hooked up with Yoko Ono. Not long ago I happened to watch two television events that brought back memories of why I felt that way.

The first show was *Rock & Roll Circus,* a 1968 concert film featuring a segment with Lennon and Ono playing in an all-star band. During one song Ono rolled around inside a black sack in front of the

---

[1]Gerard Kelly, *Retrofuture* (Downers Grove, Ill.: InterVarsity Press, 1999), p. 12.
[2]Ibid., p. 17.

stage. During another number she wailed and screamed incoherently while the band played. At one point guitarist Eric Clapton gave Ono a bewildered look that seemed to say, "Lady, just what are you doing over there?"

The second was VH1's rebroadcast of five episodes of *The Mike Douglas Show* from 1972. The week's worth of shows was cohosted by Lennon and Ono. Each show featured the couple's unique friends, including writers, philosophers and political activists. This time, Mike Douglas was the guy with the "this is *really* weird" look on his face.

At the dawn of a new millennium, John and Yoko's strangeness isn't all that strange. Although few, if any, knew it at the time, those shows offered a sneak peek into a fundamental change that was taking place in the way people thought and lived. The curtain was closing on the modern era while simultaneously opening to expose the dawning of postmodernity. Now, thirty years later, yesterday's "unusual" is all-too-familiar and "usual."

This rapidly changing cultural situation presents unique challenges to those who love and work with today's emerging generations. Parents, educators, pastors and youth workers are among those responsible to lead young people from childhood to adulthood. Those who fulfill their calling in conscious obedience to God face a unique set of challenges, perhaps the greatest being the need to cross the expanding cultural-generational gap. On one side stand adults raised largely in a *modern* cultural context. On the other side are children growing up in a new and radically different world—a *postmodern* world never experienced by previous generations. While adults and young people long to see this cultural-generational gap closed, it continues to expand as the culture changes at breakneck speed.

Because those of us who work with young people have grown up in a different world, we find it difficult to understand and relate to today's youth. Thus we must approach our calling to work with young people as a crosscultural missions venture. Dean Borgman says that "God asks us to make the Word understandable in all cultures of the earth. This means the Word must enter the world of skateboarders, surfers, mall rats, rappers, gang members, as well as those around the country club." To do so, we need to be tested in and familiar with the "waters of contemporary culture." Why? Because postmodern youth "will open up only to those who have come into their world."[3] "Youth ministry is crosscultural work," writes Paul Borthwick. "Youth ministers require the skill of missionaries, taking biblical truths and applying them to specific cultures. Increased secularization, postmodern thinking, and our post-Christian culture have set youth in a culture distinct from that of adults."[4]

Borthwick relates the story of Vincent Donovan, a missionary from North America who went to minister to the Maasai people of East Africa. When he returned to the United States, Donovan was surprised by the crosscultural mission field he faced.

> I realized that here on the home front I had left behind me one of the most exotic tribes of all—the young people of America. They have their own form of dress, symbolized by the omnipresent blue jeans; their own food, not always the most nutritious; their own music, which I confess, I do not understand; their own rituals enacted as they listen to their music in concert; their own language; their own values, remarkably similar from New York to California. Dress, food, music, ritual, language, values—these are the things that make up a tribe, or a sub-culture as they have been called. It is to that tribe, as they are, that the Gospel must be brought.[5]

The postmodern mission field lies in the halls of our schools, in our churches and even in our own homes! As I stood at the baccalaureate podium, I faced a vast crosscultural mission field that includes all of our children.

The sad reality is that the life-shaping power of the postmodern worldview stands in marked contrast to the increased ineffectiveness of the church to communicate God's good news *and* a distinctively Christian world and life view to today's young people. George Barna

---

[3]Dean Borgman, *When Kumbaya Is Not Enough* (Peabody, Mass.: Hendrickson, 1997), p. 32.
[4]Paul Borthwick, "Cross-Cultural Outreach: A Missiological Perspective on Youth Ministry," *Christian Education Journal* 3NS (1999): 63.
[5]Vincent Donovan, quoted in ibid., p. 79.

notes that "there is evidence that spirituality has been mainstreamed into teen life without radically affecting the lifestyles and values of most teens."[6] We haven't done a good job of entering into and understanding their world.

The ministry challenge is made even more difficult by the fact that many tenets of postmodernism conflict with the foundational tenets of biblical Christianity. Our children are living and growing up in a world where, as Gene Veith says, "the only wrong idea is to believe in truth; the only sin is to believe in sin."[7] Failure to recognize this fact only makes the cultural-generational gap grow that much wider.

It's time to view the calling to reach the young as missional in nature. We must develop a deep and detailed understanding of our mission field, the values, attitudes and behaviors of our youth. This understanding is a necessary prerequisite to effective communication and contextualization of the gospel message.

God Speaks: *A Theological Framework for the New Missionary Frontier*

Our understanding of the mission field of the emerging generations is rooted in the biblical story of redemption and the mandate to fulfill the Great Commission—to "go and make disciples of all nations" (Mt 22:19) as ambassadors of Jesus Christ.

Creation was originally marked by perfect harmony between God, humans and the created order, and God's mandate to humans to exercise dominion over all the earth (Gen 1—2). Through sin, humans brought—and continue to bring—disorder to this perfect creation (Gen 3:1-7). The consequences of sin run as deep and wide as the created order itself. Nothing is left unpolluted by sin. Consequently, all creation—including our children—groans for redemption (Rom 8). As fallen beings, all people are under the wrath of God and left deeply alienated in their relationships with God and each other, and within themselves. Our punishment is separation from

---

[6]George Barna, "Teens Change Their Tune Regarding Self and Church," *The Barna Update*, April 23, 2002 <www.barna.org/FlexPage.aspx?Page=BarnaUpdate&BarnaUpdate ID=111>.
[7]Gene Edward Veith Jr., *Postmodern Times* (Wheaton, Ill.: Crossway, 1994), p. 196.

God and banishment from the Garden of Eden. All of us, whether we know it or not, long for God and the Garden. But we can't get there on our own.

God—in his good pleasure, grace and love—initiated a plan to undo the effects of sin. He promised to Eve a child who would bruise the head of the serpent (Gen 3:15). The Scriptures record the unfolding of this amazing and great plan of redemption, a plan that provides us a way back into the Garden through the Messiah.

The New Testament begins with Matthew's account of the coming of the promised Messiah. He is Jesus, the Lamb of God who has come to undo the effects of the Fall. During his life and ministry, Jesus made it increasingly clear that his followers were to be ambassadors who carry out his mission by serving as agents of redemption in the fallen world. On the night before he was crucified, he prayed, "As you sent me into the world, I have sent them into the world" (Jn 17:18), and after his resurrection he said to his disciples, "As the father has sent me, I am sending you" (Jn 20:21). Their mission—and ours—was to proclaim the good news to those who are lost, as many of the lost would come to believe in Christ through them (Jn 17:20).

The God-ordained mission of the church throughout all time has been to fulfill the Great Commission of Jesus to "go and make disciples of all nations" (Mt 28:18-20). The Lord has sent the church to preach the gospel to people who are "harassed and helpless, like sheep without a shepherd" (Mt 9:36). They are people desperately needing reconciliation to God through Jesus Christ. The purpose of our missionary calling is to work as instruments in the hand of God by proclaiming good news so that sinners might be restored to an intimate relationship to God, living under his sovereignty as his disciples in this world and in the world to come.

The Great Commission applies to the crosscultural mission field of the emerging postmodern generations. We are called to live out our faith in the postmodern world as crosscultural missionaries. We must not only understand the unchanging Word of God but also those to whom we are called to minister.

Doing Our Homework: *Three Crucial Steps for the Crosscultural Missionary*

The church has much to learn from the world of advertising. Marketers create needs that are only satisfied by the products they sell. In their quest to become experts in crosscultural communication, they spend millions of dollars annually on market research. They become "missionaries," communicating their message across generations and cultures. Perhaps the greatest lesson the church can learn from marketers is the peril of attempting crosscultural communication without taking the steps necessary to ensure that the intended message will be heard and understood.

Consider the case of Pepsi. When the company decided to expand their market by selling their soft drink in China, they concluded that the simplest and most cost-effective approach would be to use their successful U.S. marketing slogan of the time—"Come Alive with the Pepsi Generation!"—for use in the Chinese market. A series of ads were developed featuring the slogan translated word for word into Chinese. The Chinese folks who initially saw the ads were shocked. The slogan translated into Chinese as "Pepsi Brings Your Ancestors Back from the Dead!" Someone hadn't done his homework!

A similar situation occurred when the Coors brewery decided to expand their market into South America. When Coors translated their slogan "Turn It Loose!" into Spanish, the ads promised to help people "Suffer from Diarrhea!"

The church risks a similar muddling of its message to the emerging generations and plugging their young ears when we don't take the time to know them, their language, their culture and their world. In order to effectively communicate the gospel with clarity in today's cultural setting, we must take three necessary steps. These steps reflect elements that were present in the earthly ministry of Jesus and in the missions endeavors of the apostle Paul. They have also been alternately present and absent throughout the history of Christian missions. When present, the gospel has gone forth with power; when absent, the gospel is difficult if not impossible to hear.

Step 1: Know the unchanging Word. John Stott reminds us that the word *evangelism* comes from the Greek term meaning "to bring or spread good news." "It is impossible, therefore, to talk about evangelism without talking about the content of the good news. What is it? At is very simplest, it is *Jesus*. Jesus Christ himself is the essence of the gospel."[8] If our mission is to lead young people to him, we must know him ourselves.

Therefore, the first step is to know the message—inside out and upside down. We must know the incarnate Word, our Redeemer, Jesus Christ. To know the risen and living God-man means that we have entered into a growing relationship with him. The apostle Peter admonishes us to "grow in the grace and knowledge of our Lord and Savior Jesus Christ" (2 Pet 3:18). We are to read, listen to and study God's written revelation of himself, the Bible—the primary and principle way that God speaks to his followers today.

We have been called by God to testify through our words and deeds to his Son, the one through whom our salvation has been mediated and secured (Acts 4:12). God has "committed to us the message of reconciliation. We are therefore Christ's ambassadors, as though God were making his appeal through us" (2 Cor 5:19-20). To communicate Christ crossculturally, we must know Christ.

Knowing Christ means that we view all of life through the framework and lens of God's Word. Knowing the Word keeps us grounded and less prone to be influenced by the world and unknowingly slip into betrayal of Jesus. Stott warns that "the main reason for every betrayal of the authentic Jesus is that we listen with exaggerated deference to contemporary fashion, instead of listening to God's Word."[9] We risk spiritual stagnation, loss of vision and apathy if we fail to listen to God's Word.

The first and greatest need of the missionary to the emerging generations is to know God and his Word, for that Word is "the power of God for the salvation of everyone who believes: first for the Jew, then for the Gentile" (Rom 1:16)—and for the young person at the dawn

---

[8]John R. W. Stott, *Authentic Christianity,* ed. Timothy Dudley-Smith (Downers Grove, Ill.: InterVarsity Press, 1995), p. 323.

[9]John Stott, *The Contemporary Christian* (Downers Grove, Ill.: InterVarsity Press, 1992), p. 24.

of the new millennium. God has chosen to disclose himself through his Son and his written Word.

Step 2: Know young people and their rapidly changing culture. Not long after I had landed in Belfast, my host warned me about what *not* to say as I spent the week speaking to parents, pastors and youth workers. These were English words familiar to both Americans and the Irish. However, I needed the warnings since to the Irish these words are filled with sexual meaning. If I used these words—even naively— my audience would be preoccupied with meaning I never intended. I was deeply thankful to my host for helping me better understand my audience.   *receptor oriented communication*

A basic principle of effective communication is that the message sender must know the receiver, particularly how and what the receiver thinks. The basic message of God's Word doesn't vary from culture to culture. But the words used in communicating the unchanging Word must always be chosen with deep sensitivity to the receiving culture. This requires not only an intimate and growing knowledge of the message but also of the receiver and his or her culture.

The model for this type of crosscultural adaptation is the incarnation of the God-man, Jesus Christ. God sent his Son, Jesus, a particular man, into a particular world at a particular time to a particular place. "The Word became flesh and blood, and moved into the neighborhood" (Jn 1:14 *The Message*). Jesus lived among those he ministered to. He embraced their lives by sharing in their day to day activities. He became intimately familiar with their language, values, beliefs, customs and thoughts.

The apostle Paul is an excellent model of someone who adapted his presentation of the unchanging message to his audience. In the book of Acts we see how his presentation changed from audience to audience. This man who became "all things to all men" had, as Jerram Barrs says, "done his homework. He respected his hearers sufficiently and had a deep enough care for them that he had worked at understanding their ideas and their religion."[10] He learned their "language"

---

[10]Jerram Barrs, *The Heart of Evangelism* (Wheaton, Ill.: Crossway, 2001), p. 216.

so that they were able to understand the message he was called to communicate.

To know the emerging generations that make up our youthful audience, we must take the time to know them at three different yet equally important and necessary levels.

First, we must know them individually, in terms of both their unique personality and abilities (nature), and their lifetime of experiences (nurture). Our resolve to know them should move us to seek answers to several questions: What is unique and special about their personality? What makes them get up in the morning? What do they value? What are their interests? How do they make decisions? What skills do they possess? What is their socioeconomic background? What is their ethnic/racial heritage? What is their religious background? Is there anything unique about their physical, mental or emotional condition? Where do they live? What is their gender? Who or what is the authority in their life? What have they experienced in their home? What is their family like? Who are their peers, and how are they influenced by them? Who do they spend time with in school? What major events have shaped their life, both positively and negatively? What are their hopes, fears, dreams and plans for the future?

Gary Parrett, in *A Many Colored Kingdom: Multicultural Dynamics for Spiritual Formation*, offers guidance on how to become a "culturally sensitive minister." He relates a helpful real-life example of the importance of an exhaustive and multilayered approach to getting to know a young person individually:

> To illustrate, let us consider the case of a young woman who was part of a church project that I and several others worked on years ago. I will call her Sandy. Suppose I was a new pastor in Sandy's church and desired to minister to her in a culturally sensitive way. How could I equip myself for the task? As a shepherd, I would be committed to knowing my sheep, each one, individually, seeking the same spirit in which our Lord Jesus, the Good Shepherd, ministers to his own (see John 10:10-30). I might ask the question, "Who is Sandy anyway?" How might I answer this query? Sandy

is a Korean-American teen-aged girl. These few descriptive words, by themselves, evince the complexity of the challenge. I must understand something about the meaning of "American" and of "Korean" and of the hybrid form, "Korean-American." But there is also the matter of being a teenager in America. Thus, I must also know something about so-called youth culture and the various potential influences it can have on Sandy. She is a young woman, not a young man, and this too is a critical piece of who Sandy is. But the case is more complex still. Sandy lives in a particular geographical region of the United States. She is part of an evangelical church youth group. It is a Korean-American youth group. She reports to me that it is very different from the other Korean-American youth groups in her area. She thinks the "climate" is more spiritual in her church than it is in others she has visited. She attends a particular high school and, at that school, "hangs" with a particular group of friends. We could, of course, continue the exercise, but the point should be clear. A person's culture is multilayered and exceedingly complex.[11]

Second, we must know them developmentally. In just a few short years teenagers grow from the dependence of childhood into the independence of adulthood. These are confusing years filled with unprecedented change. During this time they are seeking answers to the basic developmental questions such as "Who am I?" "Who are my friends?" "What does my future hold?" We must listen to and communicate with them in ways that reflect a deep understanding of the particular place they're at developmentally. "Youth ministry's cross-cultural nature necessitates the understanding of the phase of life that [they] are going through in all of its experiential dimensions."[12] We should know them so well developmentally that we understand them better than they understand themselves. If our expectations and understanding are too high, then we will overshoot our target with the

[11]Gary Parrett, "Becoming a Culturally Sensitive Minister," in A Many Colored Kingdom: Multicultural Dynamics for Spiritual Formation, ed. Elizabeth Conde-Frazier, S. Steve Kang and Gary A. Parrett (Grand Rapids: Baker Academic, 2004), pp. 145-46.
[12]Borthwick, "Cross-Cultural Outreach," p. 66.

message. If our expectations and understanding are too low, the opposite might occur.

Third, we must know their changing cultural context. They are powerfully molded and shaped by the world around them. In today's postmodern, media-driven cultural context, they are bombarded with messages that shape their understanding of and interaction with the world. To understand them, we must understand their culture.

Step 3: Take the unchanging Word to young people growing up in a rapidly changing culture. Once we know the message and the "address" of those awaiting the delivery, we need to get on our way and deliver the good news. If we have done our homework, our presentation of the gospel will be understandable to the youth we've been sent to reach.

The foundation for this type of effective communication is what John Stott calls "double listening," the ability and resolve to listen to two voices at one time. He says that all Christians are called to "stand between the Word and the world, with consequent obligation to listen to both. We listen to the Word in order to discover evermore of the riches of Christ. And we listen to the world in order to discern which of Christ's riches are needed most and how to present them in their best light."[13] With our understanding of the Word *and* the world as a foundation, we can then contextualize the gospel by sharing it in a meaningful way to the emerging generations.

Contextualization is defined as "taking the gospel to a new context and finding appropriate ways to communicate it so that it is understandable to the people in that context,"[14] and "the practice of declaring or depicting and living out the gospel message in cultural forms and terms drawn predominantly from the frame of reference of those you are communicating with."[15] The book of Acts and Paul's letters show the apostle's consistent commitment to contextualizing his message to his hearers, shaping his presentation to each unique audi-

---

[13]Stott, *Contemporary Christian*, pp. 110-11.
[14]A. Scott Moreau, Gary R. Corwin and Gary B. McGee, *Introducing World Missions* (Grand Rapids: Baker, 2003), p. 12.
[15]Steve Scott, *Like a House on Fire* (Chicago: Cornerstone Press, 1997), p. 6.

ence in order that they might have the opportunity to hear the good news. He was "faithful and relevant, not merely trendy."[16]

Deaf Culture or Dumb Church? *The Danger of Missing a Step*

Imagine that one Sunday morning your pastor delivers a rousing call to missions involvement. As the sermon draws to a close, your pastor invites everyone to consider whether God might be calling them to proclaim the gospel somewhere. During the closing hymn, a young man can hardly contain himself. Steve steps out of a pew, makes his way to the front of the sanctuary and obviously has something to say. Your pastor quiets the singing, and Steve steps forward. "Pastor, the Holy Spirit has stirred my heart this morning. I am feeling an unmistakable call to take the gospel to China." Steve obviously has gifts that match his new calling. He is a mature Christian who is serious about his faith and studying God's Word. He also shares his faith with others. As the elders come forward to lay hands on Steve and pray for him, the pastor pulls one aside and instructs the elder to go to the church office, log on to Orbitz.com, and book Steve a one-way ticket to Beijing for the following weekend. Then the prayer begins.

Fast-forward a few days. Steve's one-way flight to Beijing lands, and after a good night's sleep he heads to the streets with his Bible in hand. Steve begins his new missions venture on a busy street corner, preaching to passersby.

How effective do you think Steve will be at communicating God's Word to the people of Beijing? His call is genuine. He knows the Word. He is taking the Word right to the Chinese people. But Steve has a problem. While he knows the Word and he's taken it to the Chinese people (steps one and three), he has skipped step two. He hasn't taken the time to know the Chinese people, their language and their complex culture. As a result no one hears or understands what Steve is saying. Steve is "answering questions nobody is asking, scratching where nobody is itching, supplying goods for which there is no

---

[16]Stott, *Contemporary Christian*, p. 27.

demand—in other words," he is "being totally irrelevant, which in its long history the church has often been."[17]

Steve's pastor should have directed him to do what responsible and effective foreign missionaries and their churches have done for decades. Steve would have spent not just weeks or months but years in preparation for mission in China. His call would be evaluated and confirmed. He would have diligently learned the Chinese dialect of the people he was called to reach. He would have spent lots of time studying the Chinese culture and its unique spirituality.

Sadly, this illustration serves as an accurate description of how the church has tried to engage the emerging generations. Yes, we know the Word and have a genuine desire to share the gospel with them. But we haven't taken the time to know them and their changing culture. When it becomes obvious they aren't responding to our efforts, we lament the fact they have turned a deaf ear to the church. But is that really the case? I don't think so. More often than not, their ambivalence to the church is rooted in the fact they can't hear anything we're saying. Because we haven't taken the time to know them and their world, they don't hear or understand any of it. They're not deaf—we're dumb. In the end, we've done an "injustice to people whom Christ loves and for whom he died."[18]

John Stott says that in our current cultural situation the

> feeling of the remoteness, obsolescence, and irrelevance of Christianity is widespread. The world has changed dramatically since Jesus' day, and goes on changing with ever more bewildering speed. People reject the gospel, not necessarily because they think it false, but because it no longer resonates with them. Can the church survive the challenge . . . or will it suffer the ignominious fate of the dinosaur, equally unable to adapt to a changing environment, and become extinct?[19]

Francis Schaeffer knew all too well the importance of taking all the

---

[17]Ibid., p. 222.
[18]Duane Elmer, *Cross-Cultural Conflict* (Downers Grove, Ill.: InterVarsity Press, 1993), p. 17.
[19]Stott, *Contemporary Christian*, p. 17.

steps and missing none. At times, he was criticized for his engagement with the world. People would ask him, "Why don't you just
preach the simple gospel?" He answered, "You have to preach the
simple gospel so that it is simple to the person to whom you are talking, or it is no longer simple."[20]

When Worlds Collide: *Lessons from a Toy Gun*

Sometime during the mid 1960s a missionary couple serving in India
came to stay with my family. They had visited us before, and I was especially fond of the husband, who I remember as fascinating, warm and
engaging. But I'll never forget the day when my younger brother, no
more than five or six years old at the time, passed through the kitchen
and innocently pointed a toy gun at our missionary friend and said
"bang, bang." I was shocked—as was my younger brother—when our
missionary friend's demeanor suddenly changed to anger. He looked my
brother in the eye, grabbed the gun and pointed a finger in my brother's
face, exclaiming, "Don't ever point a gun at me like that again!" I'm not
sure if my brother cried, ran away or did both. I was unaware of anything but my feeling of horror. When the dust finally settled from his
outburst, the man turned and looked at me. Seeing my wide-eyed surprise, he offered a simple explanation: "I was once shot at in India."

That incident is my first conscious memory of the collision between
two different cultures. In this case it was how those cultures viewed
and perceived guns. For me, my brother and all the boys on our block,
a plastic pistol was simply a toy used in our everyday neighborhood
games of cops and robbers. To our older friend from India a toy gun
mustered up feelings and memories of conflict, fear and fright. In our
worldview a plastic gun held by a child was entirely normal and appropriate. In his worldview guns represented something entirely different.
We were all looking at the same toy pistol, but we were viewing it
through very different windows.

---

[20]Francis A. Schaeffer, *He Is There and He Is Not Silent*, in *The Complete Works of Francis Schaeffer: A Christian Worldview*, vol. 1, *A Christian View of Philosophy and Culture*, 2nd ed.
(Wheaton, Ill.: Crossway, 1985), p. 285.

The collision of worldviews is inevitable whenever those on either side of the cultural-generational gap engage the other. We must understand how the emerging generations have been influenced by and embraced postmodernism. Thus we must understand postmodernism as a worldview.

What in the World Is a Worldview?

What is a worldview? Simply stated, it's the framework every human being has through which we understand and interpret life. Scholars and cultural critics have defined *worldview* in a variety of ways. James Sire offers a concise and helpful definition: "A worldview is a commitment, a fundamental orientation of the heart, that can be expressed as a story or in a set of presuppositions (assumptions which may be true, partially true or entirely false) which we hold (consciously or subconsciously, consistently or inconsistently) about the basic constitution of reality, and that provides the foundation on which we live and move and have our being."[21] Another definition is that it "is simply the sum total of our beliefs about the world, the 'big picture' that directs our daily decisions and actions."[22] A "worldview is variously described as a lens, a model, a picture, or a framework consisting of fundamental beliefs through which we view the world and our calling and future in it."[23]

The Christian worldview is rooted in the story of what God is doing in the world. James Sire says that story follows the flow of creation, Fall, redemption and glorification. A Christian's personal story is a "tiny chapter" in that master story. When we think about what we believe about God, humanity and the universe, "the result is a set of presuppositions that [we] can express in propositional form."[24] These presuppositions may accurately reflect or be mistaken about the way things really are. We may consciously come to these conclusions, or

---

[21]James W. Sire, *The Universe Next Door: A Basic Worldview Catalog*, 4th ed. (Downers Grove, Ill.: InterVarsity Press, 2004), p. 17.
[22]Charles Colson, *How Now Shall We Live?* (Wheaton, Ill.: Tyndale House, 1999), p. 14.
[23]William D. Romanowski, *Eyes Wide Open* (Grand Rapids: Brazos, 2001), p. 47.
[24]Sire, *Universe Next Door*, p. 18.

we may—as is probably the case more often than not—assimilate them without ever consciously pondering them. In addition, our assumptions may be consistent or inconsistent with each other. Finally, Sire says our worldview is our foundation for living that is shown by our words and actions. Consequently, the worldview we actually live might not be the worldview we understand ourselves to hold. Belief— or worldview—is expressed in behavior.[25]

Picture for a minute the face of a young person you know. Now, put a set of glasses on that face. Those glasses represent his or her worldview—the lenses through which he or she views and interprets all of life. Those glasses shape his or her presuppositions, principles and convictions. They color every thought, decision, value, attitude and behavior in their world.

The unique set of glasses young people wear today is the postmodern worldview. Like all other worldviews, the postmodern glasses provide individuals with a perspective on every aspect of life. Postmodernism functions as their "compass or road map."[26] As it becomes the predominant worldview in North America and beyond, more and more of our children will find in postmodernism answers to life's basic questions—questions whose answers shape how young people look at and live their lives. By understanding these questions, we can gain a deepened understanding of the needs, hopes, dreams, concerns and problems of the young people we know and love. The questions are

- "Where am I?" "What is real?" "What is the nature of the world?"

- "Who am I?" "What is my purpose for being on this earth?"

- "What's right and what's wrong?" "How do we explain the bad things that happen in the world?" "How can we differentiate between the bad and the good?"

- "What happens when I die?" "Is that it? Or is there something else awaiting me when my heart stops beating?"

---

[25]Ibid., pp. 18-19.
[26]Albert M. Wolters, *Creation Regained* (Grand Rapids: Eerdmans, 1985), p. 4.

- "Is there a cure for the evil and brokenness in the world?" "Will things get any better? If so, how?"[27]

In reality, we can expect that only a very small segment of young people—or adults for that matter—have ever thought consciously about these questions and sought answers in a consistent and organized fashion. John Fischer calls a worldview the one thing that "everyone has but most people don't know what it is."[28] Even though it might not be consciously formed and embraced, it's still there, providing our young with "a model of the world" (the way the world is), guiding them through the world (how to conduct themselves and live life), and telling them how the world "ought to be."[29]

To know their worldview is to know them. It is a prerequisite to effectively engaging them in a discussion of how God's Word provides consistent, compelling and truthful answers to each of these foundational questions. This is the avenue by which the church can travel to avoid the mistakes of Pepsi, Coors and Steve.

---

[27]For a more in-depth explanation and discussion of the worldview questions, see Sire, *Universe Next Door*, pp. 20-22, and J. Richard Middleton and Brian J. Walsh, *Truth Is Stranger Than It Used to Be* (Downers Grove, Ill.: InterVarsity Press, 1995), pp. 11-12.
[28]John Fischer, *Finding God Where You Least Expect Him* (Eugene, Ore.: Harvest House, 2003), p. 65.
[29]Brian J. Walsh and J. Richard Middleton, *The Transforming Vision* (Downers Grove, Ill.: InterVarsity Press, 1984), p. 32.

3

POSTMODERNISM

[handwritten: Definition of PM - good/bad/etc]

A Worldview Without a Center

AS WITH ALL PHILOSOPHICAL MOVEMENTS and world-views, the postmodern worldview didn't suddenly emerge or sponta-neously appear in a vacuum. It has a history. To fully understand what it is, how it functions and why it's been embraced by the emerging generations, we must take time to understand its development in its historical context.

The simplest way to understand human history is to divide it into three major epochs or time periods: *premodern, modern* and *post-modern.* Each of these periods is marked by a distinctive worldview (and many unique subviews that won't be addressed here), and result-ing developments in the values, attitudes and behaviors of the people living in those unique times.

Premodern period. From the beginning of time until roughly A.D. 1700, people believed in the supernatural realm. It was a given that God (or the gods) exercised absolute authority, power and control over every area of human life. "Life in this world owed its existence and meaning to a spiritual realm beyond the senses."[1] There was cer-

---

[1]Gene Edward Veith Jr., *Postmodern Times* (Wheaton, Ill.: Crossway, 1994), p. 29.

tain consistency across cultures as each "society was generally united under one religion, which prescribed rules and roles and beliefs."[2] It was a theistic world where the existence of deity was unquestioned.

The premodern era was God- (or god-) centered; every society recognized and worshiped some sort of supernatural power. Some saw the deity as personal; for others, it was impersonal. But for all, there were powerful entities beyond the realm of the senses. Premodern societies recognized that truth was absolute and objective. Because truth came from God (or gods), it was not a matter of conjecture. Those who had knowledge of divine things became authorities who taught the masses how to worship or appease the gods. "They were thus agents of truth, its promoters and practitioners."[3] Truth was "out there," and it was communicated to the people by the priest, shaman or witch doctor.

The premodern world was a deity-centered world in which humans had faith or belief in a supernatural reality that existed beyond themselves. Premodern people believed that "there is a God; therefore conform to him."[4]

Modern period. At the dawn of the 1700s, human understanding of the physical sciences began to expand and accelerate. This new era of rapid scientific advance ushered in a growing sense that by exercising the newly discovered vista and power of human reason through scientific study and exploration, humanity was limitless in its ability to bring about positive change and progress to a world marked by disease and decay.

Historians refer to this period of heightened reliance on reason and the marginalization of faith in the supernatural as "the Enlightenment." Knowledge itself was seen as "certain, objective . . . and inherently good."[5] Rapid advances in science and technology fueled the belief that science—apart from divine revelation or reliance on God— could not only explain the nature of the world but improve it in the

---

[2]Douglas Groothuis, *Truth Decay* (Downers Grove, Ill.: InterVarsity Press, 2000), p. 33.
[3]Marva J. Dawn, *A Royal "Waste" of Time* (Grand Rapids: Eerdmans, 1999), p. 41.
[4]Peter Kreeft, *Back to Virtue* (San Francisco: Ignatius Press, 1992), p. 23.
[5]Stanley Grenz, *A Primer on Postmodernism* (Grand Rapids: Eerdmans, 1996), p. xi.

process. The industrial and scientific revolutions ushered in a new era of hope in the capacity of human reason and its ability to make the world a much better and more hospitable place.

In modernity "man" had become the measure of all things, and human reason rather than revelation was now the "final arbiter of truth."[6] Divine revelation was not only irrelevant but unnecessary. "In the modern period, human reason would take the place of God, solving all human problems and remaking society along the lines of scientific, rational truth."[7] Man replaced God, and science replaced religion. As a result, "Christianity was pushed into the background, put on the defensive. Many churches compromised, reinterpreting the faith according to Enlightenment dogmas. Liberal theology was invented. Nothing was excluded from the sovereignty of the human intellect."[8]

The modernist's hope was also redirected. Hope now rested not in the God who existed outside the self but in the rational mind within. Proponents believed that knowledge would lead to progress that would free humanity from the bonds of natural and relational oppression. Humanity had its destiny and fate resting in its own hands, and the promise and hope of a world void of problems and suffering led to increased reliance on science and the scientific pursuit. As long as people were learning more about the world and harnessing the world according to that knowledge, it was believed that humanity would continue to move forward. In addition, it was believed that the resulting economic advances and higher standard of living would result in "personal happiness and social harmony."[9]

Religious belief and practice didn't suddenly disappear. They were still present, but they no longer shaped the culture. They were moved from center stage to the periphery. The supernatural was displaced by the natural. Ecclesiastical authorities, while they still existed, no longer served as the guides to life and its meaning. God and faith were marginalized

---

[6]Ibid., p. 62.
[7]Veith, *Postmodern Times*, p. 27.
[8]Ibid., p. 35.
[9]J. Richard Middleton and Brian J. Walsh, *Truth Is Stranger Than It Used to Be* (Downers Grove, Ill.: InterVarsity Press, 1995), p. 22.

solely to offer personal comfort or to temporarily fill in the gaps until the inevitable advances of science would plug the holes. It was a period that was optimistic about the future because man was "self-assured and in control of his own destiny."[10] Soon modern people were living as if "there is no God; therefore we play God to the world."[11]

Postmodern period. Postmodernism dawned as a popular movement in the West in the 1960s. Some have suggested that it took root in mainstream America when President John F. Kennedy was assassinated on November 22, 1963. It was then that Americans began to wake up to the fact that the modernist promise of progress and a better world had failed. Not long after, America was fully engaged in the Vietnam War. All one had to do was turn on the evening news or pick up the morning paper to see that the human race hadn't taken itself to a better and more civil place. Instead, we had only used our increased knowledge to equip ourselves to cause death and destruction on a much-larger scale. Modernism was an empty promise.

The evidence was overwhelming. Crime was on the increase. Conflict and war raged on virtually every continent. Poverty and hunger existed for a growing segment of the world's population. Urban centers were rocked by scandal and decay. Pollution filled the skies and rivers. "In spite of real advances in medicine and convenience, people now sense that technology and progress have given us a society of useless products, deforested countryside, polluted water, extinct species and fragmented social structures."[12]

While it's far too early to predict how the postmodern worldview will ultimately manifest itself or how long it will last, some things are certain. In just a few years, society has moved—and continues to move—from a spirit of optimism about the future to a dark skepticism and nihilism that has little room for hope. Just as the Enlightenment led to a rejection of the supernatural beliefs of the premodern period, postmodernity has rejected the ideals and assumptions of the Enlight-

---

[10]Ibid., p. 14.
[11]Kreeft, *Back to Virtue,* p. 23.
[12]Alan J. Roxburgh, *Reaching a New Generation* (Vancouver, B.C.: Regent College Publishing, 1998), p. 11.

enment. Now, "postmodernism pervades everything, and none of us can escape it."[13] It is the worldview that is increasingly shaping the emerging generations.

Postmodernism: *A Worldview with Distinctives*

By its very nature, postmodernism has a tendency to defy definition or categorization. How can one absolutely define a worldview that claims there are no absolutes? How can one list characteristics of a view of the universe that actually views the world as a "multiverse"? Add to that the fact that postmodernism is an emerging worldview marked by transition, and the task becomes that much harder. Stanley Grenz says that "postmodernism defies definitive description. . . . In a sense, postmoderns have no worldview. A denial of the reality of a unified world as the object of our perceptions is at the heart of post-modernism."[14]

But there are common threads that run through the tapestry of postmodern thinking and expression, whether that thinking and expression are consciously lived or not. I have isolated some of the most foundational features of the postmodern worldview. These are the big changes that have taken place in how people think and live. Of course, each person is different. These elements exist at various levels and in a variety of combinations both individually and collectively. Each person and institution in the area of our ministry and mission efforts should be thoroughly observed and evaluated in order to determine which elements are present, and how they've combined to formulate the unique worldview of that individual or institution. In the postmodern world we can expect consistent inconsistency from person to person and within each individual as he or she changes from moment to moment.

Stories and words are power grabs. When I first visited my friend Ryan in his art studio, I was fascinated by his sculptures. At various

---

[13]Veith, *Postmodern Times,* p. 177.
[14]Grenz, *Primer on Postmodernism,* p. 40.

stages of development, each one looked like . . . something; I just wasn't sure what. Ryan seemed to enjoy my inquisitiveness and obvious confusion. Frustrated, I finally asked, "What is it?" His answer frustrated me further: "What does it look like to *you?*" "I'm not sure, that's why I'm asking," I responded. Ryan smiled and said, "It's whatever *you* want it to be." "But what is it to you?" I asked. His response captured the spirit of the emerging postmodern worldview: "For me, it's whatever *you* want it to be." Ryan believed that my "story" about his sculpture was as equally valid and important as his "story," or anyone else's.

Prior to our present postmodern time, there were systems, laws, traditions and principles that served as a kind of glue to hold society together and keep everyone on the same page. These combined to form a metanarrative or "overarching story that gives focus, cohesion, commonality, and meaning to life."[15] A curious viewer could ask an artist to explain the meaning of a work and get a straightforward explanation.

In the postmodern world there is no room for an overarching story or metanarrative that binds society together. Instead, each community has its own "myths" or narratives, but these should not be misconstrued as universal. All stories are equally valid and have meaning only for the community that possesses them. Nothing exists to integrate life and pull a society together at the level of the most basic foundations.

For postmoderns, metanarratives are oppressive. In a play for power, metanarratives force a dominant group's worldview on others. They are all-inclusive in the sense that they are seen as the one and only way. Postmodernism often appeals to history as a way of proving this by pointing to political, religious and racial oppression as being legitimized and justified by metanarratives.

The language and words used in metanarratives are constructed and employed by one culture or group in an effort to suppress another. Particular words are employed to perpetuate the belief systems and ideas of those using them. Language is used to construct mean-

---

[15]Dawn, *Royal "Waste" of Time*, p. 45.

ing. Postmodernists believe that language is used to imprison. In order to escape, we must "deconstruct" language so that we can "undermine the walls" and "break out."[16] In the end all narratives are equally valid, with no one overarching metanarrative explaining once and for all the meaning and purpose of life.

This fundamental shift explains why the biblical metanarrative of creation, Fall and redemption is so quickly rejected in the postmodern world, and why my friend Ryan welcomes and celebrates everyone's individual interpretation of his art as equally valid.

Uses feelings, not reason. In 1964 the world of advertising was still modern in its approach to marketing products. One television commercial at that time captures that modern marketing in unmistakably clear fashion. The ad was designed to show men how Aero Shave shaving cream was far superior to competitors' brands through the "Aero Shave Moisture Test." Two men simultaneously lathered up with different shaving creams, and Aero Shave was proven, through time-lapse photography, to outlast the leading competitor by hydrating and remaining on the face longer. "Aero Shave keeps drenching your beard while others dry out!" Marketers knew that objective proof was needed to convince people of the value of their product.

Not so today. Contemporary ads typically aren't designed to appeal to reason. Rather than preaching the superior nature of a product, marketing creates a desirable experience or positive feeling that is associated with their product. For example, an ad for Norelco electric razors says little about the quality and shaving performance of the razor. Instead, two Norelco electric razors are displayed in a manner clearly meant to evoke an image of two people performing oral sex on each other. In small text off to the side are the words "Get a close, comfortable shave whenever you're in the mood."

A classic example of how advertising reflects this shift from reason to feelings is the case of James J. Smith, a child psychologist who spent six years helping advertisers research how to sell to children. Children want love and acceptance, and like adults, they are willing to

---

[16]Veith, *Postmodern Times,* p. 53.

spend their money to get it. The basic premise of advertising to kids involves "luring children" with a basic felt need and "cloaking the message." Smith cites an Oreo cookie ad as a perfect example. The ad flashes thirty images of happy children, but the product logo is shown only once. The intended result is to have children associate the cookie with feelings of love and happiness. Nothing is mentioned about the cookie's taste or nutritional makeup. The appeal is entirely emotional.[17]

The postmodern world has rejected modernism's rationality and reason. Today, "the intellect is replaced by the will. Reason is replaced by emotions."[18] The way that we now know what we know is not through observation and scientific inquiry. People choose to believe in "what I like" or what "feels good to me." Ravi Zacharias says the postmodern generation "hears with its eyes and thinks with its feelings."[19] Consequently, everyone is free to construct or choose their own reality as subjective experience supersedes objective facts in the decision-making process. Gerard Kelly notes that "the generations of the post-industrial twenty-first century will increasingly evaluate every product, including public faith, in terms of their experience of it."[20] Or as Leonard Sweet says, "experience is the currency of postmodern economics."[21]

This profound shift is subtly reflected in the titles of two popular Christian books. For a long time J. I. Packer's *Knowing God* was a foundational text, particularly among new converts and university students. While still popular, Packer's book has been somewhat displaced in recent years by Henry Blackaby's *Experiencing God*. The titles reflect this shift from knowing to experiencing. In a postmodern world, emotions are the final judge of what makes something good, true and right.

---

[17]Susan Campbell, "Hidden Hooks in Children's TV Ads," *Philadelphia Inquirer*, December 2, 1990.

[18]Veith, *Postmodern Times*, p. 29.

[19]Ravi Zacharias, "An Ancient Message, Through Modern Means, to a Postmodern Mind," in *Telling the Truth*, ed. D. A. Carson (Grand Rapids: Zondervan, 2000), p. 26.

[20]Gerard Kelly, *Retrofuture* (Downers Grove, Ill.: InterVarsity Press, 1999), p. 69.

[21]Leonard Sweet, *Postmodern Pilgrims* (Nashville: Broadman & Holman, 2000), p. 32.

Embraces moral relativism. For over fifty years Billy Graham circled the globe as a gifted evangelist proclaiming the truth of God's Word. Whenever Dr. Graham, leather-bound Bible in hand, would speak the words "the Bible says," his audience knew that it was time to listen. Among both the "found" and the "lost" there was a sense of respect for God's Word, a respect that for some, carried over from premodern times when people believed what God said through the prophet Isaiah: "I, the LORD, speak the truth; I declare what is right" (Is 45:19). For others, the respect was rooted in the modern belief that there was such as thing as unchanging, objective, transcendent truth that was rooted in something or someone outside ourselves. Either way, people were more prone to sit up and listen.

As our culture shifts into the postmodern epoch, what was once respect for Billy Graham's words is shifting to skepticism and increasing disbelief. No longer do we live in a world that believes that a single truth is out there which we're on a quest to discover. Today, "the Self is the source of truth and reality. . . . What one chooses does not matter; that one is free to choose is all that matters. . . . There are no controlling rules or norms for society; not even God has that right."[22] In the postmodern world truth becomes what people—an individual or a community—want it to be. "With no absolute canons of objective truth, the rational is replaced by the aesthetic. We believe in what we *like*."[23] As a result there are as many different realities as there are people.

Our postmodern world is marked by a new level of moral relativism, the view that each person's own personal standard of right and wrong is as legitimate, true and authoritative as any other. The end result is significant. Every individual becomes a moral nomad, wandering through life without any commonly held standard by which to measure ideas, opinions and choices. Without an underlying moral compass, everything becomes random and fragmented, with no connecting points. Instead of choosing to obey, one simply chooses. Words,

---

[22]Timothy R. Phillips and Dennis L. Okholm, eds., *Christian Apologetics in the Postmodern World* (Downers Grove, Ill.: InterVarsity Press, 1995), p. 13.
[23]Veith, *Postmodern Times*, p. 176.

books, films, music, art and the Bible all take on personal meaning. Fashion, art, spirituality and reality become fluid.

Popular culture certainly reflects this changing spirit. A growing number of music videos barrage viewers with a series of fast-paced and incongruous images. The contradictory images are to be interpreted and deconstructed by the viewer who arrives at "what it means to me." Sheryl Crow captures the moral spirit of postmodernism in her song "Everyday Is a Winding Road" when she sings, "these are the days when anything goes." At the conclusion of the first film in the *Matrix* trilogy, the film's main character, Neo, describes this new world as "a world without rules and controls—a world without borders and boundaries."[24]

This morally relativistic world poses unique challenges to the church. First, institutions proclaiming the "truth" are rejected simply by virtue of the fact that they claim to have *the* truth.[25] For Billy Graham (or anyone else) to preface a proclamation with "The Bible says . . . ," meaning, "this is the truth" is perceived as the height of arrogance and a play for power. In a postmodern world, sin becomes a conceptual impossibility. Nobody has the authority to say "this way is the right way." Since individuals can't sin, they can only "act ill-advisedly" by making a poor choice or a choice that just didn't work out as planned.[26] All you can have, according to Francis Schaeffer, is "situational, statistical ethics—the standard or averages—but you cannot have morality."[27]

In the end postmodern moral relativism is a recipe for spiritual, moral and political chaos. Perhaps Richard John Neuhaus best summarizes the legacy of moral relativism when he says we are "herds of independent minds marching towards moral oblivion with Frank Sinatra's witless boast on our lips, 'I Did It My Way.' "[28]

---

[24]*The Matrix,* dir. Andy Wachowski and Larry Wachowski, Warner Brothers, 1999.
[25]Veith, *Postmodern Times,* p. 19.
[26]Harry Blamires, *The Post Christian Mind* (Ann Arbor, Mich.: Vine Books, 1999), p. 62.
[27]Francis Schaeffer, *He Is There and He Is Not Silent,* in *The Complete Works of Francis Schaeffer: A Christian Worldview,* vol. 1, *A Christian View of Philosophy and Culture,* 2nd ed. (Wheaton, Ill.: Crossway, 1985), pp. 296-97.
[28]Richard John Neuhaus, quoted in Charles Colson, *How Now Shall We Live?* (Wheaton, Ill.: Tyndale House, 1999), p. 376.

Celebrates pluralism, diversity and tolerance. There have always been great differences between peoples of different nationalities, races and religions. However, before television, world travel and massive migration to the West, we weren't aware of the extent of the differences in the world. Everyone was pretty much like us. But immigration and technology have combined to shift the makeup of our neighborhoods, churches, schools and even homes. While this in and of itself isn't a negative thing, it has fostered an environment where we can no longer assume that our closest neighbors will think, talk and act like we do. The potpourri that was once the world "out there" is now a mark of our own immediate lives as diversity meets us around every bend. Such diversity is not a bad thing as God is the author of diversity in many areas, including race and culture.

Our pluralistic world has subtly softened the plausibility that "our way" is the right way and "our truth" is the only truth. In the postmodern world, where everyone is encouraged to think and do what's right in their own eyes, differences in values and behaviors that once were seen as wrong are now permissible—even celebrated. The postmodern worldview has gone beyond encouraging diversity that's good to encouraging a type of diversity that allows sin to be celebrated, or at the very least tolerated.

The natural outcome is "the breakdown of social and religious consensus, or rampant pluralism, which tends to fray social cohesion."[29] Since it's impossible for anyone to claim their view is true, those who hold to "antiquated" views of sin are viewed as intolerant, judgmental and narrow-minded. Thus tolerance becomes necessary: it allows those with diverse and mutually conflicting beliefs and behaviors to safely coexist.

While God is the author of diversity, he is not the author of sin. Nor does his holiness allow him to tolerate sin. There is a danger in elevating tolerance over biblical truth. Compassion for the sinner risks being replaced by the acceptance of sinful behavior as normal. One example is the growing acceptance of homosexuality and other alternative sex-

---

[29]Groothuis, *Truth Decay,* p. 53.

ual lifestyles as a normal expression of human desire and behavior. Christina Aguilera's Grammy Award-winning video for her song "Beautiful" extends the song's lyrical call to self-acceptance and condemnation of bigotry—a positive message—by visually including a pair of homosexual male lovers and a transvestite into the mix of characters. The unmistakable message to viewers is that these are people whose lifestyle choices are "their own business" and "right for them." These differences should be tolerated and celebrated by those who don't choose to participate in those behaviors themselves. The message is clear—those in the wrong are not the homosexual and the sexually confused cross-dresser, but those who believe the homosexual and the cross-dresser are engaging in sinful behavior.

Replaces immorality with amorality. An edition of *What Is Enlightenment?* magazine caught my eye on a recent trip to our local bookstore. The cover trumpets the periodical's mission as "redefining spirituality for an evolving world." Inside, the magazine's purpose statement says: "We are in search of a radical new moral and philosophical architecture for twenty-first century society. We believe that finding this framework for transformation—rooted in the timeless revelation of enlightenment, reaching toward a truly coherent ethics for the postmodern world—is imperative, not only for the evolution of our species, but for our very survival."[30] The edition's lead article—with title and photo prominently displayed right there on the front cover—says it all: "Morality Bites! Searching for Ethics in a Postmodern Age." Under those words sits a partially eaten apple and the head of a serpent. The magazine recognizes the seismic moral shift and resulting change and confusion that has come with the dawn of the postmodern worldview. But the article's quest is for naught.

In a postmodern world where shared standards of morality don't exist, immorality becomes an impossibility. In the absence of commonly held absolutes, all behavior is *amoral:* neither right nor wrong. A lack of moral norms erases the possibility of sin, guilt and personal responsibility for one's actions. Fewer and fewer people have a sense

---

[30]*What Is Enlightenment?* February-April 2004, p. 4.

of having done something wrong. We already see this in our justice system. Increasingly, our courts are filled with "victims" sitting at the tables of both the prosecution and the defense.

A few years ago our local television station ran a grainy black and white security video that happened to catch the robbery and shooting of a local grocer in his small corner store. The gruesome clip showed three hooded figures committing a horrible crime that left the grocer on permanent life-support. A week later the three perpetrators—ages thirteen, fourteen and sixteen—were caught. The day after their capture the front page of our local newspaper ran a photo of the thirteen- and sixteen-year-old boys as they sat handcuffed in the back of a police car. Their demeanor spoke volumes. The camera caught the sixteen-year-old with a defiant smirk on his face and his hand raised, making an obscene gesture to the world. The thirteen-year-old, sitting next to him, appeared to be "yukking it up" for the camera. The photo left the unmistakable impression that neither boy thought he had done anything wrong. In a world without a moral center, they hadn't. In effect, they were only being true to their postmodern worldview.

Promotes an agonizing pessimism. The modernist soul—having placed its faith in technology, reason and science—longed for and optimistically expected the inevitable unfolding of a better world. It was believed that with each new day, the world would become a more comfortable and inhabitable place. The postmodern worldview recognizes that the world isn't getting better. In fact, it's getting worse. Human reason and scientific advances have polluted the earth and depleted its resources. Humanity cannot solve the world's problems.

There is a certain nihilistic flavor to the postmodern worldview. Modernism lied, and the world isn't going to get any better. Where there was once something to look forward to, now there is nothing. At best, we are spinning our wheels, going nowhere. "If all ideas are equally valid, as postmodernism insists, then no idea is really worth our allegiance; nothing is worth living or dying for—or even arguing about."[31] Heidegger's *Angst*, or dread, is the feeling that gnaws away

---

[31]Colson, *How Now Shall We Live?* p. 23.

at those whose wheels never move forward. This spirit is captured in Alice In Chains's hit song from the early 1990s, "Them Bones":

I believe them bones are me.
Some say we're born in to the grave.
I feel so alone.
Gonna end up a big ole pile of them bones.

We see the end result woven in and through the fabric of our contemporary culture. People with nothing to look forward to pursue diversions in an effort to get their minds off the inevitable.

Displaces hope with despair. Shortly after the fall of communism, I watched Barbara Walters interview the former Soviet leader Mikhail Gorbachev. At one point during that interview Walters asked Gorbachev about his philosophy of life. After pondering her question for a moment, Gorbachev responded, "My philosophy of life is this: people are born, people suffer, people die."[32] A short period of silence followed, allowing those harrowing and hopeless words to sink in. Millions of Western television viewers were probably not too surprised. After all, communism was so oppressive that anyone living under it couldn't help but be filled with hopelessness and despair. What millions of television viewers didn't realize was that Gorbachev's words captured the essence of how a growing number of Western young people were actually feeling about life. Even though their lives had been filled with economic opportunity and freedom, they still shared his despair. Why?

When modernism is displaced by postmodernism, hope is replaced by hopelessness. There is a symbiotic relationship between the postmodern worldview and personal despair. Gene Veith points out that the postmodern mindset has had a "devastating impact on the human personality. If there are no absolutes, if truth is relative, then there can be no stability, no meaning in life."[33] Consequently, we have moved into what social theorists call a state of anomie. "*Anomie* is the

---

[32]Mikhail Gorbachev, interviewed by Barbara Walters. I have only my notes from watching the interview and so quote Gorbachev from my handwritten notes.
[33]Veith, *Postmodern Times,* p. 72.

loss of a *nomos*—the loss of any secure sense of a meaningful order to the world."[34] If the postmodern worldview continues to grow, a growing number of young people will attempt to numb their pain by "escaping" through diversionary pursuits or by taking their own lives through suicide.

8. *Fosters a longing for connections and permanence.* During his high school years, my son Josh and his football teammates worked together with a shared sense of mission and purpose. During the winter and summer months they would spend time together in the weight room, working and sweating as they encouraged each other to become physically stronger. They would also gather informally on the practice field, parking lot or in the school gym to run pass patterns and catch balls. They hoped that repetition would result in flawless execution once the season began. In mid-August they began formal practice sessions. They listened to their coaches, memorized plays, followed instructions and learned the rules of the game. When the first game of the season arrived, they were of one mind. They were going to work together to accomplish their goals. These young men and their coaches shared a "worldview" that unified them and made them a team. They were all on the same page. Stepping off that page meant you were alienating yourself from the team and would no longer be a part of the football family. When the final gun sounded at the end of Josh's final game as a senior, I watched my son stand alone in the center of the field as the rest of his teammates celebrated their victory. Josh was the last player to walk off the field. I met him at the sidelines and saw the tears streaming down his face. The victory was great, but he was feeling the pain of no longer being a part of this football "family."

A shared worldview is like the glue that holds people together on a team or in community. But in postmodernism there is no unifying factor that gives one a sense of being connected to a team. Everyone stands alone. In effect, the postmodern world is marked by alienation and homelessness.

Theologian David Wells offers insight into this loss of connections

---

[34]Middleton and Walsh, *Truth Is Stranger,* p. 36.

and community in a world lacking permanence. He says that in days gone by, we lived in an *integrated* society where we were taught and held accountable by people we knew, and we had boundaries that were shared by others. Increased mobility, a booming economy and technological advance has destroyed this sense of community and created a *disintegrated* society. Today, we are taught by an impersonal media machine. Because we wander alone, we make up our own rules and do what we want. The only boundaries we have on our behavior are legal; voluntary self-restraint is disappearing. Wells notes that the stability that comes with permanence is also disappearing. Families break up. Marriages fail. Friendships are broken. In our highly mobile society people rapidly move in and out of community. Beliefs are up for grabs. Everything is disposable. As a result, we are attached to nothing. In our postmodern society people wander from place to place looking for others to connect with, a group to belong to and a place to call home.[35]

The recent phenomenon of the underground rave culture has been fed by this longing. Hundreds, sometimes thousands, of disconnected young people gather in abandoned warehouses or on fields to lose themselves in a community that dances to pulsating electronic music while high on ecstasy or other club drugs. The parties might last for a few hours or up to a few days. Hard-core ravers admit they're wanting to experience community and connections that offer them four elements, signified by the acronym P.L.U.R.: Peace, Love, Unity and Respect—adding up to "total acceptance." As our postmodern society becomes increasingly fragmented, their longing for connections, community and permanence will grow. People will continue to look for a place to call home.

Advances interest in spirituality. Michael Stipe, lead singer of the band R.E.M., captures the yearning so many postmoderns feel: "We are floundering more—culturally, politically, spiritually—than I can imagine anyone has been in several centuries. It's hard to imagine that so many people are confused about who they are, what their dreams,

---

[35]This is a summarization of a lecture presented by David Wells at Gordon-Conwell Theological Seminary, January 2001.

hopes, aspirations and desires are—and who's pulling the strings."[36] Hopeless and despairing individuals who live in a decentered post-modern world seek to satisfy their hunger and thirst for God through "spirituality." Ultimately, the heart's longing for home is a spiritual search and a cry for redemption. The need for God is driving more and more people to consciously search for spiritual fulfillment.

While modernist rationalism had slammed the door on spirituality, postmodernism has nourished a fast-growing and refreshing interest in mystical and spiritual reality. People are on a quest for transcendence. The postmodern culture is a "very spiritual culture, and many desire an experience of something that is beyond them. . . . [O]ur culture is hungry and needy and knows it is looking for answers."[37]

This trend is confirmed in a 1998 survey from the National Opinion Research Center at the University of Chicago. The researchers found that among eighteen to twenty-two-year-olds, only 16 percent had any contact with organized religion. Still, they had a significantly higher interest in spiritual issues than those who were the same age twenty years earlier. Today, 82 percent are asking questions about life after death, as compared to only 69 percent in 1978.[38] The culture—particularly pop culture—is more than ready to provide "answers."

Unfortunately much of the new postmodern spirituality rejects propositional truth and is drawn instead to mystical experience. The pendulum that had swung to the side of reason in modern times appears to be swinging to the other extreme. Hence the present interest in books on angels, the rising fascination with Wicca and other neo-pagan religions, popular music and film featuring spiritual themes, and television shows that offer crossover "connections" between the living and the dead.

Alister McGrath says of this deep fascination with unorthodox spirituality that never fulfills:

---

[36]Michael Stipe, cited in "The Party 2000," *Rolling Stone,* December 30, 1999-January 6, 2000, p. 110.
[37]Mark Gauthier, "Church/Campus Connections," in *Telling the Truth,* ed. D. A. Carson (Grand Rapids: Zondervan, 2000), p. 208.
[38]See Dick Staub, *Too Christian, Too Pagan* (Grand Rapids: Zondervan, 2000), p. 15.

Many people feel that any kind of fulfillment has eluded them. "Whatever it is that has the power to satisfy truly and deeply, I have yet to find it." For some, it is something that is for ever beyond human grasp. Some of the things that seem to assure fulfillment fail to live up to their promises. . . . The great certainty of our time seems to be that satisfaction is nowhere to be found. We roam around, searching without finding, yearning without being satisfied.[39]

In spite of this fact, the good news is that the search goes on. *Dismisses Christianity.* Kristen, a solid Christian and bright, young college student, was about to spend a summer planting trees in an overseas reforestation effort. Before she left, her campus minister challenged her to spend time asking her overseas peers this simple question: "What do you think about Christ?" While planting seedlings, she queried her coworkers and recorded their responses. Her findings were rather simple. First, she discovered that her peers are very spiritual, but there is no central truth that they follow. Second, she learned they are looking for truth everywhere, but they are repulsed by Christianity because it is too exclusive. Finally, Kristen discovered that her friends seemed to want to know Christ, but they didn't want to have anything to do with the church. Christians seemed to be hypocritical, unreal and undevoted. But they had never seen real Christian faith in action. Kristen's unscientific survey reveals that while spirituality is fashionable, there is a very real bias against Christianity.

Postmodernism sees Christianity's assertion of truth as a play for power. While modernists argued rationally that Christianity isn't true, postmodernists disagree with Christians because Christians think they alone have spiritual truth. As a result, the emerging generations reject Christianity not on the basis of the claims of Christ, but because Christians say those claims are universally true. They can't get beyond its exclusivity.

In a normal environment, this would be troubling enough. But it is even more troubling that this rejection is taking place in a time when

---

[39]Alister McGrath, *The Unknown God* (Grand Rapids: Eerdmans, 1999), p. 8.

interest in spirituality is on the rise. While an interest in spirituality may initially lead them to investigate Christianity, they are prone to quickly dismiss it as too constricting and archaic. Pop singer Alanis Morissette, in true postmodern fashion, defines and reinvents God on her own terms:

> Over the last few years, though, I've realized that God is compassionate and has no preference about how we live our lives. I think that is communicated through the fact that we're given free will. There are definitely universal laws, the laws of consequence and cause and effect, but I don't think God prefers one choice over the other. He or she or it notes rather than judges. Once I realized that, it immediately made me feel more responsible for my own life. If God doesn't judge us, all of a sudden it puts the onus on us humans. We're the creative force. We're creating what our world looks like right now and will look like down the road.[40]

These, my friends, are postmodern, post-Christian times.

Sees faith as a smorgasbord. I live in Lancaster County, Pennsylvania—a place widely known as "Dutch Country." Our county is a popular tourist attraction, the main draws being our Amish communities and an abundance of good food. When I'm traveling and people who have visited Lancaster find out that's where I'm from, they typically ask me about one of the many smorgasbords we have in our area. Visitors make a point of filling up at one or more of these popular all-you-can-eat buffets when they come to Lancaster.

Perhaps our most well-known smorgasbord is the Shady Maple. Every Monday through Saturday its large parking lot is filled with buses and cars that bring thousands of diners looking to fill up on breakfast, lunch or dinner. The Shady Maple boasts an amazing food bar advertised as "200 feet of Delicious Pennsylvania Dutch Cooking." (That doesn't include the bread bar, salad bar, beverage bar and dessert bar!) The choices are endless. Every plate is custom made by

---

[40]Alanis Morissette, cited in "The Party 2000," *Rolling Stone,* December 30, 1999-January 6, 2000.

the individual customer. No two meals are alike.

The emerging postmodern worldview has fostered an environment that encourages individuals to fill their own spiritual "plate" according to their own taste. The postmodern generations are taught to build their own faith systems based on what they like or feel they need. "Spirituality becomes more of a consumer item than a matter of facts, arguments and truth."[41]

Religion in today's postmodern world is a matter of personal taste and individual choice, not just in the sense of what system people choose to follow but in the content of that system itself. Their deep interest in spirituality leads them to combine elements of Christianity, New Age religions, neo-paganism, the occult, Near Eastern religions, pop psychology and mysticism in new and unique ways. These post-Christian faith systems are part and parcel of what Gerard Kelly has labeled "God 'R Us Spirituality."[42] Consequently, today's individual-ized, postmodern "spiritual journey is increasingly carried on outside organized religion"[43] and without regard for timeless and unchanging biblical truth.

Looking for Bus 119

I speak English and *only* English. That's why I became increasingly frustrated while standing on a cold, dark street corner in downtown Prague a few years ago. It was 6:30 a.m., I was stumbling under the weight of three bags of luggage, and I had little time to find my way to the airport to catch a plane home. Even I was getting sick of hearing myself ask, "Excuse me, do you speak English?" All I got was a succession of negative responses and confused looks.

All I needed to get started on the long journey home was someone who could understand my question, "Can you tell me where to find bus 119?" Finally, a young woman spoke the most beautiful words I had ever heard as a foreign traveler, "Yes, I speak English. You can get

---

[41]Groothuis, *Truth Decay,* p. 28.
[42]Kelly, *Retrofuture,* p. 162.
[43]Staub, *Too Christian, Too Pagan,* p. 15.

on bus 119 down at that corner." Finally, I was on my way home!

While some of them are consciously aware of it and some are not, today's postmodern youth wander through our cultural landscape in search of the way home. Many of us in the church wonder why their search doesn't lead them enthusiastically into our pews and willingly onto the road to life. Perhaps our unwillingness and lack of enthusiasm to go to them as a mission field by learning their language and understanding their postmodern worldview is to blame. In other words, it's not a case of the postmodern generations consciously turning their back on the church but the church (unconsciously or consciously) turning its back on the postmodern generations. If that's the case—and I think it is—their negative opinion of Christ has been shaped not by the God-man himself but by those called to be his ambassadors in the world.

In his book *Between Two Worlds,* John Stott challenges preachers to become bridge builders by relating the unchanging truths of God's Word to the existential situation of those longing to hear good news. Stott's challenge is relevant to those who want to effectively communicate to the emerging generations.

> Now a bridge is a means of communication between two places which would otherwise be cut off from one another by a river or a ravine. It makes possible the flow of traffic which without it would be impossible. What, then, does the gorge or chasm represent? And what is the bridge which spans it? The chasm is the deep rift between the biblical world and the modern [or postmodern] world. . . . Our task is to enable God's revealed truth to flow out of the Scriptures into the lives of the men and women [and children, teens, and young adults] of today.[44]

The emerging generations need people of faith who are willing to bridge the chasm. They need to be in relationships with people struggling to relate God's unchanging Word to today's rapidly changing world. They need directions from people who are unwilling to sacrifice

---

[44]John R. W. Stott, *Between Two Worlds* (Grand Rapids: Eerdmans, 1982), pp. 137-38.

truth to relevance *or* relevance to truth. Isn't that what Jesus did when he bridged the chasm between heaven and earth?

I finally caught bus 119. I made it home because a foreign national had taken the time at some point in her life to learn my language. Then, she took the time to listen to my question. Finally, she was willing to answer my question in a way that I could understand, pointing me in the right direction.

There are a lot of people wandering aimlessly in our world. They're asking questions about how to get home. I doubt they'll find their own way into the church. Instead, the church—one that listens to them and understands their postmodern worldview and how it's shaped their lives—must go to them.

4

WELCOME TO THEIR JUNGLE

ON A RECENT TRIP TO DOWNTOWN Manhattan I gained a sense of what it must be like to be a young person standing at the noisy and confusing crossroads of adolescence. It was 5 p.m.—the peak of rush hour. We were walking through Times Square. My senses were overloaded by activity happening in every direction. My field of vision was filled with people, cars, buildings and advertisements. The smells of hot dogs and soft pretzels were making me hungry. The hustle and bustle, everything from taxi horns to barking street vendors to loud music pumping onto the street from storefronts, enveloped me. Even my sense of touch came into play as I got bumped and brushed-up against in the rushing river of people. My friend Mike turned to me and said, "This is amazing, isn't it? It's known as the crossroads of the world!" I thought to myself, "If I didn't already know where I was heading, how would I know where to go?"

Adolescence is a crossroads. It's a time marked by overwhelming change, numerous questions and a search for answers. Not sure which direction to take, the emerging generations are presented with confusing messages and options. Usually, the signposts they choose to follow are the most attractive, loud and convincing in response to their unspoken teenage cry of "Show me the way." The choice is made easier when they see their peers moving en masse in one direction. The automatic assumption is, "That must be the way."

The signpost of the postmodern worldview is attracting far more youthful attention than others. And why not? It's big, bold and convincing. No matter where young people position themselves at the crossroads or which direction they gaze, this signpost fills their field of vision, saying "This is the way!"

A Mission Field Molded by Postmodernity

Most people I meet through my ministry—young and old alike—have been shaped in some way by the postmodern worldview. It's in the air we breath. But *the point at which* our experience with the postmodern worldview commenced plays a significant role in *how* and to *what* extent we've been shaped and influenced by that worldview.

We can assume with reasonable certainty that those of us who were adolescents during the period dominated by the modern worldview would have followed, to a significant degree, the "signpost" of modernism. This includes members of the "G.I. Generation" (born 1901-1924), the "Silent Generation" (born 1925-1942), and the "Boom Generation" (born 1943-1960). The first generation to embrace postmodernism at a significant level is alternately known as busters or Xers. These are members of the adult population born between 1961 and 1981.[1] But it's the generation that followed, the Millennial generation, that has been shaped and molded most powerfully by the postmodern worldview.

Marva Dawn summarizes the "postmodern slogans" that bombard this generation from all directions. These have found a home in their collective psyche, thereby shaping the behavior of the Millennials as they find their way through the impressionable years of childhood and adolescence.

---

[1] These generational designations vary in title and parameter from scholar to scholar. Determining generational designations and parameters is an inexact and relatively recent endeavor. For the sake of our discussion here, I have chosen to use the designations and parameters established by William Strauss and Neil Howe. For more information see, Neil Howe and William Strauss, *The Fourth Turning: What the Cycles of History Tell Us About America's Next Rendezvous with Destiny* (New York: Broadway Books, 1997), p. 17.

- The Enlightenment project is a bust—there is no such thing as progress.
- Life has no meaning—it's just a game.
- You are the only one who cares about you.
- No story is universally true.
- There is no such thing as truth except what you created for yourself.
- Every claim to truth is a power play.
- Therefore, everything must be mistrusted (or deconstructed).
- There is no order—all is random.
- You only go around once, so do it with gusto.[2]

While the extent of influence and intensity of these messages vary from community to community and individual to individual, we can reasonably assume and generalize that they *do* influence every member of the emerging generations due to the fact that no matter who they are, where they live or where they turn, the signpost of the postmodern worldview is in sight. As a result, those of similar age will fall under the postmodern influence and adopt similar values, attitudes and behaviors during their teenage years.

Our ministry effectiveness with the Millennials (and subsequent generations) demands that we understand the unique way that postmodernism shapes their values, attitudes and behaviors.

What the Researchers Tell Us

I first watched *Saving Private Ryan* in a packed movie theater. Before the lights dimmed, I looked around the room and noted the diverse crowd that had gathered to watch the critically acclaimed film that took viewers on a visually graphic trip through the horrific realities of World War II. Some of the attendees were old enough to have been through the war themselves. Even though I grew up during the war in

---

[2]Marva J. Dawn, *Is It a Lost Cause?* (Grand Rapids: Eerdmans, 1997), p. 23.

Vietnam, I had never been in battle. Two twenty-something young men had come with me to watch the film. Their fathers had been to Vietnam, and they wanted to gain a deeper understanding of the emotional fallout their fathers were still experiencing from combat. Finally, there was the usual Friday night movie crowd—kids looking to escape through some entertainment.

When the lights came up after the film's conclusion, I watched as hundreds of people slowly walked up the aisle to exit the theater. The older folks were visibly shaken and largely silent, tears streaming down the faces of some. It appeared that the film had stirred emotional memories of a battle they or someone they knew had been through. Some from my generation were also teary-eyed. Many of them were quietly discussing this visually realistic depiction of war. My twenty-something friends were also crying. For the first time they understood the unspoken and haunting war memories their fathers had been harboring. But by far the most interesting and disturbing response came from a group of high school boys. As the credits rolled and the lights came up, one loudly proclaimed, "That was cool!" Then they discussed the special effects. They had missed the entire point of the movie. While nobody said anything, I noticed a couple of older gentlemen sneering at the boys.

I learned a lot by watching four generations respond to *Saving Private Ryan*. Each one had viewed the film through the filter of their life experiences and worldview. Each one had processed the film in their own unique collective way based on who they were and how they had been shaped by their past and present life context. The differences in their responses were roughly indicative of differences in their ages and respective generations.

In recent years increasing attention has been paid to the uniqueness of each generation. While these generational distinctives have been studied for a variety of reasons, two of those reasons stand out. First, there are those—sociologists, anthropologists, historians and futurists—who study generations to be able to *track* and *predict* social trends. Their work is primarily academic in nature. Second, there are those who study generations to effectively *market* product. These researchers don't stop at understanding; they exert a growing and powerful influence that actually shapes and reshapes the values, attitudes and behaviors of people. A basic understanding of the purpose, methodology and fruit of each of these approaches is helpful to those of us in ministry so that we might more clearly understand the Millennials and subsequent emerging generations and set them in their missional context.

Those who engage in generational study for the sake of social research are best represented by researchers William Strauss and Neil Howe. Their cyclical view of history has led them to develop a popular paradigm that views generational traits as shifting in distinctive ways every twenty years with the advent of a new generation. Then, each of those generations is linked with one of four generational archetypes that appear again and again in recurring sequence throughout the cycle of history. In other words, history repeats itself in a "what goes around comes around" orderly fashion about every 80 years. The pair's cyclical paradigm plays out most recently beginning in 1925 at a time when America was asserting itself as a global presence. Their "*Artist*" generations are born during a crisis. The Silent Generation served that purpose most recently as "they applied their expertise and sensitivity to fine-tune the institutional order while mentoring the passions of youth."[3] Howe and Strauss believe that "a *Prophet* generation is born during a High."[4] In our times, the Prophet generation is the baby-boomers born into the "high" of the post-WWII economy. A "*Nomad*" generation follows during a period of Awakening.[5] Generation X'ers are today's Nomads as they wander through a "busted" and broken world. The next cycle sees the arrival of a "*Hero*" generation that is born during an Unraveling.[6] Howe and Strauss optimistically view the Millennials as today's hopeful Heroes.

While Howe and Strauss's cyclical theories are well-researched, fascinating and helpful in many ways, I'm skeptical about how well they will

---

[3]Howe and Strauss, *Fourth Turning*, pp. 17, 19.
[4]Ibid.
[5]Ibid.
[6]Ibid.

hold up when they fail to adequately take into account the monumental worldview shift that is occurring as society becomes less and less modern, and more and more postmodern. Because of the nihilistic nature of the postmodern worldview, those who look at the world through the framework and reality of a biblical world and life view can't share Howe and Strauss's sense of optimism for the Millennial generation. After all, how can postmodern nihilists be fully hopeful outside of Christ? I think they too quickly make the mistake of equating the Millennials' youthful idealism with a hope that will bring lasting personal peace and purpose enduring into adulthood. In the end, Howe and Strauss look back at history and offer a helpful paradigm that is *descriptive*. However, the recent advent of postmodernism's increased and powerful influence limit the paradigm's *predictive* reliability.

Still, Howe and Strauss do us a huge favor by helping us understand the uniqueness of different generations. They define a generation as "a society-wide peer group, born over a period roughly the same length as the passage from youth to adulthood (in today's America, around twenty or twenty-one years), who collectively possess a common persona."[7] Their description of a "generational persona" is especially helpful for those of us looking to discover the distinctives of the mission field of the emerging generations:

> What is a generational persona? It is a distinctly human, and variable, creation embodying attitudes about family life, gender roles, institutions, politics, religion, culture, lifestyle, and the future. A generation can think, feel, or do anything a person might think, feel, or do. It can be safe or reckless, individualist or collegial, spiritual or secular. Like any social category (race, class, religion, or nationality), a generation can allow plenty of individual exceptions and be fuzzy at the edges. But unlike most other categories, it possesses its own personal biography. It can feel nostalgia for a unique past, express urgency about a future of limited duration, and comprehend its own mortality. As a generation ar-

---

[7]Neil Howe and William Strauss, *Millennials Rising: The Next Great Generation* (New York: Vintage, 2000), p. 40.

rives, advances, and recedes, this core persona invariably reveals itself. Not every member will share it, of course, but every member will deal with it, willingly or not, over a lifetime.[8]

According to Howe and Strauss, if we want to identify the persona of a generation, we should be looking for three attributes. First, the members of a common generation will share *perceived membership*. Sometime near the dawn of adolescence, they realize they're part of a group that shares an identity distinct from those who are older. Second, they will share *common beliefs and behaviors*. Howe and Strauss believe that in this respect, the Millennials have made a clear break from prior generations. The reason for this, I believe, is their postmodern worldview context. And third, they share a *common location in history* marked by a unique blend of trends and events.

The categories and definitions proposed by researchers Howe and Strauss are helpful guides for those who correctly understand that like cultures, generations reflect dominant worldviews and ideas which must be understood as a prerequisite for effective crosscultural missions in today's youth culture.

Those who engage in generational study for the purpose of market research are numerous and influential. The emerging generation is the most targeted market segment in history. It's as if youth walk around with targets on their backs. Research on children and teens confirms several facts. First, they have more discretionary money to spend than any other age group. Second, they're also spending family money. Third, children influence their parents' spending decisions. Seventy-three percent of youth marketers surveyed "strongly agree" or "agree" with the statement "Most companies put pressure on children to pester their parents to buy things."[9] That explains the three-page minivan ad I saw in *Sports Illustrated for Kids,* a magazine targeting ten- to fourteen-year-olds. Marketers know that kids work hard at convincing their parents what to buy. Fourth, marketers want to de-

---

[8]Ibid., pp. 40-41.
[9]John Geraci, Dana Markow and Osa Hirsch, "Harris Interactive/Kid Power Poll of Youth Marketers: Summary Report," *HarrisInteractive,* 2004, <www.harrisinteractive.com/expertise/pubs/KidPower_Poll_Results.pdf>.

velop "brand loyalty." Kids become adult consumers. Develop allegiance to your brand now and chances are you'll have them for life. Fifth, kids are a powerful sales force. If a brand or product achieves the coveted status of "cool," young people will talk about it, wear it and "sell" it. Finally, the Millennial generation is huge.[10]

But it's not enough to know *why* marketers target the emerging generations. It's important to know *how* that marketing affects young people and *how* that knowledge can increase our understanding of distinctive generations, particularly those who are children and teens today.

The marketing onslaught in today's world began shortly after World War II. As the G.I.s returned from war, there was a sudden increase in marriages and a subsequent rise in births. Marketers smelled opportunity. They researched boomers and developed marketing plans targeting them. The formula worked. Today marketers develop and sell their products by "segmenting" the generations from each other through fostering a generational persona.[11] Regarding this Andy Crouch writes:

> For maximum effect, one must create a self-consciousness in the consumer that encourages him to segment his own world— because once you have a customer with a pre-fabricated sense of where he fits in the consumer universe, the cost of pitching a new product goes down dramatically. The complex and expensive process of convincing your customer that your product meets one of his needs is much less important if you can appeal to a pre-existing set of identity markers. Simply invoke the telltale signs of his chosen segment, and he will know that your product is for people like me.[12]

In his book *Creating Ever-Cool* Gene Del Vecchio teaches marketers how to sell to kids. Del Vecchio views the kid marketplace as a battleground—a place where the "battle will be won by the company that

---

[10]For more information and analysis on marketing, see Peter Zollo, *Wise Up to Teens* (Ithaca, N.Y.: New Strategist, 1999), pp. 8-21.
[11]See Howe and Strauss, *Millennials Rising*, p. 40.
[12]Andy Crouch, "For People Like Me," *Regeneration Quarterly,* February 2000 <www .regenerator.com/5.3/crouch.html>.

best understands kids, their emotional needs, their fantasies, their dreams, their desires. Such knowledge is the mightiest weapon in a marketer's arsenal to win a child's heart." According to Del Vecchio, the way to win those hearts is through attaining "ever cool," the holy grail achieved through the formula to "satisfy a kid's timeless emotional need(s) but routinely dress it up in a current fad or trend." Marketers are shaping a child's "psyche, . . . that part of each of us that governs our thoughts and feelings, both consciously and subconsciously. It is the intangible, yet ever-present entity that shapes what we think, how we behave, what we dream. It is, when all is said and done, who we are."[13] Marketers are crosscultural "missionaries" peddling their material "gospel." By getting to know the emerging generations and speaking their language, their product and accompanying worldview have been welcomed and assimilated into the collective psyche of the young.

Those who study generations and generational theory are explaining *and* shaping the young people we've been called to reach with the gospel. They serve us in our effort to get to know this mission field by deepening our understanding of the fact that each generation has those differences magnified and exploited by a marketing machine bent on creating segmented generational identities that translate into higher profits. Looking at the fruit of their marketing research and efforts opens our eyes to the unique features of the emerging generation known as the Millennials. As the marketing machine grows, it will function in the same powerful life-shaping way with succeeding generations.

The Unique Marks of the Emerging Generation

The generation of children and teens born after 1982 shares Howe and Strauss's attributes of commonly perceived membership and common location in history. In addition, they have been corporately and individually shaped by living in a rapidly changing world, which has filled their developmental years with powerful life-molding experi-

---

[13]Gene Del Vecchio, *Creating Ever-Cool* (Gretna, La.: Pelican, 1997), pp. 24, 28, 34.

ences resulting in some distinct generational beliefs and behaviors. While the Millennials are diverse, there are some identifiable marks that must be recognized and understood if we are to effectively reach them with the gospel.

Before examining each of these Millennial marks, it's important to recognize that many are partially shared to varying degree and intensity with individuals and groups who are members of preceding generations. Yes, the Millennials are a unique group. But just as not all members of the Millennial generation share all of the marks and traits to the same degree, there are those in the previous generations whose life context and experience overlap more with those who are younger, than with those of their own generational category and age. In that way, it is sometimes helpful to look at the Millennials and other emerging generations as a mindset shaped by shared experiences rather than an age group with strict parameters. There will always be some overlap.

Without a moral compass. My trip to the store for a pair of new running shoes was an educational experience. My head was spinning from the vast array of shoes facing me when a group of three shoppers on a similar mission arrived and stood next to me. Two of the shoppers were boys, perhaps fourteen or fifteen years old. The third shopper was one of the boys' father. In a matter of moments, two things became abundantly clear. First, Dad was simply there to drive and pay. Second, his son lacked the character to keep his mouth and behavior in check. Upon arriving at the store, Junior and his friend immediately went to the most expensive sets of running shoes. When Junior picked one up, Dad very calmly suggested that the price was out of his range. Immediately, the boy yelled, "Dad, shut up! You are so annoying." The boy then turned back to his friend and continued his conversation.

The father tried a second time, and the scene played itself out again. While Junior used the same disrespectful words to address his dad, his tone and volume were both more intense. When all was said and done, the scene occurred three times before Dad gave up and handed his credit card to the cashier. She rang up a bill for the most expensive pair of running shoes in the store. Granted, there were numerous dynamics taking place, and I was an uninformed observer. But one thing was abundantly clear: Dad had little or no authority in Junior's eyes.

Young people growing up in the postmodern culture have lost their sense of right and wrong. They have been molded by a postmodern media culture and a circle of peers that are equally lost and confused. "Many of our children's friends and our neighbors have no reference point, no guiding standard by which to assess life," says Marva Dawn.[14] Without an external standard to define right and wrong behavior, Junior was free to respond to his father any way he desired. Thus there was nothing wrong with humiliating his father in public. For Junior, and others like him, "moral authorities have lost their appeal. . . . Logical systems, theological proofs, and legitimate authority no longer count."[15]

The ever-growing moral void is manifest in behavior in every corner of our society. Our schools have been especially hard-hit by the rise of postmodern amorality. Teachers spend a growing amount of time dealing with students' behavioral problems. This has necessitated the creation and implementation of school-based "character education" programs. One of the leading proponents of character education, Thomas Lickona, is convinced that "our society is in deep moral trouble" and "schools must do what they can to contribute to the character of the young and the moral health of the nation."[16] Lickona notes that while many of our kids are committed to causes like human rights, the environment and global awareness, the general trend is very alarming.[17]

I believe that as the postmodern worldview continues to take root and grow, we will continue to see a rise in a variety of school behaviors Lickona lists as indicators that our society is failing to provide for the moral development of our young. These include violence and vandal-

---

[14]Dawn, *Is It a Lost Cause?* p. 23.
[15]Dean Borgman, *When Kumbaya Is Not Enough* (Peabody, Mass.: Hendrickson, 1997), p. 25.
[16]Thomas Lickona, *Educating for Character* (New York: Bantam Books, 1991), p. 5.
[17]Ibid., pp. 12-19.

ism, stealing, cheating, disrespect for authority, peer cruelty, bigotry, bad language, sexual precocity and abuse, increasing self-centeredness, declining civic responsibility and self-destructive behavior.[18] Sadly, research continues to document the rise in these behaviors among our emerging generations. If the trend goes on, we will continue to see a decline in civility and increased loss of respect for authority. We can also anticipate a rise in violence on the streets, in the classroom, on the athletic field and in the home.

Culturally diverse. I grew up in the northeast suburbs of Philadelphia, and between kindergarten and fifth grade, the only faces I saw in the school were white. But my elementary classmates and I were exposed to racial and cultural differences in the world in three ways. First, there was the generic "Children of the World" poster that hung on the wall of our classroom. The only place we might "meet" these children was on the pages of our social studies books or on a grainy 16 mm black-and-white movie. Our second avenue out of our white ghetto was TV. Third, there were the school fieldtrips to the city museums. The bus rides to and from our destination took us into an urban setting that seemed like another world. And my experience as a child was not unique. The world of previous generations was largely racially and culturally segregated.

Not so today. Immigration, emigration, increased mobility, transportation advances, economic opportunity and the pervasiveness of the global media machine have brought about a major shift in the makeup of neighborhoods, communities and schools. Urban and suburban schools increasingly reflect the multicultural and multiethnic flavor of surrounding neighborhoods and communities. More and more schools are multilingual. And for those who only rub elbows with people like themselves on a daily basis, the media and the Internet provide unprecedented access to the cultures and diverse cultural fruit of the world. How else can one account for the spread of hip-hop music and culture to the plains of mid-America as rural teens embrace a way of life rooted in and flowing out of urban streets they've never walked down themselves?

Racial diversity is part of our children's world. In 1976, 85 percent

---

[18]Ibid.

of the teen population in the United States was white. By 1998 that number had decreased to 67 percent. It is estimated that by the year 2050, white teens will be a minority.[19] Unlike my own childhood experience, three-fourths of today's children have friends who are of a different ethnic origin.[20] "Kids today are being exposed to more ethnic and cultural influences than at any other time."[21]

God is the author of racial, ethnic and cultural diversity. Crosscultural missions theorist Duane Elmer says "this fact calls all of us to deal with cultural diversity, see it as he sees it—as good—and honor it as the handiwork of the wise and sovereign Creator."[22] But Elmer believes that these very forces can also be very destructive as "differences can build stronger bonds between people or it can break them. Broken relationships often result from a failure to understand and adjust to the differences we have inherited from a wise God."[23] As our young adjust to differences, we must likewise adjust to the reality of their world.

Sadly, racism and prejudice will continue to exist with great intensity among some members of the emerging generation. We can be certain that sinful expressions of disunity will manifest themselves among some as this emerging generation comes of age. But for most, these barriers are starting to crumble.

Pluralistic and tolerant. There is a new openness to cultural diversity. This trend is positive when it decreases hostility and enmity between groups, and lays the groundwork for conversation and cooperation. But this movement is negative and destructive when used as a justification of sinful and immoral behavior. Os Guinness says, "Ours is world in which 'Thou shalt not judge' has been elevated to the status of a new eleventh commandment. Many people today consider judging evil to be worse than doing evil."[24]

---

[19]Nathan Cobb, "Generations 2000: Meet Tomorrow's Teens," *Generation Y Papers,* April 28, 1998, <http://home.pix.za/gc/gc12/papers/p2020.htm>.
[20]Ibid.
[21]"Ten Youth Trends That Are Changing the Face of Food and Beverage Marketing," *Kid Power Exchange,* March 16, 2004, <http://iqpc.nac.net/2003_nl/0304_article2.htm>.
[22]Duane Elmer, *Cross-Cultural Conflict* (Downers Grove, Ill.: InterVarsity Press, 1993), p. 23.
[23]Ibid., p. 24.
[24]Os Guinness, *Long Journey Home* (Colorado Springs, Colo.: Waterbrook, 2001), pp. 56-57.

This new way of thinking will continue to work itself out in a variety of behavioral choices facing the young. How they handle a host of moral issues, including cheating, stealing, infidelity, dishonesty, pornography and sexual perversion, gives us insight into how pluralistic they are. Even if they don't engage in those behaviors because "that's wrong for me," they might tolerate the participation of others, who are free to choose "what's right for them." Unfortunately, even professing Christians are apt to accept, embrace and exhibit these attitudes as their own.

Broken relationships. Junior high was a difficult place for me. While I'd love to have a shot at some "do overs" in order to make some better choices, I don't think I'd like to relive my junior high years again. My most positive memory of it was the end of the school day. It felt great to be leaving the jungle and going to a place filled with comfort and love. While my home certainly wasn't inhabited by perfect people, I knew that my parents loved each other and me.

If junior high was a jungle then, it can't be the least bit enjoyable today. Research reveals that today's adolescents face a growing number of difficult problems. For many, the best time of day is not when that final bell rings and they head home, but the moment they leave their home at the start of each day. When the school day ends and they head home, many are walking into a mess. Growing up has become much harder.

Gen-Xers inherited a relationally broken world. Much of that brokenness came from their family relationships. But the Millennial generation actually has it worse. Judith Wallerstein, an expert on the effects of divorce, cites the following statistics regarding families in America today:

- Nearly half of all first marriages end in divorce, and 60 percent of second marriages end in divorce.

- Since 1970 at least a million children a year have seen their parents divorce.

- Half of all children whose parents divorce are under the age of six when the breakup occurs.

- Twenty-five percent of all children will spend part of their childhood in a stepfamily.

- Forty percent of all marriages in the 1990s involve one or both people who have been married before.[25]

Many of the Millennial children will never live in a home with both biological parents. According to the U.S. Census, there were 10 million single-mother families in the United States in the year 2000. That figure reflects 26 percent of all families where the children reside with a parent or parents. In addition, there are 2 million single-father families in the United States.[26] Far too many children are living in a home where mom and dad have never married each other. There are 11 million people living with an unmarried partner in the United States; 1.2 million of these are living with an unmarried same-sex partner. A total of 41 percent of America's cohabitating households have children under eighteen living in them.[27] These trends will continue as cohabitation becomes more acceptable. George Barna reports that during the period in which they were single, one out of every three adults has lived with someone of the opposite gender other than family members or relatives.[28] A full 44 percent of the nation's adults under the age of thirty-five have cohabitated.[29]

Add to these sobering statistics the current realities of family-time famine, alcoholism, parental pressure and sexual abuse, and it becomes abundantly clear that the emerging generations face life in a relationally broken world that outdoes the broken world of Generation X. These sad facts reveal the source of the "homelessness" so many young people feel.

Alecia Moore lived with her feuding parents until she was seven years old. That was the year her favorite person—her dad—moved

[25]Judith Wallerstein, Julia Lewis and Sandra Blaskeslee, *The Unexpected Legacy of Divorce* (New York: Hyperion, 2000), pp. 162, xxvi, 160, 239.
[26]"Statistics on U.S. Families," Women's Educational Media, <www.womedia.org/taf_statistics _print.htm>.
[27]"Statistics," Alternatives to Marriage Project, <www.unmarried.org/statistics.html>.
[28]"Born Again Adults Less Likely to Co-Habit, Just as Likely to Divorce," *The Barna Update*, August 6, 2001, <www.barna.org/Flexpage.aspx?PageCMD=Print>.
[29]Ibid.

out. She's described her home as being like World War III. Her teenage years were marked by hurt, pain and confusion that manifested themselves in anger and rebellion. Known to teenage music fans as "Pink," Moore sings of her pain as a form of self-therapy. In her song "Family Portrait," she sings:

It ain't easy growin' up in world war III.
Never knowin' what love could be. You'll see,
I don't want love to destroy me like it has done
my family.

Pink's words speak for her generation.

While the long-term fallout is yet to be fully realized, we can be sure that the Millennials will "beget" more of the same as they struggle to understand love, sexuality, commitment, marriage, parenting and other relational issues. Wallerstein has discovered that "the major impact of divorce does not occur during childhood or adolescence. Rather, it rises in adulthood as serious romantic relationships move center stage."[30]

Perhaps *alienation* is the word that best describes this sense of homelessness. Gerard Kelly believes alienation is the most common and strongest thread woven through the tapestry of today's youth culture: "The irony of the 'new global youth club' is that the one thing young people most share the world over is this sense of lostness."[31]

In their challenging book *A Generation Alone*, William Mahedy and Janet Bernardi examine the fallout of these relational realities on Gen-Xers. Mahedy has a background in counseling veterans of the Vietnam War as they struggled with post-traumatic stress disorder. When he began working with students in campus ministry, he realized that many of the students exhibited the same emotional and spiritual difficulties of Vietnam veterans. Their experience of "war" in the home was taking a huge toll.[32] With the Millennials just now entering adult-

---

[30]Wallerstein, *The Unexpected Legacy of Divorce*, p. xxix.
[31]Gerard Kelly, *Retrofuture* (Downers Grove, Ill.: InterVarsity Press, 1999), p. 151.
[32]William Mahedy and Janet Bernardi, *A Generation Alone* (Downers Grove, Ill.: InterVarsity Press, 1994).

hood, we can assume that many will struggle with the same problems Mahedy saw in his students. We can also assume that many will adapt in true postmodern fashion, handling a brokenness that never should have existed in the first place by assimilating and accepting the various types of family breakdown as normal and right. Gone will be any remnants of stigma or immorality associated with divorce, cohabitation, homosexuality, gay marriage, adultery, abuse, infidelity, fornication and a host of other behaviors that lie outside the bounds of God's intention for his gifts of personhood, sexuality, marital covenant, fidelity and family.

Media saturated. My children and their peers are the most media-saturated generation of all time. In a survey conducted in 2003, the Kaiser Family Foundation discovered that 35 percent of children up to six years old have a TV in their bedroom, 27 percent have a VCR or DVD player, one in ten have a videogame player, and 7 percent have a computer. Amazingly, 30 percent of those three and under have a TV in their room.[33] The significance of this media saturation is enormous. For those without positive input from parents and other adults, the media is a surrogate parent. Media's content shapes their worldview. Get to know their media and you're getting to know them.

MTV understood this phenomenon and the unique and powerful role it was playing when the network decided to solicit a new wave of advertising in the early 1990s. The music network ran a print ad that asked readers, "Ever hear anyone refer to the NBC generation?" The bold statement referred to the fact that researchers were calling young people "the MTV generation." The ad's fine print read: "MTV is not a TV channel. It's a cultural force. People don't watch it. They live it. MTV has affected the way an entire generation thinks, talks, and buys."

In addition to shaping *what* they think, the media is shaping *how* they think, and thereby distinguishing them even further from previous generations. Millennials are passive, easily bored, uneasy with quiet, often impatient and expectant of immediate gratification. Me-

---

[33] "New Study Finds Children Age Zero to Six Spend as Much Time with TV, Computers and Video Games as Playing Outside," Kaiser Family Foundation, October 28, 2003 <www.Kff.org/ent-media/entmedia102803nr.cfm?RenderForPrint=1>.

dia saturation has led them to be less word-oriented and more visually engaged by images. Educators note an overall decrease in their verbal and written skills. Gerard Kelly calls these kids "screenagers," a phenomenon he describes as "a generation so impacted by the transition to postliteracy that image has taken precedence over word."[34] This means they are communicating, learning, perceiving and processing information in new and different ways.

Experience- and feeling-driven. Lucky Strike cigarettes have been around for ages. When my grandfather was young, the brand was marketed with the same slogan that's being used today: "Lucky Strike Means Fine Tobacco." But as we have shifted from the modernity to postmodernity, Lucky Strike's advertising changed. For my grandfather's generation and the next two that followed, Lucky Strike's advertisers appealed to the mind, thinking, "When faced with a choice, smokers will choose our better tobacco." Fast-forward to the new millennium. A recent print ad for the brand featured only the foil top of a Lucky Strike pack set against a dark background. Stamped on the foil are the initials "L.S./M.F.T." All that's left of the slogan are its initials, leaving uninformed readers to wonder, *What do those initials mean?* However, readers don't have to wonder long. Featured prominently beneath the foil top near the center of the ad is "What does it mean to you?" In other words, it means whatever the reader *feels* it should mean.

Void of any objective, universally held standards of truth and morality, young people are left to make decisions based on how they *feel.* What it means to me now may not be what it will mean to me tomorrow. It all depends on how I feel. One of Diet Coke's most recent marketing campaigns seizes on this postmodern bent toward feelings and experience. "You get a good feeling from great taste without the calories," reads the ad. "Do something with it. Do what feels good."

The determining standard is what *works* for me and what *feels* good at this moment. Kelly refers to this as "an increasing hunger for experience." He believes that in the consumer world—the world of

---

[34]Kelly, *Retrofuture,* p. 96.

our children—the experience of buying actually becomes more important than the product purchased.

What is true in commerce and industry is also increasingly true in leisure, in relationships and in religion—it is *experience* rather than *content* that provides the criteria by which a social transaction is evaluated. The generations of the post-industrial twenty-first century will increasingly evaluate every product, including public faith, in terms of their experience of it.[35]

Suspicious of truth. Young people are suspicious of Christianity for the simple reason that it claims to be true. We shouldn't be surprised that those who make no claims to faith reject Christianity. But it's alarming to see the number of *Christian* young people who accept some aspects of biblical truth while rejecting others. George Barna reports that in 2001, 33 percent of U.S. teenagers claim to be born again. When pressed, only 4 percent of teenagers claim to be born again and also believe in "the accuracy of the Bible, personal responsibility to evangelize, believe in salvation by grace alone, and possess orthodox biblical views on God, Jesus and Satan." Barna says "there is evidence that spirituality has been mainstreamed into teen life without radically affecting the lifestyles and values of most teens."[36] If left unchecked, these beliefs and the rejection of truth will lead to personal and societal chaos.

Overwhelming options. Every aspect of postmodern youth's lives is filled with a growing number of options regarding everything from clothes to food to cars to lifestyles. The college dining hall serves as a powerful example of how extensive the choices have become.

During my undergraduate years at Geneva College, my choices were limited to two or three options at each meal. Salads were pre-prepared, but we were able to choose from three dressings. When my daughter Caitlin headed off to her freshman year at Geneva twenty-eight years later, the dining hall had been reconfigured to accommo-

---

[35]Ibid., pp. 28, 69.
[36]George Barna, "Teens Change Their Tune Regarding Self and Church," *The Barna Update*, April 23, 2002 <www.barna.org/cgi-bin/PagePressRelease.asp?/PressReleaseID=111&Reference=E&Key=youth>.

date the amazing amount of culinary options. I was overwhelmed by the changes. There were four or five menu options in the main line. Another line served up sandwiches and wraps constructed according to the student's wishes. There was a pizza bar and an ice cream freezer that rivaled Baskin and Robbins. Omelets were made to order. The salad bar seemed endless and the days of three dressing choices were long gone. Instead of five or six choices of breakfast cereals, there were dozens. But talk to today's students about the food and many complain that there isn't enough variety. Are they being selfish and unappreciative? Not consciously. Compared to what they're used to, the world of the dining hall is certainly limited in its choices.

A recent ad marketing Nokia cell phones accurately trumpets the fact that "people like choices." The ad sells a phone that comes with a variety of additional "fashionable faceplates" that snap on and off, facilitating a quick change in the phone's appearance and color. Six different photos feature a model striking the same pose, but each time wearing a different colored dress with a phone to match. Readers are invited to "choose the one that fits you."

The problem with these many options is that we aren't likely to develop loyalty to any one product, behavior or idea. Charles Colson describes this when he notes that since postmodernism insists that all ideas are equally valid, "then no idea is really worth our allegiance; nothing is worth living or dying for—or even arguing about."[37] With so many choices and forces coming at them from every direction, it is inevitable that today's emerging generations are constantly changing their values and behaviors. Consistency and stability are absent both individually and collectively in a world where there are no absolutes.

Globalized youth culture. Just eight years after the fall of the Berlin Wall I traveled to Eastern Europe to speak about contemporary youth culture. I had been invited by Youth for Christ to train their European staff. Initially, I balked at the invitation, wondering what I might be able to teach them. Their staff spoke several languages. They came from a wide range of political, economic and historical contexts. But

---

[37]Charles Colson, *How Now Shall We Live?* (Wheaton, Ill.: Tyndale House, 1999), p. 23.

their leadership was convinced that if I spoke about North American youth culture, it would be relevant to their situations. Even though I decided to go, I was still hesitant about my ability to connect. After spending only a few hours in the Polish conference center, I knew that we have effectively exported our North American youth culture to the world.

After checking in to the hotel, I went to my room and was shocked to see a brightly colored Disney bed set. I asked one of the hotel staff if I was mistakenly placed in a child's room. She enthusiastically said, "No, all our rooms look like that. We love your Walt Disney!"

I went back to my room, climbed into bed and set the clock radio. When the radio woke me, I thought for a minute I was waking up at home. The song blaring from the radio was Aerosmith's "Janie Got a Gun." After showering, I turned on the small black-and-white TV and found the one station broadcasting in the area. To my surprise the show was *Married with Children*. I was shocked.

Our export success was further confirmed throughout the week as I spoke to the audience of youth workers. While every word I spoke had to be translated into over a dozen languages, the heads nodding in agreement confirmed that North American marketing had effectively spread our youth culture's products, values and worldview around the world.

Pervaded by violence. Violence and bullying are major problems affecting the youth population. Schools and communities have had to create programs to address this reality. The root causes are many. Traditional support systems have failed. Young people are hurried and stressed. They are angry. Many have been raised by a steady diet of media violence that encourages aggressive solutions to their problems. In a postmodern world increasingly void of moral restraints, many young people see violence as a valid way to solve their problems.

The story of fifteen-year-old Kip Kinkel's 1998 shooting rampage offers compelling evidence of our culture's violent bent. After killing his parents, he killed two of his Springfield, Oregon, classmates and wounded over twenty more. Kids knew Kinkel desired to shoot cats, kill people, build bombs and blow up the world. One journalist even discovered that students in Kinkel's literature class laughed when he read them a journal entry about his plans to "kill everybody." During investigations after the shooting, Kinkel's teachers said they hadn't reacted with alarm since *a lot of kids in the school and around the country were saying the same things.* In other words, killing talk has become so commonplace that it doesn't shake us up anymore.

Crime and violence may be the biggest problem faced by the emerging generations, particularly in North America. That reality struck me in a brief conversation I shared with a mother in Northern Ireland. While I was standing on a Belfast street corner, waiting for the traffic light to change, I turned to a woman—who was standing with a teenage girl—and asked, "What is it like to be raising your daughter in this place that has been riddled with violence for so many years?" Without hesitation she answered, "Your accent tells me where you're from. I can only tell you that I'd much rather raise my daughter here in Belfast, than in your country. You are from the most violent and dangerous nation on the face of the earth." I was stunned by her answer.

Violence has created a youth culture that lives in fear. Sometimes that fear serves as a catalyst for further violence, when the victim becomes a perpetrator in order to survive. Those who feel powerless will seek power. For some, that power comes through involvement in the occult or Wicca. Others may choose to respond through violent means. Still others choose to inflict violence on themselves. The recent rise in teenage self-injury (also known as "cutting") is a way that young people deal with their emotional pain. The most extreme form of self-inflicted violence is suicide—the horror of death is actually more attractive than the everyday horror of their lives.

Pushed, hurried and frazzled. Recently, a story about a local soccer team caught my attention. It told of the team's success at an invitational tournament 400 miles away. The tournament featured Junior Olympic Development teams from across the country. These were young people who had their sights set on developing into world-class soccer players. But as I read, I began to wonder if it was the kids or the parents whose sights were set on soccer greatness. You see, the team was an under-six team. These kids were barely into kindergarten and they were already playing high-pressure soccer, most likely on fields surrounded by screaming parents.

When asked, "What are the biggest problems Millennials face?" Howe and Strauss respond, "Pressure. On Time. On achievement. On living up to the high expectations of adults and friends."[38] Pressure from parents, teachers and themselves is constant; there is a fear of being left behind. Their lives are sometimes structured to the point where there is little "free time."

The pressure is typically applied to "encourage" young people to achieve greatness in three primary areas. First, there's the academic pressure and the goal of getting into the "right" college. It's one step toward a career that promises a lifetime of "success." Second, there's the pressure to achieve athletically. Our culture worships athletes as heroes. Third, there's the pressure to be beautiful. This is fueled by a media and marketing machine that promises redemption through makeup, clothing and hair products.

When asked what they are bothered about the most, teenagers say they are most anxious about grades, having enough money, how they look and planning for their future.[39] Gone are the days of just "hanging out" after school. Kids no longer have time to just be kids.

2. *Materialistic.* Since the Fall, humans have worshiped and served "created things rather than the Creator" (Rom 1:25). But the materialism of the emerging generations is set apart from previous generations in its form and function.

In the early 1990s culture critics speculated that the "Me Decade" fueled by Reaganomics was over. As a result, it was assumed the emerging generations would be far less materialistic and selfish than previous generations. Social scientists who predicted this change failed to take into account three factors that would render their predictions wrong. First, self-centeredness and sin are timeless problems that infect the human heart. The emerging generations are no different than prior generations in their basic longings. Second, the emerg-

---

[38] "Q&As from Howe and Strauss, authors of *Millennials Rising*," <www.millennialsrising.com/qa.shtml>.
[39] Peter Zollo, *Wise Up to Teens* (Ithaca, N.Y.: New Strategist, 1999), p. 228.

ing generations have a higher amount of discretionary income than prior generations. Third, marketers have increased their marketing efforts. The emerging generations have more money and more choices, and are influenced by marketing more than prior generations. And the greater the emerging generations' spiritual emptiness, the more they are prone to fill the void with material goods.

Street wise. The differences between generations became painfully obvious through observing the responses of parents and their children to identical media stimuli. Take the highly publicized and thoroughly analyzed 2004 Super Bowl halftime show produced by MTV.

My family was watching the game and the halftime show. As is my normal practice, I was giving a running commentary during the show in an effort to help my kids think critically about what they were seeing and hearing from the media. My kids endure my rants as one of the liabilities of having a cultural analyst for a dad. About halfway through the show, I commented on Nelly's performance, complete with a series of crotch grabs that for some performers have become normal, macho hip-hop fare. Nelly's antics, combined with those of the dancers moving to the beat of his anthem "Hot in Here," prompted my comment that this is why Islamists are so upset with the United States and our constant display of moral filth. Their world is different from mine. That fact was certainly undeniable when just a few minutes later, Justin Timberlake tugged at Janet Jackson's wardrobe to expose her right breast before a live television audience of millions. My kids' comments—"Come on, Dad. It's only a halftime show" and "He's only singing a song"—are not unique to them. They represent their entire generation, a generation that's seen it all, done much of it and is lacking in the naiveté of previous generations.

This reality became abundantly clear to me when three years ago I spoke on contemporary media influence to a group of doctoral students in a seminary classroom, which included baby boomer and Gen-X pastors. I watched their reactions as they screened an episode of *Jackass,* an MTV program of young adult males engaging in a variety of high-risk stunts that often results in broken bones, blood and vomiting. The older members of the class had difficulty watching. One gentleman even removed his glasses and looked away. On the other end of the spectrum were the young men in the room who had been raised watching this sort of thing. They laughed so hard at some of the stunts that they were crying. Their familiarity had long since desensitized them to the shock.

Sadly, there is little the emerging generations haven't already seen or heard. Typically, they are more tolerant of the behaviors previous generations find to be immoral or shocking. Familiarity breeds acceptance.

Concerned with appearance. Magazine covers are a window into the soul of the emerging generations. They reveal the cares, concerns and aspirations that consume our kids and fuel their consumption. Our teens are obsessed with appearance. The standard is set by a never-ending parade of magazines that send the unmistakable message: "you're only as good as you look."

A 2003 edition of Twist, a magazine popular among middle-school girls, featured a cover photo of three media heroes: Beyonce Knowles, Cameron Diaz and Kate Hudson. Their images are surrounded by words that tell readers what "paths to happiness" they will find inside. "What Guys Find Irresistible," "Magical Makeup, Sensational Smiles, Lustrous Looks," "Foolproof Flirting Secrets: Celeb Tested, Guy Approved," "Trends on Trial: Today's Hottest Styles: Do's and Don'ts." The cover also touts "Free Style Cards" and the inclusion of a "Sexy Centerfold" of male heartthrob Justin Timberlake.[40]

A recent edition of Men's Health serves as a good example of the appearance orientation of young guys. A chiseled male model stands hip deep in water. He has muscles everywhere. The cover reveals that inside, readers can find the following life-shaping secrets: "Lose Your Gut! A Beach-ready Body in 15 Days," "23 Fat-burning Superfoods," "Build Great Biceps Fast," "Dress for More Sex," and "Sure Signs She Wants You."[41]

The constant barrage of these images and messages has left a deep impression on children and teens. The fact that they have come to

---

[40]Twist, September 2003.
[41]Men's Health, August 2003.

value the outward over the inward is evident in their obsessions with clothing, make-up, hair, dieting and body image. Their continued dissatisfaction with themselves and growing emptiness are evident in the ever-growing epidemic of eating disorders. This is a generation preoccupied with and defined by their exteriors. For them, "what I see, is what I am."

Despairing and hopeless. There is a general sense among researchers that the post-Xer generation is more hopeful and optimistic, and will set the world on fire with their enthusiastic activism. Howe and Strauss say:

> Surveys show that—compared to Xer teens a decade ago— today's teens are more upbeat about the world in which they are growing up. Nine in ten describe themselves as "happy," "confident," and "positive." A rapidly decreasing share worry about violence, sex, or drugs—and a rapidly increasing share say that growing up is easier for them than it was for their parents. Teen suicide rates are now falling for the first time in decades.[42]

Granted, many of our young people are concerned with and active in causes including environmentalism and global peace. But my sense is that the researchers are being far too optimistic. I say this for several reasons. First, it's presently difficult to compare and contrast the Xers and Millennials. Xers have been adults for some time, and researchers conducted longitudinal studies looking back over their entire lives. The research was reflective. In contrast, the research on Millennials, the oldest of whom are just entering adulthood, is predictive. With many of the more destructive social trends that negatively affected the Xers still present and on the rise, are we to assume that these same trends won't have a similar effect on succeeding generations? I agree with Gerard Kelly's prediction that the Millennials will be "more X than X."[43]

Second, Howe and Strauss's paradigm is built on historical examinations of generations that grew and developed in times shaped by

---

[42]Howe and Strauss, *Millennials Rising,* pp. 7-8.
[43]Kelly, *Retrofuture,* p. 40.

the modern worldview. The Millennials have grown up in a world and culture shaped by the more nihilistic postmodern worldview. One is hard-pressed to understand how postmodernity can foster a deeply ingrained spirit of hope and optimism.

Third, we hope our children will grow up to make the world a better place. But our hope may cause us to mistake youthful idealism for a more mature and lasting reality. Optimism is important, but we shouldn't be so optimistic that it blinds us to reality. From a biblical perspective, hope not placed in the one, true Creator and God of the universe, is only an empty hope that can never weather the reality of the storms of life.

My analysis is confirmed in the results of a Harris Interactive/Kid Power Poll. As part of the survey, a group of 643 Millennials were asked to compare themselves to Gen-Xers. The poll discovered that today's teens say they are (1) more stressed and busy—75 percent, (2) more unsupervised—69 percent, (3) more depressed—68 percent, (4) more angry—64 percent, (5) more rebellious—63 percent, (6) more selfish and self-centered—59 percent, (7) more immature—50 percent, (8) more distrustful of adults—50 percent, and (9) more unstructured in their upbringing—50 percent.[44] If these answers accurately reflect the emerging generation, the reality is they are less than hopeful.

There is a symbiotic relationship between despair and the postmodern worldview. Despair leads youth to embrace postmodernism. Postmodernism feeds the notion that there is no hope. Gerard Kelly recognizes this relationship: "Despair and hedonism, suicide and escape—in reality these are two sides of the same coin of angst, and postmodernity is providing more and more places to spend it."[45]

While the younger members of the emerging generations may appear to have "hope" today, it cannot be a lasting and truly meaningful hope unless it is built on the foundation of a restored relationship with their Creator through Jesus Christ. Francis Schaeffer's work sheds more

[Handwritten marginal notes: "True but what it means is a hope in something absolute. Need to recapture the possibility of absolute. Need to challenge the presupposition that there were no absolute. Need to come up w/ an apologetic."]

[44]John Geraci, Dana Markow and Osa Hirsch, "Harris Interactive/Kid Power Poll of Youth Marketers: Summary Report," Harris Interactive, 2004 <www.harrisinteractive.com/expertise/pubs/KidPower_Poll_Results.pdf>.
[45]Kelly, Retrofuture, p. 119.

light on this fact. Schaeffer believes that when society stopped believing in absolutes, it slipped below "the line of despair." But even though society has slipped below the line of despair, its members might not yet consciously manifest hopelessness, despondency, and emotional anguish. In Schaeffer's thinking, "They have given up the expectation of giving a rational basis to their hopes and values, but they may not yet have experienced the full significance and implications of this. They may continue to function very well with such a situation."[46]

Deeply spiritual. Today's young people are wearing their interest in spiritual things on their sleeves. This interest can be seen in film and television. It can be heard in the music. Spirituality is everywhere. But they are increasingly disinterested in conventional religion, especially Christianity.[47]

With its deemphasis on rationality, postmodernity has reawakened a cultural interest in and fascination with all things spiritual. In true postmodern fashion the spirituality of today's emerging generations is entirely subjective, with each person choosing elements from a variety of faith systems and incorporating them into their own "religion." Even though those elements may be highly incompatible or mutually exclusive, it doesn't seem to bother Millennials.

Gerard Kelly offers a helpful summary of what he calls a "Gods R Us post-Christian spirituality."

- The primary influence on popular spirituality is no longer orthodox Christianity.
- In its place, new generic spiritualities are emerging that prioritize personal experience, pluralism and self-made creeds.
- The influence of these perspectives is pervasive, touching many who do not call themselves religious and sparking a revival in spirituality.
- The new emphasis on spirituality will shape the way individuals choose and express a faith, but will also impact the way in which

---

[46]Francis Schaeffer, cited in Millard J. Erickson, *Postmodernizing the Faith: Evangelical Responses to the Challenge of Postmodernism* (Grand Rapids: Baker, 1998), p. 67.
[47]See Borgman, *When Kumbaya Is Not Enough*, p. 32.

popular culture perceives and judges the Christian church.[48]

Pluralism and relativism mark the faith of the emerging generations. This personalized, postmodern, "whatever" spirituality is captured in the words of Hoobastank's song "Same Direction":

> So why does there only have to be one correct philosophy?
> I don't want to go and follow you just to end up like one of them.
> And why are you always telling me what you want me to believe?
> I'd like to think that I can *So, you can find infinite truth?*
> Go my own way and meet you in the end

17. *Crying out for redemption.* At the root of the Millennials' groan is a deep hunger for God that is a natural part of being made in God's image. They are separated from him and don't know how to reconnect. Every other aspect of their brokenness is rooted in this separation. Consequently, we must do all we can engage them in ways they can hear and understand, pointing them to the redemptive and transforming message of the cross.

The emerging generations stand confused at a crossroads. Which way should they go? We must stand with them and point them in the right direction.

---

[48]Kelly, *Retrofuture*, p. 164.

5

UNDERSTANDING CULTURE

I GREW UP IN PENNSYLVANIA. I went to college in Pennsylvania. You might assume from those two facts that my choice to stay in my home state would make my transition to college life a bit more easy, but that wasn't the case. My difficulty was rooted in the fact that even though I was attending college in my home state, I had moved to a place that felt like another world.

In August 1974, when we loaded up the family car to head to college, my familiar, "normal" surroundings of shared habits, customs and passions in suburban Philadelphia became a thing of the past. Our drive took us 325 miles west. Geneva College was located in Beaver Falls, a small town north of Pittsburgh. Not long after my parents got in the car to head back home, I realized my childhood was rather limited in scope. I had been used to the soft rolling hills of eastern Pennsylvania. For the next four years I would be hiking up and down the steep hills that marked our campus and all of western Pennsylvania's terrain. At night I would lie in my room listening to the rumble of freight trains echoing through the valley as they carried steel and coal. I was breathing air that carried a unique blend of unfamiliar odors from the many factories and steel mills that dotted the area. Cars were sometimes covered in rust from overexposure to the salt that kept the roads ice-free during the cold and snowy months.

When I'd proudly wear insignias of my beloved Philly sports teams, I was ridiculed by the native Pittsburgh fans. In my new world, people thought I was crazy for putting mustard on my pretzels, yet they put ketchup on their eggs! A cheesesteak was something they had never heard of. They would laugh when I talked about eating hoagies; they ate subs. When I'd ask for a soda, I'd get a funny look. They drank pop. Scrapple was something they had never heard of. Their neighborhoods looked markedly different from the one I knew as a child. And if I summoned a new friend with "Yo!" I would get a befuddled look. In the midst of western Pennsylvania normalcy, I was suddenly out of step and abnormal.

My adjustment to moving into another culture would have been much easier if I had understood the differences that exist among cultures and the function that culture plays in our lives. Those called to engage the emerging generations with the message of the gospel must approach their calling as crosscultural missionaries. Like my move across the state, they move from an adult culture to the unfamiliar world of postmodern youth. Their world is not our world. Their culture is not our culture.

If we answer God's call to the mission field of the emerging generations, we will experience two inescapable realities. First, our journey will be crosscultural in nature. Second, we will experience culture shock. But the level and intensity of that shock can be buffered by taking the time to understand culture and how it functions.

As the new and different postmodern culture unfolds around us, God's people unfamiliar with this new way of thinking and living must get beyond an uninformed "we're right and they're wrong" approach that inevitably leads to their forfeiting positive influence and engagement for the sake of the gospel. Instead, we must develop a set of skills that help us to listen to the emerging generations, understand them and their world, and then reach them with an explanation of the gospel that takes into account, understands and uses the familiar language, categories and concepts unique to their culture.

In the first four chapters of this book, we've examined the rapidly changing, postmodern world. Each of us is responsible to know not only the broad outlines of postmodernity but also how it is subtly changing as it develops, and how it is affecting the individual young people God places in our lives.[1] According to Dean Borgman, one of our main tasks "is to make divine revelation (the Bible and especially Jesus Christ) relevant and coherent to any particular age and society. To fulfill that task with regard to young people, we must learn a great deal about culture."[2] We must become like "the men of Issachar, who understood the times and knew what Israel should do" (1 Chron 12:32). Missions theorist Sherwood Lingenfelter says that "we must be learners and let them teach us before we can hope to teach them and introduce them to the master Teacher."[3]

What Is Culture?

Our first meeting took place in the foyer of the church back in the mid-90s, and was planned by a mutual friend who knew we shared an interest in the music of Marilyn Manson. I was there to speak and was dressed in my typical "speak to a group of conservative adults" attire—khaki pants, button-down shirt, tie and navy blue blazer. As I stood reading a bulletin board, I heard a friend greet Bekah as she entered the room. I spun around in time to see him point Bekah in my direction and say, "There's Walt over there. Let me take you over to meet him." As Bekah, a recent convert to Christianity, turned in my direction I quickly realized that Marilyn Manson had played a very significant role in her life. She was dressed from head to toe in Gothic-style black clothing and accessories. Her bare arms revealed a series of large and interesting tattoos. Her extremely short hair was colored or-

---

[1] We can reasonably assume that the same postmodern worldview will shape subsequent generations in similar but not totally identical ways. The rapid nature of change will continue to create differences between generations. It will remain the responsibility of God's people to listen to and understand the emerging generations. The principles laid out in this book will remain relevant in our quest to understand and engage any culture to which we are called to minister.
[2] Dean Borgman, *When Kumbaya Is Not Enough* (Peabody, Mass.: Hendrickson, 1997), p. xiii.
[3] Sherwood G. Lingenfelter and Marvin K. Mayers, *Ministering Cross-Culturally: An Incarnational Model for Personal Relationships*, 2nd ed. (Grand Rapids: Baker Books, 2003), p. 22.

ange. Her black eye-liner set her eyes deep into her lily-white face. Those eyes were looking me up and down, and it was obvious from her silence that she couldn't imagine how a middle-aged man dressed like me could have any knowledge of or interest in any type of popular music, let alone hers.

She took a step back as she cynically asked, "You're the guy who's written about Marilyn Manson?" I answered in the affirmative. "Have you ever listened to any of his music?" she asked in doubt. "Yes," I replied. I then proceeded to name every one of his albums and mentioned individual songs that I had found to be especially interesting. The more I talked, the closer she moved toward me. Eventually, we wound up sitting on a bench discussing her music, her life and her story. By the end of a long conversation we were friends.

When we parted ways, even though we both spoke English and shared a common faith in God, we understood that we had just met someone from a different culture. Permission to enter Bekah's world was given to me only because I had listened to and understood her culture. Even though I could have let her appearance put me off, I wasn't frightened or threatened by it.[4]

Culture is what we believe, what we do and how we live our lives from day to day. It binds us to those who think and live in a similar manner. John Stott describes *culture* as "a tapestry, intricate and often beautiful, which is woven by a given society to express its corporate identity."[5] Bill Romanowski offers a simpler and more direct definition: "culture refers to the way that we define and live in God's world." It is "a collection of ideals and beliefs, values and assumptions, that makes up a kind of master plan for living and interpreting life."[6] For our purposes, culture is the "soup" the emerging generations swim in

---

[4]Because the differences between Bekah and myself were visually obvious, our encounter was unmistakably crosscultural in nature. At times, the temptation for those working with the emerging generations is to *wrongly* assume—consciously or unconsciously—that the absence of obvious outward differences other than one's age means that few, if any, inward or attitudinal cultural differences exist. It is important to understand and approach *all* encounters and relationships with members of the emerging generations as crosscultural in nature as their values, attitudes and behaviors are being shaped by the predominant emerging worldview.
[5]John Stott, *The Lausanne Covenant* (Minneapolis: World Wide Publications, 1975), p. 26.
[6]William D. Romanowski, *Eyes Wide Open* (Grand Rapids: Brazos, 2001), pp. 36, 42.

every day.[7] Consequently, if we want to engage the young for the sake of the gospel, we'd better take the time to know what's in the soup.

In one of our local restaurants, the soup bar typically features three selections. I've watched how people choose their soup. As they arrive at the bar, they grab a bowl. Then they step back and scan the names of the soups in each of the large soup tureens. Before placing soup in their bowl, they lift the lid off the tureen, stir the soup, lift the ladle and examine the soup's ingredients. If they like what they see, they fill their bowl.

If we are to effectively engage our children with the truths of the gospel, we must step up to their world, lift the lid, and look carefully at the unique and ever-changing mix of cultural elements they "swim" in. We can't escape the reality that those elements, as strange and frightening as they may seem—shape their worldview and govern their lives. We might even be tempted to close the lid because we don't like what we see. But if we hope to effectively communicate the good news, we can't avoid the ingredients of that culture.

The Characteristics of Culture

What are the main characteristics of culture? First, we must understand that culture has been created by God and given to humanity to use and enjoy. In the book of Genesis, we read that God made humans in his own image (Gen 1:26-27) and gave them the responsibility to enjoy, care for and develop all he had made (Gen 2:15). Theologian Al Wolters says:

> People must now carry on the work of development: by being fruitful they must fill it even more; by subduing it they must form it even more. Mankind, as God's representatives on earth, carry on where God left off. But this is now to be a *human* development of the earth. The human race will fill the earth with its own kind, and it will form the earth for its own kind.[8]

---

[7]For a more technical definition of *culture* see Harold Netland, *Encountering Religious Pluralism* (Downers Grove, Ill.: InterVarsity Press, 2001), p. 328.
[8]Albert M. Wolters, *Creation Regained* (Grand Rapids: Eerdmans, 1985), p. 36.

Engage presentation

In effect, "we are called to participate in the ongoing creational work of God, to be God's helper in executing to the end the blueprint for his masterpiece."[9] Our creativity results and is expressed in human culture. Culture is the good gift of God entrusted to us to develop as responsible stewards.

Second, culture is universal. While culture differs from place to place and time to time, everyone participates and shares in culture.[10] Where there are people, there is culture. Both the songwriter who prayerfully constructs her music to the glory of God *and* the unredeemed songwriter who brings glory to himself are making culture. Bill Romanowski says that "culture is our common human endeavor, a historical process carried on from generation to generation that binds us together in the community of humankind."[11]

Third, culture is shared[12] as a system for living by those in a particular society. The same is true for subcultures within a society. A visit to a local high school would reveal that while there is a general culture of students sharing values, attitudes and behaviors, there are also unique subcultures: the band kids, the athletes, the scholars, the Goths and the cowboys. Each particular group is marked by a unique mix of beliefs and behaviors that bind them together and distinguish them from others. Each individual finds identity and security in a particular group.

Fourth, culture is learned. Missiologist David Hesselgrave points out that culture "is not biologically determined or restricted by race."[13] We unconsciously assimilate the culture that surrounds us. It becomes normal to us because "it's always been that way." But in the postmodern world of globalized media promoting numerous options, young people are consciously choosing to adopt cultures and subcultures that are markedly different from those they've been raised in. There's the rural farmboy who's never set foot in an urban

---

[9]Ibid., p. 38.
[10]David J. Hesselgrave, *Communicating Christ Cross-Culturally,* 2nd ed. (Grand Rapids: Zondervan, 1991), p. 100.
[11]Romanowski, *Eyes Wide Open,* p. 49.
[12]Hesselgrave, *Communicating Christ Cross-Culturally,* p. 100.
[13]Ibid.

ghetto, but who talks, dresses and lives like a hip-hop gangsta.

Fifth, culture is an integrated whole.[14] Like a living organism, culture's different parts are interrelated. Each part affects the others. If a culture places high value on human life, that will be reflected in its human relations, in its medical and business practices, and so on. If humanity is devalued, that will be reflected as well. In a postmodern world where contradictions aren't an issue or problem, culture is increasingly marked by the consistency of inconsistency. The responsibility of the cultural observer is to discover and understand each part of the cultural soup and how those parts combine as a whole.

Sixth, culture isn't static. Cultures evolve as the years go by. They develop new elements on their own, assimilate elements of other cultures and discard those elements that are either outdated or no longer necessary. Consequently, those who desire to understand the culture of the emerging generations can never assume that their job is done. Every minute brings change.

Two Levels of Culture

As the missionary to the emerging generations stirs the soup, there are certain ingredients to look for. While they might seem small and insignificant, these ingredients offer us valuable insight into who young people are and how we can best reach them with the gospel.

A simple illustration from my time in youth ministry reveals the need to examine two levels that exist in every culture. Our son Josh was only three years old and loved coming with me to youth group. On one occasion our group was on a winter youth retreat. I walked outside to find the guys showing Josh how to make and throw a snowball. Knowing I was watching, Josh's instructors told him to start throwing snowballs at the girls. At that point I felt a responsibility to step in and explain to Josh why this was a "bad" thing. Josh understood that "bad" meant it was wrong and he was to stop.

A short time later, the guys decided to play basketball, so they took

---

[14]Ibid.

Josh with them into the gym. He was impressive enough in his drib-
bling skills to get everyone staring. One of the guys enthusiastically
said, "That's *so* bad!" Just minutes before, I had reprimanded Josh by
using the word *bad* to describe behavior I didn't want to see from him.
Now, Josh's behavior was being described with the same word, only
this time it meant the exact opposite.

This illustration exemplifies two cultural ingredients that we should
look for. There is the level of culture that we can empirically observe
every day. In my illustration, it is the spoken word *bad*. But there is a
deeper level. The second, foundational level lies beneath what we observe. It is the underlying meaning. I used *bad* to indicate to Josh that
his behavior was wrong and it should stop. My young friend used *bad*
to indicate that Josh's behavior was good and it should continue.

Our examination of *both* levels of cultural helps us not only understand the meaning of the outward expressions of another culture that
are unfamiliar to us but also the tension that exists when the same
expression—whether a word, behavior and so on—is used and understood by different people from different cultures in different ways.

Cultural analyst Patty Lane likens these two levels to an iceberg. The
"objective culture," or observable parts of the culture, are the part of
the iceberg that can be seen above the water's surface. The hidden aspect that lies beneath the surface is what Lane calls the "subjective
culture." "This is the internal part of culture that drives or motivates
the visible, objective culture."[15] I've found it helpful to understand
these two levels this way: the underlying level of a culture is best described as a *worldview,* and the visible level is best described as what
the *world views* when it observes everyday life. It includes everything
we do and make. Because it is visible, it's easier to recognize and describe, but it can be strange and difficult to understand. Sometimes,
our assumptions about the meaning beneath what we see can be totally off base, thereby jeopardizing our ability to connect. Patty Lane
refers to this as "misattribution." It's the tendency to assume or assign

---

[15]Patty Lane, *A Beginner's Guide to Crossing Cultures* (Downers Grove, Ill.: InterVarsity Press,
2002), pp. 18-22.

our own meanings and motives to someone's behavior.[16] If we fall into this trap, we will miss what those meanings and motives really are.

My friend Bekah and her tattoos serve as a powerful example. Bekah wears her objective culture up and down her arms. I'm sure that most adults Bekah encounters misattribute what her tattoos mean and why she has them. At first glance, some might think that the markings on Bekah's body are repulsive, meaningless, faddish and something she will regret later in life. If that's the case, we've fallen into the trap of misattribution and we won't come close to understanding Bekah or her culture. But if we take the time to probe deeper by asking Bekah about the meaning of her tattoos, we would learn the truth about her.

When I asked Bekah to tell me about her tattoos, her eyes lit up. My question and her excited response indicated two things. First, it told Bekah that I had an interest in her. She knew that I cared about her. Second, it told me that Bekah's tattoos meant something important to her.

I listened carefully as Bekah, pointing from one tattoo to the next, took me on a tour of significant events in her chaotic life. Bekah never knew what the next day would bring. But she did know that each morning those tattoos would be there for her. In many ways, her tattoos are the most permanent things in her life.

One tattoo really caught my attention. On her left shoulder were the words "God Help the Outcast." Bekah told me she had gotten this, her newest tattoo, after seeing the Disney film *The Hunchback of Notre Dame*. She explained that in the film the scorned gypsy characters sing "God Help the Outcasts" as a prayer for deliverance from their pain and suffering. As the characters sang, Bekah was reduced to emotional rubble; their words reflected her own desire to be released from her aloneness and brokenness:

God help the outcasts, hungry from birth.
Show them the mercy they don't find on Earth. . . .
God help the outcasts or nobody will.

---

[16]Ibid., p. 27.

Later that night Bekah's heart was gripped by God and she came to faith. Within hours she was at the tattoo parlor getting the song's title stamped on her shoulder. The tattoo is a permanent reminder of the night that God transformed her life.

After we had looked at this, her latest tattoo, Bekah pulled down the collar on her shirt, pointed at a bare spot between her shoulders, and said, "This is where I'm going to get my last tattoo. It's going to be three simple words—'Jesus Loves Me.' " I asked her about what this tattoo would mean to her. "It's the last tattoo I'll ever need," she said. "It represents the last chapter and the end of the story that my tattoos tell. My life is now complete." I was moved. To understand what I saw on her arms I had to know about the world beneath the skin-deep ink. Once I knew that world, I better understood and knew Bekah.

The subjective level of the postmodern culture is being expressed in the objective culture in a variety of ways. We must look for and analyze those behaviors that will give us further insight into who young people are, how they think and how they live. The following list highlights a few of the objective ingredients in the youth-culture soup that warrant our attention. Like Bekah's tattoos, each can give us great insight into their culture.

- language and slang
- mannerisms, gestures and habits
- dress and clothing style, piercings, tattoos, body markings
- facial expressions
- peer group, social organization and hierarchy
- music, radio stations and preferences
- movies and television shows
- books and magazines
- modes of transportation
- hobbies and interests
- extracurricular school activities

- heroes and role models
- art
- jobs
- websites
- food preferences
- favorite places
- spending habits
- observable behaviors
- time management

The Functions of Culture

As a child I loved to spend afternoons swimming in my friend Stuart's pool. Jumping out of the steamy summer air into the cool, clear water was heavenly. We'd swim for hours on end. When I'd head home for dinner, the effects of the pool were obvious. My body was dripping wet. My eyes were reddened from the pool's chlorine. And my fingertips were shriveled like raisins.

Swimming in the soup of today's postmodern culture isn't any different, except for the fact that our kids are in it twenty-four hours a day. To assume that culture has no influence or effect on them would be to misunderstand who they are and ultimately forfeit our ministry effectiveness.

Culture is a map. Developmentally, youth are living in a period marked by more earth-shaking change and uncertainty than they'll ever experience again. They wonder what is happening to them and where all the change is leading. Consequently, they are continually looking for a map to guide them along the way.

Unfolding before their eyes in today's world is the map of postmodernity. The map clearly guides them at both objective and subjective levels, effectively teaching them what to think and how to live in the world. The culture defines and shapes their reason for getting up in the morning, and guides their decisions on how to spend their day once they're out of bed.[17] While culture's mapping influence is always strong, our current Western cultural situation has created an environment where the volume has been turned up on culture's power to shape and teach the emerging generations. In today's world, music and media are stepping in and fulfilling the role increasingly abandoned by parents who are either physically absent by choice or circumstance from their children's lives, or emotionally or spiritually detached because they take little or no interest in the emotional and spiritual nurture of their kids.

By nature and developmental stage, children and teens are like sponges. This fact can be seen in Deuteronomy when God charges parents and the community to live out his commandments and to "impress them on your children" by talking about his commandments everywhere and at all times (Deut 6:4-9). But when parents and the community fail to keep these "mapping" responsibilities in a deliberate and unified manner, the lessons about a biblical worldview can't and won't be heard. Of course, even though the lessons are absent, young people continue to probe, question and learn. They seek out maps and teachers who speak into their needs. George Gerbner has found in his ongoing analysis of media that its power to teach young people has increased vigorously in recent years. He says:

> For the first time in human history, the stories are told not by parents, not by the school, not by the church, not by the community or tribe and in some cases not even by the native country but by a relatively small and shrinking group of global conglomerates with something to sell.[18]

Not only are the conglomerates selling product, they are selling a worldview that will live on in the hearts and minds of young people long after the product's been used and forgotten.

One area where developing young people are looking for guidance is sexuality. Sadly, the family and the church have largely refused or

---

[17]For more explanation of these basic principles, see Steven Garber, *The Fabric of Faithfulness* (Downers Grove, Ill.: InterVarsity Press, 1996).
[18]George Gerbner, quoted in Romanowski, *Eyes Wide Open*, p. 56.

forgotten to map out God's design for sexuality to the emerging generations. But that doesn't stop them from seeking answers.

One highly popular song from 2003 and 2004 reveals how the media is mapping out sexuality for our children. "Stacey's Mom," a catchy tune by the group Fountains of Wayne, is sung from the perspective of a middle school boy who hangs out with Stacey—a cute female classmate—in order to fulfill his desire for her attractive single mother. The video visualizes the fantasies of the youngster, portraying Stacey's mother seductively encouraging his desire. He watches her undress, get a back rub while naked and pole dance on the kitchen table. His conclusion? "Stacey's mom has got it going on!" The video comes to a conclusion with a surprised Stacey catching the boy masturbating while fantasizing about her mother.

What should we make of the video? Theologian Darrell Guder gives some guidance: the "primary issue . . . is to identify, name, and critique the ways in which various social realities form or make—cultivate —a people."[19] In other words, we are not only identifying the objective stuff of culture, but we must discover *where* it's sending them and *how* it's telling them to get there. We will be hopelessly ineffective if all we say to our kids is, "I saw the 'Stacey's Mom' video. It's wrong. Now, this is what God says about sex . . ." We must first ask, "How is it shaping our youth, and what is it teaching them to think? How is it forming their worldview?" In the case of "Stacey's Mom," a young audience is directed to a place where there are no boundaries. The song is promoting a postmodern ethic. God is absent from the picture. Sexuality is purely an individual pursuit. Impressionable and curious young viewers are being told to act any way they deem appropriate. "Stacey's Mom" is a map pointing the way to understanding, expressing and practicing not only their sexuality but a complete lifestyle.

The map of culture teaches a way of life. It is our responsibility as crosscultural missionaries to deconstruct the map and understand how it guides the young. To know their map is to know them. Then, and only then, can we challenge the map's inaccuracies, affirm what's

---

[19]Darrell L. Guder, *Missional Church* (Grand Rapids: Eerdmans, 1998), p. 151.

right and correctively guide them with the map of a biblical world and life view.

Culture is a mirror. For several days in November 2002, Jenna's mom and dad halfheartedly watched the TV updates on actress Winona Ryder's shoplifting trial. It was news that really didn't interest or concern them. But then they got the phone call. They were in absolute shock. Their seventeen-year-old daughter was caught shoplifting. They had modeled and taught her a Christian worldview. Jenna professed faith in Christ, seemed to be growing in that faith and was active in her church youth group. While Jenna felt the normal amount of peer pressure, she usually stood strong against many of the temptations she and her peers faced. Then this. Jenna's blindsided parents drove to the police station looking in vain for answers to their questions.

As part of their effort to help Jenna stop shoplifting, her parents knew they had to go beyond simply stating, "Jenna, that's wrong. Don't ever do it again." They had communicated those values to her continuously while she was growing up. Instead, they had to discover the underlying reasons for Jenna's shoplifting. Their task was to understand how Jenna's objective, visible behavior served as an expression of the underlying subjective worldview. They needed to get to the root in order to fully understand what motivated her. Then they could look for ways to address those root causes through sharing biblical truth that speaks directly to those underlying assumptions.

Denis Haack believes that one of the reasons Christians should be monitoring and understanding culture is because it can be "a window of insight into a worldview we do not share."[20] I like to picture myself standing behind young people as they look into the window, or mirror, of their culture. As I look over their shoulders at the reflection, I want to look at *their* music, magazines, movies, websites and so on. What is reflected back helps me understand them at a deepened level.

Haack encourages us to seek out these "windows of insight" into cultures for two reasons.

First, it will give us information about that worldview, about the

---

[20]Denis Haack, "Christian Discernment 202" <www.ransomfellowship.org/D_202.html>.

ideas and values which it contains, and second, it will help us to see life from the perspective of that worldview. If we are to understand those who don't share our deepest convictions, we must gain some comprehension of what they believe, why they believe it, and how those beliefs work out in daily life.[21]

When we stand behind Jenna and her shoplifting peers to look into the mirror, the observable behavior reveals their deep needs and offers insight into a worldview that is unique to their culture. Let's see what their reflection tells us.

- Some teens say they shoplift because they love the "rush" or the "high." Bored with life, they are looking for some excitement. Research indicates that the serotonin-induced rush can actually become addictive for these thrill-seekers, leading them to steal again and again in order to get high.

- Other teens see shoplifting as a way to rebel against an adult-run system they see as constrictive and oppressive. Many of these kids have been squashed or forgotten by the adults who should have taken an interest in their lives. Angry and hurting, they try to outsmart the system. If they succeed, they feel that they've pulled one over on adults.

- With so many kids shoplifting and talking about it, more and more feel the pressure to do it themselves. They want to be a part of a group. Some social groups even see shoplifting as a form of initiation or hazing. If someone refuses to shoplift, they are excluded from the group.

- Shoplifting is sometimes used by teens as a substitute for loss. A broken relationship, parents' divorce or the death of a loved one can leave a teen feeling as if they were unfairly deprived. Some shoplift to exercise some control in their lives (even if only in a small way).

- Many kids describe their lives as "depressing." The adolescent years are also filled with the anxiety associated with so much

---

[21]Ibid.

confusing life change. As crazy as it sounds, stealing becomes a way to find relief in the midst of the turmoils of the teen years.

- Envy might be driving some to shoplift. We live in a materialistic culture where young people are under a constant barrage from advertisers who tell them that you are what you have and what you wear.

- We live in a postmodern culture where there is no commonly held standard of right and wrong. This attitude increasingly affects children, even those who profess faith in Christ. In their mind there's nothing wrong with being a Christian teen and shoplifting.

Looking into the mirror of Jenna's culture opened windows of insight and redemptive opportunity to her mom and dad. Based on what they saw, they evaluated Jenna's situation and applied practical and scriptural responses to the real—not assumed—issues and needs. Understanding culture as a mirror served them in powerful ways.

Culture is always moving and never neutral. "What is that supposed to be?" While I don't remember the specifics of what it was we were looking at, I do remember where I was: the Philadelphia Museum of Art. My fifth grade class was on an educational trip. All we saw lining the walls were confusing images that appeared to be no different from the random scribblings we had made when we were first graders using finger paints. Our museum guide referred to what we were viewing as "modern art."

People have scratched their heads over modern art since its advent. Most have walked away believing that there is no intended meaning to what they've seen. But art critic Hans Rookmaaker challenged our faulty view. "Modern art is a complex phenomenon," he writes. "But in the final analysis one thing stands out just as much as with 'old art': each work of art has its own message, its own quality, its own form. And each has to be 'interviewed' for its own individual peculiarity."[22] Rookmaaker correctly understood, as should we, that just as Jesus said

---

[22]H. R. Rookmaaker, *Modern Art and the Death of a Culture* (Wheaton, Ill.: Crossway, 1994), p. 135.

that "out of the overflow of the heart the mouth speaks" (Mt 12:34), it's out of that same overflowing heart that the brush of the painter paints, the pen of the screenwriter writes, the hands of the songwriter compose, and on and on. Rookmaaker goes on to apply this truth to all of us who missed the point of modern art:

> Too many have bypassed modern art with a shrug of the shoulder, failing to see that it is one of the keys to an understanding of our times. For many of these works, particularly the more extravagant ones, are signs of the crisis of our culture. They embody new ways of thinking. They proclaim the meaninglessness of all we may think sacred.[23]

Ironically, the meaning of much modern art is found in its meaninglessness.

Those who are older too often fail to look at the soup of the emerging generations and see that every ingredient has meaning. Because its meaning might not be obvious, we erroneously assume that it has no meaning at all. When we believe there's no meaning, we automatically fail to understand how it functions as a map, and we bypass our opportunity to use it as a mirror. In addition, we forfeit our opportunity to understand the very heart to which the gospel speaks.

Culture is never neutral. It was created by God as something good. But it is marred and polluted as a result of the Fall into sin. Paul tells us that creation joins humanity in "groaning" for liberation from its "bondage to decay" (Rom 8:18-23). Until that time, culture will be involved in a process of pushing and pulling as its various elements either bring glory to God or to the world, the flesh and the devil. C. S. Lewis said there is "no neutral ground in the universe: every square inch, every split second, is claimed by God and counterclaimed by Satan."[24]

Albert Wolters offers helpful clarification as he differentiates between the "structure" and "direction" of culture. Wolters says that "structure refers to the order of creation, to the constant creational

---

[23]Ibid., pp. 135-36.
[24]C. S. Lewis, *Christian Reflections*, ed. Walter Hooper (Grand Rapids: Eerdmans, 1967), p. 33.

constitution of any thing, what makes it the thing or entity that it is."[25] The structure of something is positive and good. In its substance, essence and nature it was brought into existence by God at creation and was part of his perfect created order. "Direction, by contrast, designates the order of sin and redemption, the distortion or perversion of creation through the fall on the one hand and the redemption and restoration of creation in Christ on the other."[26] In other words, all the ingredients in the cultural soup are either moving in the direction of obedience or disobedience to God's will. They are never neutral. "To the degree that these realities fail to live up to God's creational design for them, they are misdirected, abnormal, distorted. To the degree that they still conform to God's design, they are in the grip of a countervailing force that curbs or counteracts the distortion."[27]

We must discern between those ingredients in the postmodern soup that are moving away from God's order and design, which must be challenged and renounced, and those that are worth celebrating, retaining, transforming and enriching because they are moving in the direction of God's will for his world.[28]

Many people have difficulty understanding and practicing this concept. For example, in the early 1990s I began showing adults the Pearl Jam music video "Jeremy." The song and video tell the story of a thirteen-year-old boy who is cut off relationally from his parents and peers. At the song's climax, the lyrics tell us that "Jeremy spoke in class today." The video shows him "speaking": he walks into the classroom, throws an apple on the teacher's desk, pulls a pistol from his pants, and shoots himself in the head in front of his classmates (the act is implied, not shown).

People often wonder what kind of sick man I am to show such a dark and violent video in church. Despite the protests, I continued to show the video. Why? First, it offers adult viewers a powerful "mirror"

---

[25]Wolters, *Creation Regained,* p. 49.
[26]Ibid.
[27]Ibid.
[28]John R. W. Stott, *Christian Mission in the Modern World* (Downers Grove, Ill.: InterVarsity Press, 1975), p. 122.

experience. The video's popularity and staying power were testimony to the fact that it was depicting the reality of many kids. Second, I always explained to the adult viewers that what they had just seen was one of the most powerful and biblical music videos of all time. No, Pearl Jam's lead singer and song writer, Eddie Vedder, makes no claims to be a Christian. But the song and video truly reflect creative excellence. The song and video, along with their creators, image God.

In addition, the song's message clearly shows the downside of what happens when God's order and design for the family is not followed. "Jeremy" brings glory to God, calling all those who view it to see how our sinful, culturally accepted distortions of family and relationships have deep and abiding negative consequences. The message is clear: something is wrong, and it must be made right. The video opens tremendous doors to discussing the biblical worldview.

Putting It All Together: *Musings on MTV's Video Music Awards*

Understanding culture is not merely an academic exercise. Rather, it's foundational to engaging and ministering to the emerging generations. But how does it all fit together? What follows are some thoughts I penned for youth workers and parents the night of the 2003 MTV Video Music Awards (VMA)—one big ingredient in the postmodern cultural soup. You'll see how this one particular broadcast serves as a map and a mirror.

> *August 28, 2003.* It's 11:20 Thursday night. Tonight I did what I do on MTV's annual Video Music Awards day—I watched and processed the show. My head is spinning from what I viewed the last three hours. This year, I had to head right to the computer to record my thoughts. The VMAs—like all popular entertainment—function in our culture as both a map and a mirror. As a map the VMAs direct and shape the developing worldview of vulnerable children and teens who look to the music industry for guidance. In that sense, viewing the broadcast put me in the same "classroom" as our kids. For those of us who want to know

what the kids are learning from these teachers, the VMAs give us a front-row seat in the classroom. It's imperative that we know what our kids are learning. That way we can affirm or correct where necessary. As a mirror the VMAs allow us to gaze at ourselves to see what we look like and what we've become. The show is an accurate reflection—although many of us won't admit or believe it—of how we've changed, what we think, how we live and who we are as a culture. Granted, the reflection I saw tonight was not something I liked. Nor was it an accurate reflection of me as an individual. But, collectively, I can't argue with the fact that what I saw is a reflection of what our youth culture has become and what our mainstream culture is becoming.

All that said, what does this year's VMA map and mirror have to tell us about our culture and our kids? What follows are some random and initial musings regarding what we can learn about youth culture and how to minister in it, from this year's VMAs.

The popular music industry is gasping for air. With the exception of the first five minutes of the show, there was very little that was eventful or new. Popular music is looking for that "next big thing"—something to spike record sales. I think the evidence of that was the fact that Justin Timberlake won three awards. (Don't get me started on that one!) Yes, Coldplay won three awards too. But overall the industry is on autopilot. I'm not sure when the next big thing is coming along. But when they find (or invent) it and it hits, it's going to make a big splash. Unfortunately, the chances are that the big splash will be made by some young performer who allows him- or herself to be remade in the image of what the industry thinks will sell (à la Justin, Britney and Christina). As a result, the big splash will probably be the result of good and effective marketing and not good and creative music.

Now, about those first five minutes. *Homosexuality and lesbianism are no longer stigmatized or seen as sinful. In fact, they are celebrated in the mainstream.* First, you've got Britney Spears and Christina Aguilera singing Madonna's "Like a Virgin" while dressed in white wedding "dresses"—actually, they looked like they had been purchased at Victoria's Secret. Don't forget that just three years ago these two were topping the charts as the reigning "good girl" queens of formulated, generic, pop music—and millions of parents were buying their albums and concert tickets for their seven-, eight- and nine-year-old girls. Today those young fans are three years older and not even into their teenage years. The Britney and Christina they're listening to are totally reinvented as bad girls. What are those young fans learning from these "maps"? Last night Madonna joined them on stage. Dressed in groom's black, she played the part of the man in the on-stage lesbian wedding fantasy. She broke into her song "Hollywood" and began to bump and grind with her two "virgin" brides. Somewhere near the end of the opening number, Madonna ended her song with the lyrics "I'm bored with the concept of right and wrong." Those lyrics were sung in the context of engaging in an open-mouthed kiss with both Spears and Aguilera. I believe that as their lips touched, a symbolic bad-girl-of-music "torch" was passed from one generation to another. And did you notice that the next generation was on stage? Yes, that was Madonna's six-year-old daughter right there in the middle of the act. The torch is being passed again. That opening number set the stage for the anti-climatic appearance of the flamboyant homosexual cast of the hit Bravo series "Queer Eye for the Straight Guy" as presenters. Remember, "map" and "mirror." What we saw is who we are.

The urban hip-hop style and ethos rule. It is stamped all over today's youth culture. The genre is number 1 among children and teens. It's flavored the commercials. (Have you watched the commercials on Nickelodeon lately?) Our kids sing and dance to the gangsta lifestyle. In our postmodern climate there's nothing wrong with that. Granted, not all hip-hop music and style promotes the thug life. But the thug life sells records, attitude and lifestyle. I think VMA host Chris Rock was pretty insightful when he joked about 50 Cent's success and the fact that nobody talks about the music. Instead, they talk about the fact that he was shot nine times. The rise of the distinctive urban lifestyle and music into the mainstream of suburban and rural white America begs another question. Now that the truly urban owners of the genre and lifestyle have seen it move into the mainstream, what will they invent and adopt as their own. As all successful youth marketers and cool hunters know, you look for the edgy stuff, steal it from the inventor and market it to the world. But once it becomes a fad, those who created and owned it start looking for something else they can call their own. Those who work in urban ministry need to keep their ear to the ground for what's coming next. But that too will eventually be stolen, packaged, marketed and sold to the mainstream.

Freak dancing isn't freaky anymore. It's been described as "having sex with your clothes on." That's certainly what it looks like and also how it functions. We saw it on stage at the VMAs, and it's an integral part of most videos. My guess is that if you cranked up those songs on a Saturday night at a middle school retreat and let the kids loose, you'd see the same thing. And if you'd challenge them as to its appropriateness, their bewildered looks would say it all. They wouldn't have a clue what you're talking about. The "normalcy" of the behavior will leave you looking like the one who's abnormal and without a clue.

When it comes to sex, there are no rules. If you were an alien sent to watch this year's VMAs from a sociological/anthropological perspective, what would you scribble on your note pad? What kept running through my mind is that the sex act and all things sexual are the reason for living, boundaryless and sacramental. Our kids are growing up in a world where the hedonistic and unbridled pursuit of pleasure is integral to life. Fornication, adultery and homosexuality aren't even seen as naughty enough to be pursued in a sneaky way. When sex becomes redemptive, it's no shock that those hungry for heaven will feast but never be filled.

Normal looking girls don't have a chance. If you taped the show, watch it again with this statement in mind. The body-image pressure continues, and we'll see more and more of our girls at younger and younger ages begin to self-destruct over appearance. Sadly, our guys are getting the message too. Did you hear the banter last night between Nelly and Murphy Lee as they lustily discussed females and their posteriors? And what about the clothing? A commonly held standard of modesty no longer exists to dictate taboos. Instead, modesty itself is taboo. The result? It's no longer just the stereotypical construction worker on lunch break who sends out the wolf whistles as the ladies walk by. Today, our eight-year-olds have been taught to stare, harass and not care. So don't be surprised next time you hear a third grade boy "complimenting" a first grade girl on the playground for her "nasty ass."

What's next for the Olsen twins? They were there tonight, and they're also on the cover of the latest edition of *Rolling Stone*. Keep your eye on them. It appears they've been positioned as the next female media darlings and teen heartthrobs. At this point they seem to have maintained some aspects of childhood innocence—at least that's what we've been led to believe. But remember, that's where Britney and Christina were just three years ago. How they grow up will set a pattern for our kids. Watch how they are marketed and reinvented. They will serve as an interesting case study.

Postmodern self-rule rules. In today's world there is no objective, transcendent authority outside of self. The "I" determines all things ethical. "I" does what "I" wants to do. For a great example, take another look at 50 Cent's performance of his hit song "P.I.M.P." It oozed postmodern individualism. But he wasn't alone. It all serves to remind us that when those of us in ministry who stand face-to-face with kids and begin sentences with "God says" or "The Bible says". . . well, you've already seen the "so what" stares in response.

Women are ornaments for men. The VMAs featured what we so often see in the music videos—singers, dancers and women who just stand around doing nothing but being scantily clad sexual objects for men. I've often used this crude analogy that isn't very pretty: so much of the music today depicts women as nothing more or less than urinals that hang on a men's room wall. As such, they are objects used by male to relieve themselves in. But the VMAs also gave us a glimpse into something else I've been noticing over the course of the last couple of years, that is, the ladies are starting to react. But rather than asking the men to stop, they're simply doing the same thing. Britney, Christina and Madonna offer just one example. Their lusty performance said to the men: "You want us to be your sexual toys? Okay, we'll steam it up for you. It just won't be with you. It'll be with each other. All you get to do is watch." Watch for the lesbian fantasy to continue to take center stage as the women seek to turn the tables and establish sexual power over the men.

Pain is mainstream. Who would have ever thought that Johnny Cash would be a video star in 2003? And even more unbelievable is that he did it with a remake of Trent Reznor's "Hurt" from the 1994 Nine Inch Nails album *The Downward Spiral.* That's one song worth discussing with your kids. The opening line—"I hurt myself today, to see if I still feel"—captures the essence of the epidemic of teenage self-abuse.

How about Jessica Simpson's suit! I stand by what I wrote about her a couple of years ago—she's the poster girl for disintegrated faith. She isn't alone. Perhaps she's an icon for what we mistakenly call "evangelism" in our youth ministries. When are we going to start teaching our kids that coming to faith in Christ is not just about going to heaven? No, it's about living the kingdom of God here on earth and integrating that faith consistently into every area of our lives.

Beyonce never once thanked God. Unless I missed it, the winner of three moonmen stepped out of character and never once thanked the Lord. In a way I'm happy, because her music and lifestyle haven't been especially spiritually fruitful lately. But don't expect her gospel roots and expressions of faith to fade away anytime soon. They'll still figure into the mix—a mix that's becoming more and more evident in the lives of those kids (and adults) we know and love, who call themselves "Christian."

Finally, here are my two personal highlights from the show. First, the Fred Durst-Jack Black parody of Michael Jackson at last year's VMAs was brilliant! Very creative and well done. And second—on a more serious note—I was thrilled to hear Missy Elliot's words after receiving the award for "Best Hip Hop Video" early on in the show. She thanked God and then said why: "for giving me the talents and the creative mind." Hey, Missy Elliot might not be bringing glory to God through her music. But her theology was dead-on right in her comments.

As I head to bed tonight, my heart aches. It's the map and the mirror that I watched tonight that make me hurt. If you watched, you're probably hurting too. Let's use the map and the mirror as catalysts to respond as Jesus would. There's not a kid in this world or a performer on that VMA show that is beyond redemption. Our prayers and our ministry efforts need to be built on that conviction.

6

UNDERSTANDING OUR PLACE
IN CULTURE

IN THE SPRING OF 1998, I was in Denver speaking at a youth worker's convention. Leslie and one of her friends had registered to take a two-day preconference seminar I was teaching on understanding and engaging youth culture. Both taught at a private Christian middle school and felt that my seminar might be helpful to them.

Wanting to get to know my audience and their theology of culture, I typically begin these seminars the same way. I show a current music video or film clip that (1) is popular in the mainstream of contemporary youth culture, (2) accurately portrays the mainstream values, attitudes and behaviors of the emerging generations, and (3) is going to take the adults out of their comfort zone. That's how I kicked off my two days with this group.

When the clip ended and I raised the lights in the room filled with Leslie and about ninety of her youth-ministry peers, I looked at the spectrum of expressions on their faces. They looked like every group that's watched a clip that I've shown. Some were bewildered. By and large, these are people that are out of touch with youth culture. Others are squirming with excitement. They're ready to talk about how the clip serves as a map and mirror of youth culture. And then there are those who feel dirty, insulted or angry, and are ready to walk out of the room because of what they've been exposed to.

It didn't take long for me to see that Leslie and her fellow teacher were in that last group. To their credit, they didn't get up and walk out. On the second break of the first day, they had mustered enough courage to approach me. "You're asking us to compromise our faith by showing us secular things we shouldn't be looking at. You're telling us to know their culture, and that just doesn't seem right. If our students find out we've been listening to this music, won't that automatically give them permission to do the same thing? This is the very thing we're trying to teach them *not* to do."

Having encountered the same response countless times before, I sincerely applauded them for expressing their concern and encouraged them to hang in there. "Please stay and struggle with the material," I said. "It will all start to make sense to you as we move through it. Do with it what I always encourage people to do: evaluate it in light of the Scriptures. Then, if you find what I'm saying is faithful to God's Word, start to put it into practice when you get back into your school. But if you find what I'm teaching to be wrong, I want to know so we can talk about that and I can correct the error of my ways."

For the rest of our time together, the pair cautiously responded to my challenge. They asked questions and raised points of disagreement. During the breaks, they were always the first ones in line to ask for clarification or to challenge my thinking.

I appreciated these two good-natured and gracious women. But by the end of the conference, I was convinced that their theology and presuppositions wouldn't allow them to put into practice anything they had heard. Nevertheless, I hoped they would return to their school, use at least some of what they had learned and see their ability to understand and minister to their students improve.

The Culture War Within the Church

Recently, conservative Christians have rallied the troops against a host of challenging and complex social problems under the banner of fighting the "culture war." But there's another culture war that's been raging since Jesus ascended into heaven, and it's being fought inside the walls of his church among those who call themselves his followers. It's the same war that saw a battle flare between Leslie and myself, and our theologies at that youth workers convention. To use battle language, the side one takes in this war "within" will greatly influence their approach to and level of effectiveness in their interaction with the world "without." In his classic book *Christ and Culture*, H. Richard Niebuhr describes this "enduring problem" as the "many-sided debate about the relations of Christianity and civilization."[1] As we prepare to go as crosscultural missionaries into today's emerging youth culture, we need to struggle with the proper relationship between our faith and culture. What we *understand* about culture is a crucial part of the foundation on which we build our crosscultural approach to young people. But we can't stop there. The extent to which we influence or don't influence that culture hinges on *how*, as faithful followers of Jesus Christ, we choose to approach culture. How should Christians interact with culture?

While Niebuhr described five approaches to the relationship between faith and culture, I have narrowed them down to three: accommodation, alienation and transformation.

Accommodation: The church on a leash. I was excited about spending the weekend with a group of two hundred high school students, speaking at their annual retreat. Before each of my talks, various student leaders—hand-picked because of their spiritual maturity—would give some personal reflections on the topic I was going to address. Throughout the course of the weekend, I was impressed with the thoughtfulness and depth of commitment evident in the student remarks.

Saturday night arrived and I was prepared to speak about faith and sexuality, a hot topic among adolescents. The time arrived for the student testimony, and a teenage girl began by sharing how her youth pastor had asked her to speak about what it means to be both Christian and a sexual being. "Steve asked me to talk about our sexuality, the topic Walt will be talking to us about in just a couple of minutes,"

---

[1] H. Richard Niebuhr, *Christ and Culture* (New York: Harper & Row, 1951), p. 1.

she said. "As a teenager, I think about this a lot. I'm sure all of you do too. There's lots of urges, temptations and opportunities. Last year I started dating a guy and have been dating him ever since. One night last year we got a little too physical and wound up going all the way. Yes, we had sex. Right afterwards we felt dirty and guilty. That night and for a few weeks after that, we spent time praying to God, asking him to help us only do things that were pleasing to him. We also looked at the Bible. After a while, we began to realize that God made our sexuality to be a good thing. Not only that, but he wants us to be happy, feel good and enjoy our lives. Pretty soon it became clear to us that it was OK with God if we had sex with each other. Ever since that time, we've been having sex with each other. I'm glad God wants us to be happy and wants us to feel good."

Her peers erupted into applause. Before she got to her seat, her youth pastor stood and met her in the aisle. He hugged her and while patting her on the back whispered what appeared to be encouraging and affirmative words into her ear.

I sat there in stunned silence. I had heard this line of reasoning countless times before, but never in a setting like this. It became increasingly obvious to me that when it came to their sexuality, this group had listened to the world more than to the Word. When I stood to speak, I had to take a different path than I had intended. I knew I had to challenge their thinking in a positive, encouraging yet direct manner.

This young girl, her peers and even her youth pastor had uncritically followed the lead of the culture, allowing its ethos to eclipse the distinctives of a biblical view of the God-given gift of sexuality. They were on one end of a leash with culture pulling them along. Their reasoning and practice are reflected in the 2004 film *Saved*, Hollywood's disturbing yet sometimes accurate satirical look at the state of evangelical Christianity. In the film, a professing Christian woman justifies her adulterous relationship with her pastor by reasoning, "Why would God give us these feelings if what we are doing is wrong?"

Throughout the ages, many Christians have accommodated themselves to cultural values and behaviors that are contrary to a biblical worldview. Sometimes this accommodation is driven by ignorance. Perhaps we haven't been taught or studied what it means to follow Christ. All it takes is for one generation to fall into this trap, and the next generation is sure to follow. At other times cultural accommodation is driven by convenience or personal preference as we pick and choose those elements of faith and culture that we like, combining them in our personalized postmodern "faith system." Still others believe that accommodation will enhance the proclamation of the gospel. John Stott notes this compromising tradition in the lives of the Sadducees in New Testament times: "The motive for it can again be good, namely the resolve to break down barriers between the church and the world, and to be the friends of publicans and sinners, as Jesus was."[2] Of course, even though Jesus spent time with sinners, he didn't adopt their unbiblical beliefs and behavior, which accommodationists do.

Lest we pat ourselves on the back for our ability to avoid the entrapment of accommodation, we should pause and think again. While the conservative church has historically been outspoken against an unbiblical view of sexuality, there are numerous areas where we've allowed ourselves to subtly get tied on the dog end of the leash. We're marked by materialism, a problem that is the great unrecognized and unaddressed sin of the twentieth- and twenty-first-century church. Then there's American civil religion that puts guns and guts on the same level as God, leading us to believe that God has adopted America as his chosen people. When we make these and a multitude of other mistakes, we have done nothing less than make God subservient to our culture. Culture, rather than God, often sets the agenda for the church.

The website ChristianCounterculture.com includes this critique:

As we enter the twenty-first century, . . . thoughtful Christians stand in awe of the tragedy looming all around us. The *real* cultural crisis, that is:

today's Christian culture is destroying Christianity.

By today's Christian culture we mean the vast network of people—

---

[2]John Stott, *The Contemporary Christian* (Downers Grove, Ill.: InterVarsity Press, 1992), p. 263.

ministries, businesses, bookstores, magazines, musicians, TV & radio programs and the like—who claim to be followers of Jesus Christ today.

While individual differences certainly exist among them, a consistent pattern is easily detected:

the culture it represents is indistinguishable from the world it seeks "to save." It is *worldly* at its very core. . . .

Today's Christian culture so resembles the world, that standing *contra mundum*—against the world, in opposition to its culture—would amount to standing against *itself*.

Yet that is the state of things. And, what is most tragic, it has borne a multitude of misled, deluded "disciples" who are *scripturally illiterate* and *spiritually dull*.

How has this happened?

It is really quite simple:

in an effort to be influential, Christians have been trying to buy their own legitimacy from the surrounding culture by compromising the Christian world and life view.

Ironically, this has not been lost on the surrounding culture Christians sought to influence in the first place.[3]

Recent research from George Barna indicates just how many in the church take this approach to faith and culture. In a study released early in 2004, Barna discovered that only half of the United States' Protestant pastors have a biblical worldview. In addition, "the research also points out that even in churches where the pastor has a biblical worldview, most of the congregants do not. More than six out of every seven congregants in the typical church do not share the biblical worldview of their pastor even when he or she has one."[4]

When we believe that we must adapt our faith by following the

---

[3] "Antithesis: A Manifesto for the Emerging Christian Counterculture," ChristianCounterculture.com <www.christiancounterculture.com/pdf/manifesto.pdf>.
[4] George Barna, "Only Half of Protestant Pastors Have a Biblical Worldview," *The Barna Update*, <www.barna.org/FlexPage.aspx?PageCMD=Print>.

culture's lead, it is the world that is setting the agenda for the church. When we fall prey to this subtle seduction, what is viewed as "normal" or statistically "average" becomes what's right and the distinctives of the faith disappear. Regarding this Charles Colson says, "The church used to treat the surrounding society as a mission field. Now it treats it as a model. The church is climbing into the same boat as secular society, leaving its oars behind. Instead of acting as a guide to direct and challenge the culture, it is drifting with the current."[5]

While there are elements of the culture that Christians can use and enjoy, not all elements of culture are moving in a good and God-honoring direction. Thus we can't simply accommodate the world in whole.

Alienation: The church in a bunker. Throughout the history of the church, Christ's followers in different times and different places have sought to protect and defend themselves and their children from the evil and offensive influence of culture by constructing "bunkers" while awaiting their removal from this temporal world and movement on to the safe haven of eternity with God. Usually, they have believed that contact with the world or certain cultural elements would lead to corruption and the adoption of ungodly attitudes and practices. In other words, contact with the world would compromise their faith, purity and holiness. Many early Christians sought to remain pure in their devotion to Christ by separating themselves from the Greco-Roman culture. The hermits of the early church felt that a solitary existence was a path to deeper spirituality. The middle ages saw the withdrawal of the monastics from the world as they pursued spiritual purity. In my own community, the Amish continue to live a simple life of separation from the ways of the world, avoiding participation and involvement in the worldly ways of "the English."

In recent church history, many in the conservative evangelical church in America have adopted this bunker mentality. While their separation from the world has been less extreme, it is nonetheless separation. They believe that contact with the world would lead to cor-

---

[5]Charles Colson, "Church Behind Culture," *Breakpoint* radio commentary, October 28, 1991.

ruption and the adoption of ungodly attitudes and practices. Whether they consciously or unconsciously view culture as inherently evil and unredeemable, they retreat to life in a bunker.

Early on in my own life I experienced a certain degree of this type of separation. I was raised in a Christian home where my pastor-father believed that the best way to live out his love for Christ was to protect his family from many of the evils in the world. One example stands out in my mind. Every year our neighborhood held a picnic on Memorial Day. All the main activities took place in the yard next to ours. It was the one day of the year when everybody from our neighborhood—young and old alike—were together. Everyone celebrated and had lots of fun. I knew this because I sat by my bedroom window and watched the fun, wishing all the while that I could run the races, eat the food and laugh with my friends. But many of the people who were at the picnic were not Christians, alcohol was served and occasionally profanity could be heard. So we separated ourselves from our neighbors.

Typically, those who choose to be alienated from the world desire to please God and remain faithful to his Word. Their motives are right. They strive to live out their commitment to Christ and his commands, particularly the calls to "come out from them and be separate" (2 Cor 6:17), to live as "aliens and strangers in the world" (1 Pet 2:11), to "not love the world or anything in the world" (1 Jn 2:15), to "have nothing to do with the fruitless deeds of darkness" and to avoid the shame of even mentioning "what the disobedient do in secret" (Eph 5:11-12).

If we take the approach of alienation, we can fall into a legalistic lifestyle focused on outward behavior, and our church culture becomes shaped and marked by that lifestyle. Richard Mouw grew up in this sort of environment, and he has reflected on how it influences the way we live out our faith. He writes, "I was reared in an evangelical pietist culture, where a premium was placed on being 'spiritual.' This was the opposite of being 'worldly.' Our sense of the need to separate ourselves from non-Christian culture was reinforced by a fairly explicit set of rules proscribing those behaviors that were taken to be the most visible signs of worldliness."[6]

Many of the people I know who have adopted this view of culture conclude that—to some degree—non-Christian people, institutions and cultural elements are always hostile to us and our faith, that we are to be separate from the world not only in attitude but in proximity, and that life is only about surviving and enduring our time on earth until Christ returns or we go to meet him in death. And so, we build our bunkers.

While my dad's desire was good and he was motivated by his understanding of Scripture, he admittedly took his concern too far. Over time, my parents' understanding of how Christians should interact with culture changed as result of their prayerful study of Scripture. Before long we were attending and enjoying the picnic as a family. My parents then used the picnic as an opportunity to teach us that Christians are called to be in the world as Jesus was in the world, but while there, we must guard against adopting values that are contrary to God's will for his people.

Many of us pride ourselves on avoiding this type of approach to life. After all, we have striven to be "culturally relevant." But if we have established a distinctly separate Christian culture that runs parallel to the mainstream culture, and we assume that living in the parallel culture will shelter and protect us and our children from the world, then we too are living a life of alienation. Are we any less alienated when we take all the things of everyday life and culture—television, radio, music, T-shirts, jewelry, greeting cards, bookstores, coffee shops, breath mints and so on—and market them with the word *Christian* placed before each?

John Fischer believes this is exactly what we've done, calling us a generation of "cultural Christians."

> To the cultural Christian, the world is a scary place to be avoided at all costs. The products and services marketed and sold to cultural Christians help them do just that. They provide a safer alternative to the world, and as such they ensure cultural Christians keep their distance from the world. . . . It is assumed the Chris-

---

[6]Richard J. Mouw, *He Shines in All That's Fair: Culture and Common Grace* (Grand Rapids: Eerdmans, 2001), p. 2.

tian alternative will be taken wherever it applies. To not accept the Christian option is to be worldly.[7]

What are some of the problems, misconceptions and disastrous consequences of the bunker mentality?

First, many who consciously pursue a lifestyle of alienation are guilty of supporting their position by misusing Scripture. Typically, they look for passages (proof texts) to support their stance of alienation rather than prayerfully approaching the Scriptures to be shaped by what they actually teach. At times, individual verses are applied without considering their grammatical, literary, historical and cultural contexts. Rather than understanding the plain meaning of the text as intended by the author, they read into it a meaning that further cements their own theological biases.

Second, living with a bunker mentality stems from lifting those passages that rightly warn Christ's followers to avoid adopting the ways of the world out of the context of the full Bible. They avoid the tension between these passages and those that encourage contact with, living in and even enjoyment of the world.

Third, this approach forfeits the very influence Christ calls us to have on the world. In a paper presented at the 1966 World Congress on Evangelism held in Berlin, Samuel H. Moffett warned against the "sin of self-containment":

> The church that is turned in upon itself has turned its back on the world to which it was sent by Jesus Christ. . . . There may be worse sins than self-containment, but few can more quickly blunt the growing edge of the Church of Jesus Christ. The Bible counts it as the accursed sin. This is no light condemnation. Its sign is the barren fig tree (Mark 11:12-14), heavy with leaves for its own self-beautification, but sterile and without fruit. When Jesus saw it, he cursed it.[8]

---

[7]John Fischer, *Finding God Where You Least Expect Him* (Eugene, Ore.: Harvest House, 2003), p. 53.
[8]Samuel H. Moffett, "The Greatest Enemy Is Within," in *One Race, One Gospel, One Task,* ed. Carl F. H. Henry and W. Stanley Mooneyham (Minneapolis: World Wide Publications, 1966), 2:197-98.

When we retreat to the bunker, it's difficult to communicate the gospel to others.

Fourth, alienation leads to falling into the erroneous ways of the Pharisees. They were preoccupied with keeping outward appearances and in keeping themselves separate from people, traditions and activities they believed would compromise their purity. (Their very name means "separated ones.") Jesus was firm in his rebuke of their belief that ritual purity was a sign and source of inner holiness and righteousness. Instead, Jesus said that it's the things that "come from the heart" that make a person "unclean" (Mt 15:16-20). He made it clear that true righteousness consists of inward conformity to God's will.

When we stop to honestly look at the rites, rules and assumptions that are part of the separatist way of life, we can't help but see that Christ's condemnation of the Pharisees and religious leaders of his day are still eerily relevant for those with separatist tendencies today. John Stott warns against this dangerous tendency.

> Withdrawal was the way of the Pharisees. Anxious to apply the law to details of everyday life, they had a false understanding of holiness, imagining that mere contact with evil and evil people would bring contamination. And a form of Christian pharisaism or separatism has lingered in the church. It has often been due to a passionate longing for holiness and a zeal to preserve Christian culture from destruction by the wicked world.

He says that while the intent may be noble, it is nothing less than "a betrayal of Christ."[9]

Fifth, a separatist approach is often motivated by a small and erroneous view of God. Jesus promised that "the gates of Hades will not overcome" the church (Mt 16:18). Everett Cattell calls the church to "face the fact that often this withdrawal has been rationalized on the grounds of preserving the purity of the Church and of believers when actually the motivation is fear and unbelief. We simply do not trust God. We are protective of the Gospel. We lack confidence in the power

---

[9]Stott, *Contemporary Christian*, pp. 262-63.

of the Holy Spirit to preserve Christ's Church without our devices." [10]

Sixth, separatism is usually selectively inconsistent. Many separatists in the United States typically accept anything associated with "the American way" without submitting those ways to examination by the will of God as prescribed in Scripture. For example, rarely do separatists question matters of political, economic, racial or social injustice. Jesus indicted that practice of the Pharisees then and he does so now: "Woe to you, teachers of the law and Pharisees, you hypocrites! You give a tenth of your spices—mint, dill and cumin. But you have neglected the more important matters of the law—justice, mercy and faithfulness. You should have practiced the latter, without neglecting the former. You blind guides! You strain out a gnat but swallow a camel" (Mt 23:23-24).

Over the years, I've discovered an interesting yet confusing phenomenon in many of the churches I visit. Some of the churches that are most aggressive in terms of world missions are most timid and fearful about contact with their local communities. Even though they send missionaries to some of the most pagan cultures on the globe, they have chosen to separate themselves from the culture right where they live. As a result, my advice to know the postmodern culture is often met with great objections. I just don't get it. Why would they send missionaries to reach the pagan world, while at the same time, they're cloistered from the pagan world right here at home, believing it is a sign of their spiritual maturity?

John Stott is right when he calls this bunker approach of separation from the world "a perverted doctrine." When we take this approach, we are no different than the Pharisees.

> Instead of seeking to be holy in thought, word, and deed, while retaining relationships of love and care with all men, they withdrew from social contact with "sinners" and despised those who did not follow suit. They became a "holy club" . . . a pietistic enclave which had virtually contracted out of the world. They also

---

[10]Everett Cattell, "Maintaining a Delicate Balance," in *One Race, One Gospel, One Task,* ed. Carl F. H. Henry and W. Stanley Mooneyham (Minneapolis: World Wide Publications, 1966), 2:202.

became harsh and censorious; they had not pity for people in ignorance, sin or need.[11]

They moved out of the culture and into their bunkers, and they were
wrong.

Infiltration and Transformation: *The Church* in *but Not* of *the World*

When I started seminary in 1982, I had a well-thought-out plan for
getting through school quickly so that I could get back into local
church ministry as soon as possible. Newly married, I planned to have
my wife, Lisa, work full-time while I concentrated on my studies. Upon
graduation—in what I hoped would be less than three years—I would
return to full-time youth ministry, and we would start a family. When
we soon discovered that Lisa was expecting our first child, my plan
quickly changed. Now I needed to be the one working full-time while
she focused on tending to the needs of our daughter Caitlin.

I secured a thirty-six-hour-a-week job at a rather posh and historic
hotel in our town on the north shore of Boston. Over the course of my
three years at the hotel God graciously allowed me to work my way
up the ladder, from a houseman to the front desk and finally to the
management team. Consequently, I got to know each of the hotel's
150 employees and became friends with many of them.

Most everyone I worked with saw their work at the hotel as nothing
more than a job. I worked with married people who had been unfaithful to their spouses and single people who were cohabitating. Several
of the hotel's employees were open about their homosexuality. Drug
and alcohol abuse were rampant. My time spent in and around the
hotel's restaurant, pub and banquet facilities exposed me to people
and things I had never experienced before.

I can say with reasonable certainty that when I first began to work
at the hotel, I was the only professing believer on the staff. But God
made it clear to me that these were the people he wanted me to be

---

[11]John R. W. Stott, *Christ the Controversialist* (Downers Grove, Ill.: InterVarsity Press, 1970),
p. 176.

with. And it wasn't so much because of my presence in their world as their presence in my life.

For years I shied away from social contact with people who weren't "Christians" unless that contact was on my terms. Ministry contact was fine, but social contact was another matter. Now, I found myself working with them on their turf. It wasn't long before I realized that these were people made in the image of God, just like me. Their lifestyles were expressions of their fallenness. While I had no clue what God might have in store for them, I realized that none of them were unredeemable. My prayer was being answered.

Word quickly spread among the staff that I was a seminary student. Consequently, I became the "religious" counselor to just about everybody on the staff. These were hurting people with deep, deep struggles and needs. For three years I talked openly and freely about my faith, God's order and design for his world, and how God spoke to our deepest needs through the incarnation of Christ—all at their prompting and invitation. We discussed and debated moral, social and political issues. They knew exactly where I stood. But not once was I ridiculed or put down for it.

These friends provoked a new way of thinking about living my faith in the world. I learned that I could be in their midst and maintain the distinctives of my faith without compromise. Where their lives reflected aspects of God's will, I could offer affirmation. Where they strayed, I was able to lovingly challenge and confront through gracious conversation.

This way of responding to culture—infiltration and transformation—is by far the hardest and most difficult of the three options, but it mirrors the ministry of Jesus and reflects his will. It sees the culture as a mission field ripe for redemption. As God's people infiltrate the world, they are able to exert an influence that God uses to transform individuals and institutions.

The redemptive response of infiltration and transformation is the most difficult of the three because it requires diligence, wisdom and hard work. Those who choose accommodation simply do as the world pleases. Alienation leads people to escape into the supposed safety of their bunkers. But infiltration and transformation communicate God's agenda in the world. It's marked by what John Stott calls "double refusal." "We refuse to become either so absorbed in the Word, that we *escape* into it and fail to let it confront the world, or so absorbed in the world, that we *conform* to it and fail to subject it to the judgment of the Word. Escapism and conformity are opposite mistakes, but neither is a Christian option."[12] Just as Jesus willingly and obediently entered our world when sent by the Father, so he says to us, "I am sending you" (Jn 20:21). Our participation in the culture in this manner requires a balance that John Stott calls "holy worldliness." "The whole church is called (and every member of it) as much to 'worldliness' as to 'holiness.' Not to a worldliness which is unholy, nor to a holiness which is unworldly, but to 'holy worldliness,' a true separation to God which is lived out in the world—the world which He made and sent His son to redeem."[13] *Congregations, too.*

The cost of taking this Christlike approach isn't just in terms of time and effort. There's a relational cost as well. Because of its radical nature, many of our fellow Christians who take the stance of alienation will accuse you of compromising—or sometimes even dispensing with—your faith. Several years ago I was discussing my personal frustration about this reality with Dick Staub, at the time a host of a nationally syndicated daily radio talk show, in which his commitment to infiltration and transformation came through loud and clear. His daily parade of guests included high-profile people from both the evangelical subculture and the culture-at-large. He shared how he too was taking some heat from Christians who thought his commitment to listen to the world—and broadcast it!—was a dangerous and disobedient compromise of his faith. Dick then told me that he's learned that when you take that stance and humbly follow in the footsteps of Jesus, there's really no place for you to fit in. Dick wasn't wallowing around in self pity. Rather, he was stating a reality all too common for those who share his ap-

---

[12]Stott, *Contemporary Christian*, p. 27.
[13]Stott, *Christ the Controversialist*, p. 191.

proach. A few years later, he wrote a book whose title reflects that reality.

In that book, *Too Christian, Too Pagan*, Staub says:

Following Jesus today requires you to practice that same single-minded nonconformity. And it will produce the same effect in your life that it did with Jesus. If you truly follow Jesus, in addition to enjoying a most excellent adventure, you will likely end up seeming too Christian for many of your pagan friends and too pagan for many of your Christian friends. When you truly follow Jesus, you'll spend considerable time in the world like he did, and as a result, many of your religious friends will think you're too irreligious. On the other hand, many of your irreligious friends will find it odd that you are so focused on the spiritual. Thus, you end up seeming both too Christian and too pagan.[14]

When we interact with the culture in a way that truly reflects the will of Christ, we must not only examine his life, but look more closely at how he commands us to live as his followers. From start to finish the Gospels are filled with his directives to his followers. When read in their immediate and larger contexts, it's abundantly clear that God calls his people to a life of infiltration and transformation.

Jesus' prayer of John 17 makes it clear that we have been given to him by the Father out of the world. While we no longer belong to the world, we are to continue living in the world. As we live in the world, our charge is to be the hands and feet of Jesus—his presence—carrying on his mission! As Jesus prays for his followers, it becomes clear that he wants them to infiltrate the world, living in it as a transforming and redemptive presence, while maintaining their distinct identity. John Stott describes this calling as being "spiritually distinct, but not socially segregated."[15] Our attitudes, thoughts and behaviors are to reflect the will and way of the One to whom we belong. Martyn Lloyd-Jones sums it up this way:

---

[14]Dick Staub, *Too Christian, Too Pagan* (Grand Rapids: Zondervan, 2000), p. 16.
[15]Stott, *Contemporary Christian*, p. 260.

Your business and mine as Christian people is to be in the midst of this world and its affairs, and still remain true and loyal to God, and be kept from the evil. . . . The task of the Christian is to be right in the midst of this world and its affairs in order that he may do the work of evangelism, spreading the gospel and the kingdom of God, while the whole time, keeping himself unspotted from the world.[16]

We shouldn't make the mistake of believing that God's redemptive and transforming activity is limited to personal salvation. God's redemptive activity extends to every element in the cultural soup. Bill Romanowski says that

the biblical directive to be "in the world but not of it" implies that Christians ought to be both forming and reforming culture, measuring cultural developments against the principles of love, truth, faithfulness, justice, and stewardship. We have to support cultural aspects that are life affirming—promoting growth, justice, freedom, and human dignity for all—and work to reform those that are dehumanizing or oppressive.[17]

To forget or forsake this latter aspect of God's redemptive activity is to step out of the will of the Father for his church. It is this very mistake that has limited the influence and presence of the church in the United States.

Still, we don't enter the culture without precaution and protection. While there, we must keep our hearts and minds centered on God's revelation of himself, thereby guarding against becoming accommodated to the world and the culture. We take our marching orders from our Master. But while we are in that world and culture, we need not live a life of alienated fear in the bunker. Why? Because God promises to keep his own safe and secure in Christ. Even now, Christ is at the right hand of the Father interceding for us (Eph 1:20; Heb 7:25).

---

[16]Martyn Lloyd-Jones, *Safe in the World: The Assurance of Our Salvation* (Westchester, Ill.: Crossway Books, 1988), p. 14.
[17]William D. Romanowski, *Eyes Wide Open* (Grand Rapids: Brazos, 2001), p. 51.

Jesus offered insight into how he wants his followers in all times and places to live. The great French social critic Jacques Ellul described this as the "specific function" of Christians that is "decisive for human history."[18] In essence, it is a threefold calling that clearly describes our infiltrative and transforming presence in the world.

First, Jesus tells us that we are to be "the salt of the earth" (Mt 5:13). Those who first heard Jesus knew that salt symbolizes the permanent covenant relationship between God and his people (Lev 2:13). They also knew that salt was painstakingly rubbed into meat to preserve it from decay. And they used salt as a seasoning to bring flavor and life to bland food. As the salt of the earth in today's world, we function as God's people of the new covenant, united with him and representing him by being a transforming presence that brings life where there is death, and seasoning where there is no flavor. To do so, we must be *in* the world. But if we become *of* the world, our saltiness is gone and we are "no longer good for anything, except to be thrown out and trampled by men" (Mt 5:13).

Second, Jesus tells us that we are to be "the light of the world" (Mt 5:14). We are to be where the world can see us—in the midst of the darkness—ministering with mercy, grace and compassion to the lost stumbling in the darkness.

Third, Jesus tells us that we are to be "sheep among wolves" (Mt 10:16). We are defenseless as sheep in the present sinful and fallen world. It's a world that's ready to pounce on us like hungry wolves. But the good Shepherd, who watches, protects, cares for and lays down his life for his sheep is always with us (Jn 10:1-18), keeping us safe and secure as we convey his Word in the world.

The fact that infiltration and transformation is God's revealed will for us serves as reason enough for us to obediently live this approach to faith and culture without question. It needs no justification beyond that. But those who have followed the example of Christ and lived this type of life can attest to the fact that it is an approach that works. How?

---

[18]Jacques Ellul, *The Presence of the Kingdom* (Philadelphia: Westminster Press, 1951), p. 9.

First, going into the culture allows us to know both the culture and the individuals in it who are desperately in need of redemption. Before I set foot in the world of that hotel I could only imagine what that world was like and who those people were. I was surprised to learn not only that these people were people but that my previous assumptions about them were almost totally ignorant and inaccurate. As with all crosscultural work, when "speculative imagining" replaces "informed knowing," the culture and its people cannot be accurately understood and known. To return to a principle discussed earlier, we cannot understand if we haven't listened. We can't listen if we haven't entered into their lives and world. We'll be shooting our ministry efforts in the direction of a target that doesn't even exist except in our own imaginations. Consequently, ministry can't and won't happen.

To be able to take that second crucial step of "knowing changing young people and their rapidly changing culture" discussed in chapter two, we must infiltrate their world. We must know how they think, talk and act—and why. We must understand what they value, what they long for, where their allegiance is directed and why. In effect, we need to develop an understanding of their root issues and needs. Jacques Ellul, in his brilliant little book *The Presence of the Kingdom*, offers a compelling argument for the need to engage the culture in this manner:

> The will of the world is always a will to death, a will to suicide. We must not accept this suicide, and we must so act that it cannot take place. So we must know what is the actual form of the world's will to suicide in order that we may oppose it, in order that we may know how, and in what direction, we ought to direct our efforts. The world is neither capable of preserving itself, nor is it capable of finding remedies for its spiritual situation (which control the rest). It carries the weight of sin, it is the realm of Satan which leads it towards separation from God, and consequently towards death. That is all that it is able to do. Thus it is not for us to construct the City of God, to build up an "order of God" within this world, without taking any notice of its suicidal

tendencies. Our concern should be to place ourselves at the very point where this suicidal desire is most active, in the actual form it adopts, and to see how God's will of preservation can act in this given situation. If we want to avoid being completely abstract, we are then obliged to understand the depth, and the spiritual reality of the moral tendency of this world; it is to this that we ought to direct all our efforts, and not to the false problems which the world raises, or to an unfortunate application of an 'order of God' which has become abstract. . . . Thus it is always by placing himself at this point of contact that the Christian can be truly "present" in the world, and can carry on effective social or political work, by the grace of God.[19]

By infiltrating the culture, understanding will be generated and we will be able to get to know people at an intimate level. Then, and only then, can real and lasting connections be made.

Second, by going into the culture, we are able to develop credibility. While not everyone believed Jesus, the needy and lost whose worlds he entered with grace and compassion were willing to listen to what he had to say. He listened to them. He took the time to understand them. He wept with those who wept and mourned with those who mourned. They knew that he felt their pain, hurt, hopelessness and despair. As they became authentic and real to him, he became authentic and real to them. During my time at the hotel, I not only realized that my unredeemed coworkers were people, but for the first time, they met a Christian who was a real person. It still saddens me as I think of the stereotypical notions so many of them had of Christians, notions shaped primarily by our televised ambassadors of the time known as televangelists. It brought great joy to see their stereotypes slowly disintegrate while my credibility in their eyes began to rise.

Third, if we take an approach of accommodation or alienation, we forfeit our influence in disobedience. It is through our infiltration that God in his grace uses us as agents of transformation, both in individual lives and in cultural institutions. Nothing was left untouched by hu-

---

[19]Ibid., pp. 28-29.

mankind's fall into sin. Individuals, culture and God's world are fallen. Likewise, individuals, culture and God's world are redeemable. "Jesus shed his blood to rescue creation from the curse of sin. And the cleansing blood of Christ must reach not only into the hearts and lives of individuals, but into every corner of the creation which the curse has affected."[20] The whole world is the theater of redemptive activity and we are the "actors" who manifest the way and the will of Christ, both to individuals *and* in every aspect of cultural life. As we fulfill our calling to move in and through the world as salt, light and sheep in the midst of wolves, God uses us to not only proclaim good news to the captives, but liberation to the whole created order as we work to redeem the time, the culture, institutions, God's good earth and everything in it. It is only when we infiltrate or enter into the culture that we become agents of transformation, used by God as he brings souls from death to life *and* as he redeems his creation. My influence on the individuals and culture at the hotel would have been non-existent if I had not entered into that world.

Those of us who long to reach the emerging generations must prayerfully employ this approach of infiltration and transformation to open doorways for effective evangelism and ministry. In addition, we must teach this approach in our discipleship efforts with young people so that they would grow up to function in God's world as he intends. By doing so, we can help them avoid the mistakes of accommodation and alienation the church has been making for far too long.

While consistent accommodation and consistent alienation are not options for engaging the world, there will be times and situations where our faithfulness to God and his Word will require a balance that employs one or the other as a matter of obedience. It is only through living this balance that we will bring honor and glory to the One who has sent us into the world and prayed for our protection while we're there.

---

[20]Richard J. Mouw, *When the Kings Come Marching In: Isaiah and the New Jerusalem* (Grand Rapids: Eerdmans, 2002), p. 110.

7

GETTING OUT OF THE BUNKER

I RECENTLY HAD THE OPPORTUNITY to meet with a well-known, Emmy-winning actress. A group of us had been invited to hear her talk about her faith, her career and her efforts to start a new production company that would produce and release high-quality films that deal honestly with the human condition from the perspective of faith without resorting to sentimentalism or nihilism. Her deep faith in Christ and love for the arts is obvious and refreshing. When asked about how she and her vision were being received in Hollywood, her response was not what most Christians would have expected. Rather than telling us she received her greatest opposition from the Hollywood establishment, we realized that her greatest opposition came primarily from fellow Christians.

When Jesus took heat from his "religious" critics, he typically challenged them and corrected their erroneous theological beliefs and practices. On one occasion, the Pharisees were highly critical of Jesus for eating with tax collectors and "sinners." He responded with these powerful words: "It is not the healthy who need a doctor, but the sick. But go and learn what this means: 'I desire mercy, not sacrifice.' For I have not come to call the righteous, but sinners" (Mt 9:12-13).

I have learned over the years that the people who object the most to an infiltration and transformation approach are very earnest about their faith. For them, personal evangelism is typically all about seeing people come out of the world and come to Jesus. The ministry of the church is to build and fill bunkers "until Christ returns." Thus there is no need to transform the world or send new converts back into the world with and for Christ. From their bunkers these Christians some-times fire shots—typically a verse or two from Scripture—at those in the church who are attempting to transform culture. I've taken the time to listen to the corrective bullets fired in my direction. I've seri-ously considered whether their criticisms are legitimate and whether I should correct my theology and practice. The process has produced an even deeper conviction to be in but not of the world.

To reach the emerging postmodern generations with the gospel, we must challenge the bunker mentality. It has set up stumbling blocks to our obedience to Christ, thereby limiting our effectiveness as salt and light in the world. The following are some misunderstandings that keep Christians huddled in their bunkers.

Misunderstanding Scripture

It's easy to justify life in the bunker through the misuse of a few iso-lated Scripture passages. Over the years I've been challenged with the same arsenal of passages to get "out of the world" of studying and working with the youth culture. Among other things, I've been told to "have nothing to do with the fruitless deeds of darkness. . . . For it is shameful even to mention what the disobedient do in secret" (Eph 5:11-12). I've received advice to "avoid every kind of evil" (1 Thess 5:22). And I've been admonished to think only about those things that are "true . . . noble . . . right . . . pure . . . lovely" and "admirable" (Phil 4:8). I agree with all of these imperatives. To do otherwise would be disobedient. However, the problem arises when we read some-thing into these passages that was never intended.

In How to Read the Bible for All Its Worth, biblical scholars Gordon Fee and Douglas Stuart say that to correctly interpret the Bible, the reader must embark on two tasks. The first is to hear what was being said to the original hearers. Then, "you have to learn to hear that same Word in the here and now." A problem arises when we read into the Bible what we want to hear. When we do this, we engage in "selective exegesis," reading "one's own, completely foreign, ideas into a text and thereby make God's Word something other than what God really said." Fee and Stuart then state a profound truth: "A text cannot mean what it never meant."[1]

Sadly, most of the texts strung together to make a case for staying in the bunker are lifted out of their context, leading to conclusions about Christians and culture that the biblical authors never intended. Here are a few examples of how the Scriptures are misinterpreted to justify life in the bunker.

Paul's words in Ephesians 5 are often used to justify the bunker mentality. After listing several differences between those who live in light and those who live in darkness, Paul says, "Have nothing to do with the fruitless deeds of darkness, but rather expose them. For it is shameful even to mention what the disobedient do in secret. But everything exposed by the light becomes visible, for it is light that makes everything visible" (Eph 5:11-14). Does this mean that Christians are to avoid contact with darkness at all costs? Those who think so don't fully understand what Paul is saying here. Paul is telling us to avoid *doing* the "deeds of darkness." Like Jesus, we are to go as light into the world of those who are lost in darkness. However, like Jesus, we do not adopt standards and behaviors that are contrary to the will of the Father. Instead, we are to "expose" these things by letting the light— "goodness, righteousness and truth" (Eph 5:9)—of Christ shine in their midst. If we are going to be obedient and "live as children of light" (Eph 5:8), then we must not hide our light under a bunker but let it shine in the midst of the darkness.

Likewise, Paul's words to the Philippians are often used to justify a bunker mentality. Paul says, "Whatever is true, whatever is noble, whatever is right, whatever is pure, whatever is lovely, whatever is admirable— if anything is excellent or praiseworthy—think about such things"

---

[1]Gordon D. Fee and Douglas Stuart, *How to Read the Bible for All Its Worth,* 3rd ed. (Grand Rapids: Zondervan, 2003), pp. 23-24, 30.

(Phil 4:8). Separatists say that infiltrating culture is disobedient because it forces us to think about evil things. Consequently, anything "secular" should be avoided, especially entertainment. Young people particularly should avoid exposure to the movies, music and television shows that are so much a part of today's emerging adolescent culture. Instead, they should view only "Christian" alternatives that can be delivered to the safety of the bunker. Brian Godawa points out how "readers of Bible passages like this one often misunderstand the language to be express-ing a 'hear no evil, see no evil, speak no evil' approach to spirituality."[2]

But the bunker mentality is a practical impossibility. If it were to be followed consistently, those who hold to it would have to dispose of all parts of the Bible itself, those parts that refer to violence, sexuality and all sorts of evil and immoral behaviors. Godawa says that "point-ing out wrong is part of dwelling on what is right, exposing lies is part of dwelling on truth, revealing cowardice is part of dwelling on the honorable, and uncovering corruption is part of dwelling on the pure."[3] And Bill Romanowski writes:

> If Christians are to think about "whatever is true," we will have to confront the realities of our fallenness—the waste and ugli-ness of war and injustice, the depths of human despair, the chaos and confusion of life—all the while seeing these as distortions in God's world. Like the Bible itself, we must understand and feel deeply the brokenness of our world.[4]

To faithfully live in a bunker we would have the ironic task of turning our minds and hearts away from our own minds and hearts, as Jesus clearly said that it's the things that "come from the heart" that make a person "unclean" (Mt 23:25-26).

This bunker interpretation of Philippians 4:8 is applied inconsis-tently at best. While those who hold to it may ingest only "Christian" movies, TV, radio and so forth, I wonder why they don't drive "Chris-tian" cars on "Christian" highways and pump "Christian" gas. My

---

[2]Brian Godawa, *Hollywood Worldviews* (Downers Grove, Ill.: InterVarsity Press, 2002), p. 199.
[3]Ibid., p. 200.
[4]William D. Romanowski, *Eyes Wide Open* (Grand Rapids: Brazos, 2001), p. 143.

point is that not everything that isn't "Christian" is totally evil. God's common grace extends to all of humanity. Unbelievers reflect God's image and can use the gifts he's given them to engineer and create excellent cars, highways and gas! This principle extends to everything, including popular culture and entertainment. That's why an R-rated film like *Good Will Hunting* can easily reduce us to tears and draw us closer to God by clearly revealing the reality, truth, depth and consequences of abuse among the emerging generations.

But my main concern with this faulty view of Philippians 4:8 (and related passages) is not primarily with its impracticality but its faulty exegesis and application. What Paul is telling us is to "think about such things," which when properly translated means to "take into account," "ponder" and "reflect on" them. They are the values we are to treasure, continue to think about and allow to shape our everyday conduct. Paul is not telling us to avoid *looking at* the world, he is instructing us to avoid *living the ways* of the world, that is, in opposition to the kingdom of God. John Fischer says, "Paul is not talking about what we are exposed to—what we encounter in the world—but rather, what we think about. What we see and what we think about are two very different things. This is not about our field of vision as much as it as about what occupies our mind."[5]

Paul's instruction to the Thessalonians to "avoid every kind of evil" (1 Thess 5:22) is also misunderstood and misapplied. Fee and Stuart point out that these five words are at the end of a paragraph about charismatic utterances. In that paragraph Paul is telling the Thessalonians to test prophecies in order to know what to hold on to and what to reject. "The 'avoidance of evil' has to do with 'prophecies,' which when tested, are found not to be of the Spirit."[6] Commentator Greg Beale correctly states that "this verse is not primarily warning people to abstain from any kind of sinful association with the outside world . . . but to separate from false prophets within and to reject their erroneous messages."[7]

---

[5]John Fischer, *Finding God Where You Least Expect Him* (Eugene, Ore.: Harvest House, 2003), p. 136.
[6]Fee and Stuart, *How to Read the Bible for All Its Worth*, pp. 24-25.
[7]G. K. Beale, *1-2 Thessalonians*, IVP New Testament Commentary (Downers Grove, Ill.: InterVarsity Press, 2003), p. 174.

Misunderstanding the "World"

Life in the bunker is sometimes justified by an appeal to verses like 1 John 2:15: "Do not love the world or anything in the world." But what is meant by the word *world?* The Bible uses *world* three different ways: to refer (1) to the material earth made and filled by God, (2) to human beings who inhabit the earth, and (3) to any area of creation polluted by sin and therefore moving in a direction away from serving and glorifying God. David Wells defines this as "the ways of fallen humanity, alienated from God and his truth."[8] Being worldly means to adopt priorities and allegiances that are ungodly. This is the way *world* is used in 1 John 2:15. In other words we are not to separate ourselves from the created order or those who inhabit it by retreating to a bunker. We are called to live in the midst of fallen humanity, enjoying the good fruit of the cultures that fill the earth. However, we are not to adopt ways of thinking and acting that reject the lordship of Christ over all areas of life.

Removing ourselves and our influence from this sinful order is disobedient to Christ's command to go into the world of people and culture as salt and light, albeit as sheep in the midst of wolves. An accurate understanding of the *world* is fully consistent with the will and way of Father that Jesus prayed in John 17.

Misunderstanding Sacred and Secular

The objection to engaging culture is rooted in the idea that somehow our existence on earth is made up of two spheres, the sacred and the secular. While the Bible is clear that spiritual warfare is a reality, it does not teach that there's a sacred-secular split. Brian Walsh and J. Richard Middleton correctly refer to this as a "split-vision worldview" that is "at odds with the Scriptures."[9] Dualism leads people to limit God's reign to their personal spiritual lives rather than over all of creation.

---

[8]David F. Wells, *God in the Wasteland* (Grand Rapids: Eerdmans, 1994), p. 37.
[9]Brian J. Walsh and J. Richard Middleton, *The Transforming Vision* (Downers Grove, Ill.: InterVarsity Press, 1984), p. 95.

Redemption, then, is purely personal. God has no interest in creation other than redeemed humanity.

In today's church there are two kinds of dualism that are significant to our discussion. In the first, personal salvation allows a person to escape into the sacred world of the church and all things "Christian." It is assumed that this is the only path to avoiding evil and drawing closer to God. Culture is an evil to be avoided. But people in the bunker forfeit their redemptive presence and influence in the world. Al Wolters says this type of dualism is "a very great error. It implies that there is no 'worldliness' in the church, for example, and that no holiness is possible in politics, say, or journalism."[10]

The second form of dualism also separates the sacred from the secular, but its adherents don't separate themselves from the world. Believing that God is only concerned about the spiritual component of their lives, they submit their "spiritual" life to the Lord while serving other masters in the rest of life. Their disjointed worldview results in an unintegrated and stunted faith. They forfeit their redemptive presence and influence in the world because they are indistinguishable from the world. Jacques Ellul criticizes this form of dualism:

> This dissociation of our life into two spheres: the one "spiritual" where we can be "perfect," and the other material and unimportant: where we behave like other people, is one of the reasons why the Churches have so little influence on the world. . . . All we can say is: that this is the exact opposite of what Jesus Christ wills for us, and of that which He came to do.[11]

Contrary to what many in the church believe, a dualistic approach to life is not God's plan or desire for his people. The Scriptures were written from the perspective of a Hebrew worldview that didn't separate life into categories of things that were spiritual and things that were not. To them, all of the earth and its fullness were created by God. All of life was sacred. All of life was touched by the Fall. And all

---

[10] Albert M. Wolters, *Creation Regained* (Grand Rapids: Eerdmans, 1985), p. 54.
[11] Jacques Ellul, *The Presence of the Kingdom* (Philadelphia: Westminster Press, 1951), p. 14.

of life was therefore within the scope of God's redemptive activity.

It was this unity that lay beneath the apostle Paul's instruction to the Corinthians: "So whether you eat or drink or whatever you do, do it all for the glory of God" (1 Cor 10:31). In the Scriptures, the differentiation between that which is sacred and that which is secular has nothing to do with the structure of everything God created, but with its direction (whether it is serving and bringing glory to God, or serving and glorifying the world, the flesh and the devil).[12] We slip into dualistic thinking when we read the Scriptures without regard for its Hebrew perspective on reality, and we erroneously filter God's Word through the Greek worldview that separates the world into the spheres of sacred (spiritual) and secular (material), thereby imposing meanings and interpretations that were never intended.

This was the very mistake Paul was seeking to correct in 1 Timothy 4. Prior to telling Timothy that "everything God created is good, and nothing is to be rejected" (1 Tim 4:4), Paul states the reason for this statement. There were teachings on marriage and eating that were coming through false teachers. Paul calls these teachings the doctrines of "deceiving spirits" and "demons" (1 Tim 4:1). At its core, Paul's teaching refutes the false and destructive teachings of the dualistic Gnostics who, like many today, viewed life through the false categories of sacred and secular, believing that the former and not the latter was within the arena of God's care and concern.

The great Dutch theologian and statesman Abraham Kuyper recognized the errors of dualistic thinking. He wrote:

> It is not true that there are two worlds, a bad one and a good, which are fitted into each other. It is one and the same person whom God created perfect and who afterwards fell, and became a sinner—and it is this same "ego" of the old sinner who is born again, and who enters into eternal life. So, also, it is one and the same world which once exhibited all the glory of Paradise, which was afterwards smitten with the curse, and which, since the Fall, is upheld by common grace; which has now been redeemed and

---

[12]Wolters, *Creation Regained*, pp. 49-52.

saved by Christ, in its center, and which shall pass through the horror of judgment into the state of glory. For this very reason, the (Christian) cannot shut himself up in his church and abandon the world to its fate. He feels, rather, his calling to push the development of this world to an even higher stage, and to do this in constant accordance with God's ordinance for the sake of God, upholding, in the midst of so much painful corruption, everything that is honorable, lovely and of good report among men.[13]

Without even knowing it, we've been shaped by dualism in ways that keep us from effectively finding our place in culture and engaging it for the cause of Christ.

Misunderstanding Holiness

During a recent public discussion about how Christ's followers should interact with culture, one participant more or less equated the approach of infiltration and transformation I was propounding with promoting pornography.

"So what you're saying is that Christians should know the culture?" I was asked. My answer was rather straightforward: "Yes, if God in his Word charges us to reach the world with the good news about Jesus Christ, we must understand the changing cultural context in which lost people live. To do that, anyone who works with the emerging generations needs to be familiar with what they're watching and hearing—that's the stuff shaping their worldview. By doing that, we can learn how they think and what they believe. Then we'll be able to connect with them in language and categories they can understand, and the unchanging, life-changing and corrective truths of God's Word won't fall on deaf ears. In effect, we're crosscultural missionaries!"

Case closed—or so I thought. The immediate response indicated otherwise: "So you tell those who want to reach kids to watch pornography?" I was taken aback by the connection. Somehow, in his

---

[13]Abraham Kuyper, *Christianity: A Total World and Life System* (Marlborough, N.H.: Plymouth Rock, 1996), p. 43.

mind, I was promoting pornography and leading people down the compromising road to perdition. In defense, I responded as follows.

First, I clarified that pornography is an expression of sinful and fallen sexuality, and it certainly isn't a place where God wants us to go. Nor is it a place I *indirectly* suggest people go. It's not a legitimate art form that is redeemable. It's to be avoided. We know that it's left a trail of destroyed individuals, marriages and families in its ugly wake. Neither would I suggest that a parent or youth worker view pornography if they discover their kids are using it. If I discovered my son spending time in the deepest and darkest corners of the Internet, I wouldn't say, "Hey buddy, let's sit down and look at this together so we can talk about it." That would not only be wrong but ridiculous. I've seen it. He's seen it. Neither of us need to see it again. But because I know where it comes from, what it is and what it does, I *would* sit down with him and talk about it.

Second, I challenged my inquisitor's faulty logic. He had made the classic mistake of employing the flawed "slippery slope" argument. In his mind, if *A* happens (in this case, "anyone who wants to effectively share the gospel with kids should be familiar with what they see and hear"), then through a series of small steps—*B, C, D, . . . X, Y*—eventually *Z* ("you're promoting pornography") will happen too. He erroneously concludes that if there are young people viewing pornography, then we should view pornography in order to understand and reach them. Then, because it is okay for us to view pornography, we are therefore promoting pornography. In other words, because *Z* shouldn't happen, *A* shouldn't happen either. If that's the case, then Jesus, Paul and every crosscultural missionary since has messed up big time.

The conversation continued and it became clear to me that the root issue wasn't necessarily pornography. Rather, it was our differing understandings of what it means to be holy. We agreed that God calls us to be holy. But we disagreed on what that means and how we are to live and conduct ourselves in our sinful and fallen world as holy persons. In his understanding, to be holy means that we should avoid all contact with the ungodly elements of popular culture—the bunker mentality. In my understanding, to be holy requires to be *in* but not *of* the world.

Since then, I decided that I should humbly reevaluate my understanding of holiness. What if I've been wrong all this time? After all, I don't want to promote a flawed understanding that isn't faithful to God's will.

My trip back to square one had to start with the holy One. What does he say in his Word about holiness? I needed to examine the Bible from start to finish to build a comprehensive worldview. What did I find?

First, holiness is first and foremost a divine quality. In fact, the word captures the essential nature of God and includes all his attributes. When the Bible speaks of God's holiness, it means that God alone is uniquely set apart from all creation, and God alone is morally perfect. No human—apart from the God-man Jesus—is by nature holy.

Second, to be holy is to be set apart *by* God. We are declared and become holy the moment God, by grace, brings us into a relationship with himself through Christ. The source of our holiness is Jesus himself, who makes us holy by forgiving our sins (Heb 10:10). There's absolutely nothing we can do to make ourselves or anyone else holy.

Third, to be holy is to be consecrated for service *to* God. We are set apart to serve our Creator. As a result, we are to distance ourselves from the ways and values of the world that run contrary to God's will. We must prayerfully seek to separate ourselves from sin and hold fast to Christ.

Fourth, Jesus is not only the source but the standard of holiness. We are to actively express our new life in Christ, our holiness, by following his example. To be holy means that we will prayerfully and earnestly reflect the image of Christ in how we love others both inside *and* outside the church.

Fifth, holy people live the will of God, including his call to be in but not of the world. This is the great paradox of holiness—that the God who sets us apart tells us to go into the sinful and fallen world (Jn 17:15-16, 18). Looking at, listening to and understanding that world for the sake of the advancement of God's rule and reign *is not* a compromise of our holiness. This is the service for which we've been set apart.

Sixth, to be holy doesn't mean we keep a long list of behavioral dos and don'ts. This was exactly the problem with the Pharisees. Charles

Colson warns us of four problems bred by this view of holiness.

- It limits the scope of true biblical holiness to just a few but not all areas of our lives. We wind up living "out of" and not "in" the world, thereby forfeiting our mission influence.

- We fall into the trap of obeying rules rather than obeying God.

- The emphasis on rule-keeping leads us to believe that we can be holy through our efforts.

- Our pious efforts can lead to self-righteousness—an ego-gratifying spirituality that turns holy living into spiritual one-upmanship.[14]

Finally, being holy means we can't go places we can't go. Christ has never called us to deliberately sin in order to engage the world for the sake of the gospel. If you can't watch it, listen to it or read it without falling into sin, then don't. But *don't* fall into the trap of equating temptation with sin. We know that Jesus, our example of holiness, was tempted in every way but did not sin (Heb 4:15). Being tempted or plagued by evil thoughts isn't sin. If a lustful or ungodly thought enters our mind and we reject it, we have not sinned. But if we seek out, embrace or entertain those thoughts, pursuing their pleasures, we've fallen into sin. Martin Luther said that evil thoughts are like the birds that fly over our heads; they're out of our control. But we can stop them from building nests in our hair. Christ promises that we won't be tempted beyond what we can bear, nor will he leave us without a way out (1 Cor 10:13).

Yes, we are called to be holy. But our definition of holiness determines whether we're faithful to Christ's call to transform the world.

Whatever Happened to Leslie?

At the beginning of chapter six I told you about Leslie, the school teacher who struggled with how Christians should relate to culture, especially the concept of transformation. I mentioned that I thought I'd never see or hear from Leslie and her friend again. I was wrong.

---

[14]Charles Colson, *Loving God* (Grand Rapids: Zondervan, 1983), p. 127.

In the spring of 1999 the country was gripped by the horrifying massacre at Columbine High School. I was asked to travel to the Littleton area to speak to parents, students and educators in the aftermath. My office was contacted by a middle school teacher who heard that I was coming to the area and wondered if I had enough time to stop by her classroom and speak with her students about the tragedy. I arrived at the school having no idea whose classroom I was about to enter. When I walked through the door I was stunned to be warmly greeted by Leslie. Before the students arrived, she walked me over to her desk and pointed to a large stack of CDs she had borrowed from her students in an effort to get to know them and their culture. She then told me how she had decided to put into practice what she had learned from me. I was thrilled to see how she was engaging the emerging generations. I asked her to write about this amazing shift in focus so that I might be able to share it with others who were hesitant to take the same step. What follows are some of Leslie's thoughts.

I always discounted the effect that "culture" has on the students I teach on a daily basis. A veteran of youth work and education in Colorado for fifteen years, I was always confident of my ability to relate to teens on a certain level. I've known that God is able to work above all of the worldly influences teens face. I saw no real need to know anything about the culture of the kids I taught or worked with.

These were a few of the reasons "avoidance" had always been my philosophy when it came to youth culture. I would consciously steer clear of youth culture I did not understand or was afraid of. My story is evidence that you can teach an old dog new tricks, and that we always need to be ready for lessons God may want to teach us.

My re-education started back in the Fall of 1998 when I first became acquainted with Walt Mueller and the Center for Parent/ Youth Understanding at a national youth conference. The intensive, eight-hour seminar I attended was titled "Understanding

Today's Youth Culture," an area in which my expertise was complete . . . or so I thought. In this class, we were challenged to realize that today's effective youth ministry is done from "inside" the youth culture. We were introduced to the idea that culture presents a "worldview" that youth are increasingly vulnerable to. During much of the discussion I was scratching my head as these thoughts were in contrast to the way I had approached teens and their culture. Even through fifteen years of youth ministry, these were issues I considered irrelevant. Cultural influences had always been a remote, outside influence that did not directly affect the lives of my students. As a result, I stayed away from what I didn't understand.

I was resistant and skeptical, but it became obvious this was worth a try. This seminar was unsettling. Yet the class was one of basic ministry philosophy that was different from anything I'd ever heard. Fighting my fear of compromising personal holiness, I spent the next six months diving deep into my students' culture and swimming in the confusing soup of sights and sounds. It wasn't easy, but I started to feel better prepared to address my youth in areas that had formerly been uncharted territories.

Then it happened. The Columbine tragedy shook our town of Littleton to the quick, and my students put my newly developed sensibilities to the test. As our community was struggling to find answers to the violence, the teenagers in my classes were providing plenty of clues of their own. They said, "Look at our home life and the materialism we are surrounded with. Look at our unmet needs. Look at why we're angry and why we're lonely. Look at how we express ourselves and how we think. Look at what we listen to and what we see."

In the aftermath of Columbine, Walt visited my school to meet with some of my students. The discussion focused on their world and the issues and struggles these kids face. It was exciting to see how easily these young people opened up when the conversation revolved around the influences in their lives. I was again learning how to build deeper relationships with teens by knowing their world.[15]

Leslie has continued to infiltrate, observe and understand the culture of the emerging generations so that God might use her redemptively in the lives of the students she loves. Amazingly, her ministry has not only become more effective, but incredible windows of ministry opportunity have opened for her, something that wouldn't have happened had she remained in the bunker. A year after attending that first youth workers' conference, Leslie was given the opportunity to sit in on the video shoot for Korn's eye-opening music video about abuse, "Falling Away from Me." Knowing that Fred Durst, the lead singer of the band Limp Bizkit, was going to be directing the shoot, Leslie prepared herself by learning as much as she could about Durst, his music and his band.

After the video shoot was completed, I received an e-mail from Leslie encouraging me to "open the attached file." When I opened it up, my monitor screen was filled with a photo of Leslie standing next to Fred Durst, each with an arm around the other. She proceeded to tell me how she had been able to connect with Durst because she had taken the time to listen and understand. Consequently, she was given an incredible opportunity to talk with him—by entering into his world as salt and light—about his life, his music and his beliefs for an extended period of time.

Initially resistant because she found comfort in the bunker, Leslie is like so many other followers of Christ who have learned that her place is *in* but not *of* the world. She says, "My suggestions to those who may be ready to develop new tools to better work in today's youth culture are simple, yet they might revolutionize your ministry and the relationships you have with young people. Know the media and the culture of the kids you minister to. Know the markings of today's youth culture. Know the Truth. Present them with the Truth. Let God transform them with the Truth."[16] That's exactly where all of us belong.

---

[15]Leslie Bogar with Tom Piotrowski, "What's Right with This Picture?" *youthculture@2000,* spring 2000, p. 10.
[16]Ibid., p. 11.

8

THE MARKS OF THE TWENTY-FIRST-CENTURY MESSENGER

THREE HUNDRED YOUTH WORKERS, parents and pastors from all over the city had gathered to learn about the emerging generations and how to reach them with the gospel. As the evening's moderator, I sat on the stage along with four teenagers from the community who each took fifteen minutes to tell their story to the crowd. When the teens had finished, I invited members of the audience to ask questions of the young people on the stage.

As the evening was about to end, the last questioner, the youth pastor of the host church, said, "I have a question for the young man on the right." The young man, Brian, was a member of the local community who had openly stated his disinterest in Christianity. The youth pastor continued: "Every day for the last two years I have arrived here early in the morning. I park my car and walk around the building to the front entrance. Because the high school (which is across the street) is a smoke-free zone, you and many of your friends congregate on our church sidewalk to socialize and smoke before the school day begins. I walk through and around you on the sidewalk and on steps to the front door. And every morning when I sit down at my desk, I look out my window at you and your peers and ask God what I can do to reach you. It's so frustrating." At this point the youth pastor paused to think about his next words, a sure sign of his frustration. Then, he looked at

Brian and asked his question on behalf of everyone in that room: "What can we do to connect with you?"

What happened next was incredibly powerful. Brian didn't have to think about his answer at all. First, he chuckled loudly, as if to say, "You've got to be kidding! How can you *not* know the answer to that one?" Then he looked at the youth pastor and said incredulously, "That's easy! Get out of your office and come out onto the sidewalk with us!" It was a powerful and eye-opening moment for everyone in that room. In the silence, I could almost hear everyone asking themselves, *How could I have missed it?*

Many of us stare out "the window," wondering what it will take to reach postmodern youth, oblivious to the fact that the answer has been there all the time.

Our Mission Is Clear

After his resurrection and before his ascension, Jesus gathered his disciples in Galilee to give them—and his disciples in all times and all places—their charge:

All authority in heaven and on earth has been given to me. Therefore go and make disciples of all nations, baptizing them in the name of the Father and of the Son and of the Holy Spirit, and teaching them to obey everything I have commanded you. And surely I am with you always, to the very end of the age. (Mt 28:18-20)

In effect, Jesus is telling us that when it comes to the emerging generations, we are to "get out of our offices and onto the sidewalks."

Jerram Barrs notes that in the Great Commission Jesus uses words of command and comfort.[1] First, the Great Commission has the authority of Jesus, a fact that brings great comfort to those who are his followers. Jesus declares that "all authority" is his. Everything in heaven and on earth belongs to him. He is the Lord over all things, in-

---

[1]Jerram Barrs, *The Heart of Evangelism* (Wheaton, Ill.: Crossway, 2001), pp. 15-17.

cluding the powers and principalities that are at war with the kingdom of God. Barrs says of the original disciples, "They had experienced firsthand the power of the hosts of Satan as those enemies tested them and sought the death of Jesus. But Jesus assured them that just as He had conquered Satan by His death on the cross and made that adversary's plans of no effect, so He would rule the heavenly powers for them as they went into the pagan world."[2] Like those first disciples, our missionary efforts will meet spiritual resistance. But we can be sure that the risen Christ has authority over all of the opposition.

Second, the Great Commission is a command to "go and make disciples of *all* nations." Christ's authoritative lordship over everything demands a mission to *everyone* living *everywhere*. Our mission takes us not just from nation to nation but from generation to generation and culture to culture. In the original Greek text, *go* is a participle, which can be translated "as you go." The usage here "isn't a question of whether or not we are to go. This is assumed. But as we go, we are to make disciples."[3] In our efforts with the emerging generations, leading them to a life of discipleship involves telling them the good news, leading them to repentance, *and* teaching and equipping them to understand and live a faith that is integrated into all of life in obedience to the commands of Christ.

Third, Jesus comforts his disciples by promising to be with them "always." To the original disciples his promise was that "wherever they would go, however hard the road, however challenging the situation, however unwelcoming the people, whatever their feeling of weakness, He would be beside them providing comfort, encouragement, and strength, just as He had been for the past three years of their lives. They would never be alone again."[4] We too are never alone as we venture out onto the "sidewalk" of the emerging generations.

The Great Commission was not only recorded in Matthew and the other three Gospels (in various forms) but in the opening chapter of

[2]Ibid., p. 17.
[3]David M. Howard, *The Great Commission for Today* (Downers Grove, Ill.: InterVarsity Press, 1976), p. 66.
[4]Barrs, *Heart of Evangelism*, pp. 17-18.

Acts as well: "be my witnesses in Jerusalem, and in all Judea and Samaria, and to the ends of the earth" (Acts 1:8). The fact that the Great Commission is included in all four Gospels and Acts reveals its importance. As commentator Ajith Fernando has said, "This realization clearly implies that 'his last command' should be 'our first concern.' "[5]

In his letter to the Romans, the apostle Paul asks a series of questions that emphasize the necessity of proclaiming the gospel to all people in all places and times. After stating that "everyone who calls on the name of the Lord will be saved" (Rom 10:13), he asks, "How, then, can they call on the one they have not believed in? And how can they believe in the one of whom they have not heard? And how can they hear without someone preaching to them? And how can they preach unless they are sent?" (Rom 10:14-15). Called, commanded and commissioned by Christ to go into all the world, those who take the good news onto the sidewalk of the emerging generations are celebrated: "How beautiful are the feet of those who bring good news!" (Rom 10:15).

The bulk of the remainder of this book will focus on the life and ministry of the apostle Paul as a model for ministry today. As an early disciple of Jesus Christ, Paul was passionate about serving his Lord by reaching out to *all* peoples with the good news. He developed and enlisted strategies to reach out to a variety of cultures. Let's discover the characteristics of the "beautiful feet" that effectively carry the good news onto the sidewalk of the young living in a postmodern context.

First, we will look at Paul to discover how his "motivations" can serve to motivate our missionary passion for young people. Second, we will look at who we must be before we embark on our journey to the sidewalk. And third, we will examine who we must be as we live among the emerging generations on the sidewalk of their world.

The Apostle Paul: *A Model for Missionary Motivation*

Paul is passionate, enthusiastic and single-minded about his mission to

---

[5]Ajith Fernando, *Acts*, NIV Application Commentary (Grand Rapids: Zondervan, 1998), p. 57.

share the good news, which had radically transformed his life on the road to Damascus. It wasn't always that way. Previously he was "convinced that [he] ought to do all that was possible to oppose the name of Jesus of Nazareth" (Acts 26:9). When Stephen was martyred by stoning, Paul was there "giving approval to his death" (Acts 8:1). But Paul's dramatic conversion led him to stand before King Agrippa and announce: "I pray God that not only you but all who are listening to me today may become what I am" (Acts 26:29), that is, Christian.

In *Evangelism in the Early Church*, Michael Green says that this remarkable sense of missionary zeal was present not only in Paul but in all early Christians, even as they faced great opposition.[6] What was the secret of their zeal? Green has discovered a threefold missionary motivation in Paul and his contemporaries that can help us in our task to make Christ known to the emerging generations today. Each of these motivations should be prayerfully and diligently pursued by those who long to reach today's postmodern world.[7]

First, like Paul, we should be motivated by *gratitude*. Paul is overwhelmed with gratitude to "the Son of God, who loved me and gave himself for me" (Gal 2:20). Green believes that this, not a sense of obligation to fulfill the Great Commission, is the primary motivation behind Paul's evangelistic zeal. "The example of Christ and the sense of responsibility to him were very important. Mission . . . was grounded in the very nature of a God who gave."[8] As we go into the world of the emerging generations, we should count it a privilege to represent the One who has given us life, and an honor to spread the good news.

Second, like Paul, we should be motivated by a sense of *responsibility*. Paul says, "I consider my life worth nothing to me, if only I may finish the race and complete the task the Lord Jesus has given me—the task of testifying to the gospel of God's grace" (Acts 20:24). Paul knows that when he finishes the race, the Lord will reward him with "the crown of righteousness" (2 Tim 4:8). "No doubt it was this thought which, as he puts it a few verses further on, 'gave me strength

---

[6]Michael Green, *Evangelism in the Early Church*, rev. ed. (Grand Rapids: Eerdmans, 2003), p. 273.
[7]Green's three points are found in ibid., pp. 274, 282, 289.
[8]Ibid., p. 278.

to proclaim the Word fully, that all the Gentiles might hear it.' "[9] Paul is secure in his standing before God as a sinner saved by grace, and we should be too, but like Paul, we should realize that doing God's will brings the immediate reward of "a closer conformity to the character of Christ, which is itself the height of happiness."[10] Paul also feels responsible to those who are lost. "I am obligated both to Greeks and non-Greeks, both to the wise and the foolish. That is why I am so eager to preach the gospel" (Rom 1:14-15).

Finally, like Paul, we should be motivated by *concern*. Paul knows that people outside of Christ are perishing and in desperate need of rescue. These are the very people whom Christ came to "seek and to save" (Lk 19:10). The gospel saves, and Paul dispenses it as the antidote to sin. With so many in the emerging generations seeking meaning and purpose in the dead-end of postmodern spirituality, we must be motivated by urgent concern for their spiritual well-being.

What drives our service as ambassadors of Christ and his kingdom? Gratitude to God for his grace, responsibility to complete the task Christ has given us, and concern for those who are lost.

Prerequisites for Effective Ministry to the Emerging Generations

Before we venture onto the postmodern sidewalk, our lives must be consistently marked by several core commitments. These should be part of our very makeup, marking our lives every minute of every day.

Committed to be a student of the Word. The emerging generation is not ultimately seeking a relationship with another human being. It's crying out for a restored relationship with its Creator. If the crux of our ministry is to point desperate youth to that relationship, we must be in that relationship ourselves, growing in our knowledge of the Redeemer.

After twenty-five years of what most would say was a successful and fruitful ministry, Henri Nouwen came face-to-face with a simple

---

[9]Ibid., p. 285.
[10]Ibid., p. 286.

question that caused him to rethink every aspect of his ministry: "Did becoming older bring me closer to Jesus?"[11] He found himself praying poorly, being isolated from others and preoccupied with the tyranny of the urgent. In his words, he felt he was experiencing "spiritual death." This is a real danger for all of us, a danger that can leave us powerless, passionless and with nothing to give.

The antidote is to maintain a single-minded commitment to be a student of the Word—a commitment that involves three crucial and complementary elements that are essential to spiritual vitality.

First, we must prayerfully grow closer to the living incarnate Word, Jesus Christ. Nouwen says that "Christian leaders cannot simply be persons who have well-informed opinions about the burning issues of our time. Their leadership must be rooted in the permanent, intimate relationship with the incarnate Word, Jesus, and they need to find there the source for their words, advice, and guidance."[12] Nouwen believes the avenue to this intimacy is through the disciplines of contemplative prayer and theological reflection, where time spent with Christ yields the benefit of "thinking with the mind of Christ."[13] Perhaps our ineffectiveness in reaching the emerging generations is rooted in our inconsistency in these disciplines. While we may be taking the time to know the culture and developing well-planned strategies, our spiritual lifeline will be cut if we are not first and foremost committed to nurturing our own relationship with Christ.

Second, we must diligently study God's written Word. My theological reflection should be based on a systematic and disciplined study of the Bible. The failure to know and study the Scriptures as the foundation for *all* of life is a horrible mistake that serves as a recipe for ministry disaster and ineffectiveness. Perhaps without knowing it, we've allowed our faith journey to begin and end through a faulty and unconscious literal misunderstanding of Jesus' words to Nicodemus, "You must be born again" (Jn 3:7), as if birth—or getting "saved"—rather than growth is all that is required of us. Sadly, we come to faith

---

[11]Henri Nouwen, *In the Name of Jesus* (New York: Crossroad, 1989), pp. 10-12.
[12]Ibid., p. 31.
[13]Ibid., p. 66.

but fail to foster and *live* the faith in a consistent, integrated fashion. Marva Dawn speaks to the importance of knowing the written Word in today's postmodern culture if we hope to reach the young: "Raising genuinely Christian children in a culture that rejects as oppressive any comprehensive meta-narrative is NOT a lost cause IF the church stands as an alternative community formed by the meta-narrative of God's revelation to humankind."[14]

Third, we must consciously guard against the temptation to reinvent, redefine or reimagine the Word in our own image. As our culture shifts deeper into postmodernity, we will be tempted to sacrifice true biblical faith on the altar of relevance. Consequently, we need to treasure the eternal truths of orthodox, biblical faith. Thomas Oden's own spiritual journey from theological liberalism has led him to conclude that orthodox Christianity—"the consensual core of beliefs that has been held by a majority of the church throughout the span of its historical existence"—will prove to be a vital source of postmodern orthodoxy.[15]

The need to be a committed student of the Word in order to effectively minister to the emerging generations hit home hard a few short years ago. As I went into my daughter Bethany's bedroom to say goodnight, my eyes were drawn to a book she was reading. At first, it appeared to be a teen devotional book. But there beneath the title, *Conversations with God for Teens*, I noticed the words, "with a foreword by Alanis Morissette." Having been a student of Morissette and her music, I was aware that she's been outspoken about her journey to invent and practice a very personalized, smorgasbord faith. Unless something had happened to Morissette that I was totally unaware of, my daughter was "conversing" with a god that was nothing like the God of the Scriptures. I calmly asked Bethany, "Tell me about the book you are reading." She proceeded to tell me that her eighth-grade English teacher thought she might enjoy reading the book. Then Bethany went on to say, "But I'm not so sure about it Dad. I think this guy

---

[14]Dawn, *Is It a Lost Cause?* pp. 244-45.
[15]Thomas Oden, cited in Millard J. Erickson, *Postmodernizing the Faith* (Grand Rapids: Baker, 1998), p. 67.

doesn't believe what I believe." After further discussion about what she had read, I realized that Bethany was right. Even in her limited eighth-grade knowledge of God's Word, Bethany had been able to discern with accuracy that the book's author, Neale Donald Walsch, was not orthodox in his faith.

I was curious about the impact Walsch was having on the teenage population. I quickly learned that this book, as well as several others he had written, was a bestseller. I bought my own copy of *Conversations with God for Teens* and quickly devoured its contents. This book is a virtual "how-to guide" for living life as a teenager in today's world. How does God speak through Walsch's book? Walsch poses all the questions teenagers have about life to God on their behalf. The questions run the gamut from God, to sex, to drugs, to parents, to love, to school and so on. Walsch verbalizes the question to God, listens for an answer and then records that answer for kids. Of course, it is then left to the reader to discover what God might be saying to them. Walsch writes, "In my own life, God's conversations most often take the form of thoughts that fill my head, especially when I am asking for help with a serious question—and when I am willing to be quiet enough to hear the answer. God 'speaks' to me in a voice that doesn't sound like anyone's voice in particular. It is what I have called a 'voiceless voice,' something like the voice of your own thoughts."[16] He continues, "Now it might sound good if I said I ponder my questions for hours, meditating and praying and remaining in the stillness until I am brought to enlightenment and tremble with the energy of God flowing through my fingertips. But the truth is, I put down the first thing that comes to my head."[17]

It's not surprising that Walsch's methodology yields a storehouse of advice from God for teens that can be summed up in one simple sentence: "Do whatever you feel is right for you." In typical postmodern fashion, Walsch reduces spiritual "truth" and its ultimate source to one's personal preferences and self. The benediction-like words of

---

[16]Neale Donald Walsch, *Conversations with God for Teens* (Charlottesville, Va.: Hampton Roads, 2001), p. 12.
[17]Ibid., p. 13.

blessing that close the book's final chapter offer further evidence of this fact: "Go now and create your world as you would have it be. Go now and celebrate your life, and everything that makes you 'you.' Go now and recreate yourself anew in the next grandest version of the greatest vision you ever had about who you are. This is my invitation. This is your dream. This is our next grand adventure."[18]

It's not surprising that similar books that redefine spiritual truth, God and humanity—including books by Deepak Chopra and *The Da Vinci Code* to name a few—are all finding their way to the top of the bestseller lists and into the collective spiritually hungry heart and mind of our culture. With this type of thinking, believing and living increasingly serving as the worldview foundation of the emerging generations, how can we steer them in the right direction? It starts with our commitment to live in that direction ourselves by being a student of the resurrected, living, reigning and written Word. We cannot live, share or communicate what we ourselves do not have.

Committed to be a person of prayer. There's one question that I get asked more than any other: "How do you continue to maintain your faith and spiritual sanity when you immerse yourself in so much garbage?" The tone of the question is rarely one of admiration but of skepticism. My answer is always the same: I confess my reliance on the spiritual disciplines of scriptural study and prayer as the anchors the Holy Spirit uses to keep my mind and my heart from going to places they shouldn't go.

As you venture onto the sidewalk of today's emerging youth culture, you'll see and hear things that are contrary to the will of God. But there is a marked difference between (1) seeing and hearing with your guard up in order to understand and (2) unguarded seeing and hearing in order to believe and follow. The former approach is the way of the missionary. The latter the way of the impressionable seeker. Christ has promised to protect us. Still, we can't drop our guard and walk foolishly through a world that can so easily trip us up. We must be cognizant of our fallen nature, our personal weaknesses and how easy it is to cross

---

[18]Ibid., p. 236.

the line into sin. When combined with ongoing study of the Word, prayer serves as a lifeline that keeps us tethered to the truth.

Here's a great contradiction: While we know prayer is our lifeline and the means God uses to conform us to his will, we often get so wrapped up in the missions task that prayer is moved to the bottom of our priority list. It's too easy not to pray. Our passion for prayer—for ourselves and those we minister to—will be fed only by the daily discipline of seeking God, whether we feel like it or not.

Daily I petition God to fill me with knowledge, wisdom, courage, compassion, grace, kindness, mercy and humility. I also ask God to protect me from harm and to provide for my spiritual well-being. In addition, I solicit the daily prayer of friends and colaborers. At the present time, over eighty people are praying for me every day. Through regular e-mail correspondence, I inform them of my schedule, my tasks and any specific cares or concerns for which I need them to intercede. This gives me strength.

Of course, our particular mission field is always in our prayers. Regarding this, Marva Dawn says, "Children and teenagers know when their youth leader and pastor love them—and that love for them will result if the leaders devote time to praying for them."[19] God has providentially placed us in their lives. We should pray that our relationship with them grows and that God would open their hearts to receive the life-changing message of the gospel.

One of the great mysteries of prayer is that it leads us into an understanding of and conformity to God's will. It is often said that "prayer changes things." In reality, prayer also changes us as we seek God's will. Marva Dawn cites five dimensions of prayer that will lead us into active participation in the purposes of God. First, "we will come to understand and share God's burden for the world." Second, "we will comprehend what God wants us to be." Third, "we will hear what God would have us do and how to do it." Fourth, "we will be equipped to face the principalities and powers in the world around us." And fifth, "we make ourselves available to God for the effecting

---

[19]Dawn, *Is It a Lost Cause?* p. 93.

of his will through us."[20] Prayer is indispensable if we hope to reach the emerging generations.

Committed to embody and live an integrated faith. Several years ago I encountered pop culture's singing and television sensation Jessica Simpson for the first time. I had heard of her but hadn't paid much attention because she was barely making a splash on the youth culture scene. My first encounter came while I was scanning the periodical racks in a seminary library early in 2001. I spotted Simpson's all-American smile on the cover of the Salvation Army's January 2001 edition of *YS* magazine, a magazine on a mission "to help young Salvationists meet the challenge of adolescence while moving toward Christian maturity." I opened the magazine and was thrilled to read of Simpson's commitment to use her high visibility to promote her Christian faith, prayer and premarital sexual abstinence.[21] The exciting reports I had heard about Simpson's faith and witness from other sources during the previous months were confirmed. Based on what I read in *YS,* this talented daughter of a youth pastor was someone I wouldn't hesitate to promote as a positive model of someone living out their faith in the mainstream youth culture.

Then, just a few days later, I encountered Jessica Simpson on the cover of a different periodical, the November 2000 edition of *FHM: For Him Magazine,* a publication targeting 18-34 year-old men with a mission markedly different from *YS:* "*FHM* aims to be the #1 lifestyle, entertainment and fashion magazine for men, by consistently delivering an irresistible breadth and variety of information. Through quality journalism and photography, *FHM's* goal is to inform, advise, enter-

---

[20]Ibid., pp. 196-98.
[21]My citation of this incident as an example of disintegrated faith is not intended in any way, shape or form to be a criticism of The Salvation Army, their publications or their youth ministry efforts. I have and continue to be a strong supporter of The Salvation Army along with their bold and cutting-edge youth ministry efforts, particularly among young people largely forgotten or marginalized by contemporary church culture. Their ongoing strategizing and success are exemplary. Rather, my critique is solely focused on a prominent pop culture icon who consciously chose to present herself in two very dissimilar manners to two very dissimilar reading audiences. It is important to note that The Salvation Army accurately reported in *YS* magazine what they knew to be true based on the information they had and the interview they conducted with Jessica Simpson at that point early in her career.

tain, and surprise across the entire panorama of what men like and are like. It also aims to fit with the reader's needs, schedules and spending habits, constantly searching for new ways to interact with the reader-ship, and faithfully reflect the title's brand values of funny, sexy and useful." At first glance, I wasn't sure I was looking at the same Jessica Simpson. This didn't look at all like the all-American girl gracing the cover of YS. I was looking at a scantily clad and seductive vixen posed in a manner designed to catch the attention and stimulate the libido of any male who happened past the newsstand. Inside, I found more of the same, including Simpson's explanation of why she had no prob-lem with posing in a sexually provocative manner: "It's not an image. That's me—it's just who I am. . . . I will wear sexy clothes. I'm not ashamed of my body, and I am not afraid of showing it. I just do it in a tasteful way. I just turned 20 and I want to show my body, and that's okay because God gave me my body and I am proud of it and I work hard for it, dang it!"[22]

As I turned the page, I saw Simpson's "pride," "hard work" and bare posterior displayed in a photo some would describe as "soft-porn." I wondered what message her viewers were getting as their eyes darted back and forth between Simpson and the quote promi-nently superimposed on the photograph: "There are different things that people can offer, and with me, it is my virginity and the innocence of that."[23]

I was sad and disappointed. *How could Jessica Simpson do this to a generation of kids who are already struggling to find their way through the confusing moral ambiguity thrown at them by our post-modern culture on a daily basis? She's caved to the culture and is lead-ing kids down the road of glaring hypocrisy and double-speak,* I thought to myself. Jessica Simpson has become a high-profile poster girl for a twenty-first-century church that's done a terrible job of com-municating *and* living an integrated faith. We're concerned about "saving people" from their sins and the perils of spending eternity in

---

[22]Bridget Freer, "Thank Heaven," FHM, November 2000, pp. 188-92.
[23]Ibid.

hell, but we seem to care very little about modeling and teaching an integrated faith that consistently transforms all of life. Maybe those two cover photos of Simpson offer convincing evidence of the careless example we've put forth to the emerging generations.

Charles Colson says, "The church's singular failure in recent decades has been the failure to see Christianity as a life system, or worldview, that governs every area of existence."[24] He's right. Maybe we shouldn't be surprised by the fact that the world looks at the church's inconsistency and responds with repulsion, mocking laughter or simple indifference. We must have a faith that is integrated. *Integrity* describes a life that is united in a complete and consistent whole. An integrated life is one where words, thoughts and actions consistently reflect the will of God in our lives. John Stott calls this "evangelical integrity":

> There is to be no dichotomy between what we profess and what we practice, between what we say and what we are, but rather a fundamental consistency. . . . On the one hand, inconsistent Christian conduct gives people cause to "malign the word of God" and so hinders evangelism. On the other hand, consistent Christian conduct "will make the teaching about God our Savior attractive" and so will promote evangelism (Tit 2:5, 10). More briefly, bad behavior discredits the gospel, while good behavior adorns and so commends it.[25]

A disintegrated faith is not only a turn-off to the watching world, but it is abiblical and powerless. For those members of the emerging generations who need to hear the message of the gospel—those we're called *to reach*—we've offered a disjointed faith that is anything but attractive, convincing and compelling. Our disintegrated faith has led to our misrepresenting what it means to be a follower of Jesus Christ. The result? We've undermined the power and appeal of the gospel.

We need to take a long, hard look into the mirror to see what kind of lived apologetic we are offering to the world. "It does absolutely no

---

[24]Charles Colson, *How Now Shall We Live?* (Wheaton, Ill.: Tyndale House, 1999), p. xii.
[25]John Stott, *Evangelical Truth* (Downers Grove, Ill.: InterVarsity Press, 1999), p. 113.

good for us to sit here and insist that the proposition 'Jesus is Lord of the Universe' is objectively true while at the same time we live our lives in such a way that this lordship remains completely invisible."[26] It's absolutely necessary for us to demonstrate true biblical faith—a faith marked by integrity.

Committed to be a student of culture. Several years ago at a youth-ministry training conference in the Midwest, I saw a twenty-something male flipping through our Center for Parent/Youth Understanding magazine, *youthculture@today.* I introduced myself and realized that he was one of the members of a well-known "Christian band" that had been performing at the conference. As we began to chat, he confessed his growing frustration with his inability to understand and connect with young people. "I need this stuff," he said as he continued looking through the magazine. "Kids are so confusing to me, and I feel so out of touch with what's happening in their world." I was stunned. Here was a guy who definitely looked the part. Not only that, he was in front of students doing ministry every other night of the week. But he had been left in the dust. He had a heart for ministry but was rapidly losing his ability to connect.

When the apostle Paul found himself in the pagan culture of Athens (Acts 17), he first walked around the city with his mouth shut and ears and eyes open. He absorbed as much as he could about the culture so that he might not only find evidence of their spiritual hunger but so he could communicate in a language and manner that would invite the Athenians to hear the good news. Paul had it right. He realized he not only had to engage in disciplined study of God's Word but also of the culture of those he was called to minister to.

It's not enough to just know the Word, we must also know the world. Dean Borgman says, "we often overlook the necessity of an exegesis of culture or world in which we were raised and to which we minister. . . . Theology is a systematic expression of God's Word

---

[26]Phillip D. Kenneson, "There's No Such Thing as Objective Truth, and It's a Good Thing, Too," in *Christian Apologetics in the Postmodern World,* ed. Timothy R. Phillips and Dennis Okholm (Downers Grove, Ill.: InterVarsity Press, 1995), p. 169.

in a particular time and space."[27] Understanding the unique cultural situation of the audience is a necessary prerequisite to effective ministry. As Gene Veith says, "To ignore the culture is to risk irrelevance."[28]

Failing to know the music, films, television, magazines and other expressions of young people that make up their cultural soup will lead to failure in youth ministry. The current shift in worldviews and rapidity of cultural change require our diligence in cultural exegesis. Duane Elmer notes: "The better we are at interpreting culture, the fewer conflicts we will experience, the more we will be able to build authentic relationships, and the greater will be our ability to communicate God's truth."[29]

Core Characteristics for Effective Ministry to the Emerging Generations

Beyond these commitments, our lives must be marked by several core characteristics that are part of who we are and how we minister on the postmodern sidewalk. While not exhaustive, the following characteristics should be prayerfully developed as part of our ministry strategy. Not only do they reflect the will of the Creator, but they are marks of Jesus Christ, the apostle Paul and effective crosscultural missionaries throughout the history of the church.

Approach youth ministry as a crosscultural missions venture. Regardless of your age or relationship with young people (e.g., youth worker, parent or pastor), when you engage the emerging generations you must remember that there is a cultural gap *you* are responsible to span. All those working with youth must see themselves as crosscultural missionaries who employ the incarnational approach God used when he sent his Son into our world. "The Word became flesh and made his dwelling among us" (Jn 1:14). God came to us as one of us. He entered into human culture, living and using human language and customs. In effect, John 1:14 says

---

[27]Dean Borgman, *When Kumbaya Is Not Enough* (Peabody, Mass.: Hendrickson, 1997), pp. 34-35.
[28]Gene Edward Veith Jr., *Postmodern Times* (Wheaton, Ill.: Crossway, 1994), p. xii.
[29]Duane Elmer, *Cross-Cultural Conflict* (Downers Grove, Ill.: InterVarsity Press, 1993), p. 14.

that God became one of us and "pitched his tent among us."[30]

Sherwood Lingenfelter observes that Jesus didn't simply arrive on earth and start ministering. Rather, he "studied the language, the culture, and the lifestyles of his people for thirty years before he began his ministry."[31] He identified fully with those he was sent to save. Lingenfelter notes that we should love the emerging generations so much "that we are willing to enter culture as children, to learn how to speak as they speak, play as they play, eat what they eat, sleep where they sleep, study what they study, and thus earn their respect and admiration. In essence, we must leave our prison, enter their prison, and become full participants within it."[32]

Knowledge of the youth culture alone is not enough. By itself, knowledge will lead to what I call the "field of dreams" ministry mistake. In the film *Field of Dreams,* a mysterious voice repeatedly speaks to Ray Kinsella: "If you build it they will come." When he heeds the voice and turns an Iowa corn field into a baseball diamond, a group of long-dead sluggers magically show up to play ball. No doubt, knowing the emerging youth culture and creating a place for youth to gather is a noble and necessary element of youth ministry. Some young people will come. But fewer and fewer of the lost seek out the church as a source of answers. Millard Erickson implores us to take our knowledge and "cross the bridge to where the horse is, rather than standing on our side of the bridge and trying to coax the horse to come to us."[33] Our calling is to take God's unchanging Word to young people. As crosscultural missionaries, we contextualize the unchanging message in forms that are familiar to them.

Be in *but not* of *the world.* We face a crisis of imbalance. At times, we pull ourselves out of the culture, believing that contact with anything "worldly" will compromise our holiness. At other times, we are so closely aligned with the world that we uncritically assimilate values

---

[30]Howard Peskett and Vinoth Ramachandra, *The Message of Mission*, The Bible Speaks Today, ed. Derek Tidball (Downers Grove, Ill.: InterVarsity Press, 2003), p. 72.
[31]Sherwood G. Lingenfelter and Marvin K. Mayers, *Ministering Cross-Culturally* (Grand Rapids: Baker, 2003), p. 16.
[32]Ibid., pp. 24-25.
[33]Erickson, *Postmodernizing the Faith*, p. 155.

and behaviors that are contrary to God's will. We must learn to walk the tightrope of living *for* God *in* the context of the postmodern culture. By striking the proper balance we are—by God's grace—living in obedience to God, maintaining a transforming and redemptive presence in the culture, and modeling true, biblical discipleship for all those who come to faith.

Always evaluate (and where necessary abandon) methods. "That's the way we've always done it." "It's worked well for so long." These clichés can't justify using tired, outmoded ministry methods. While the content of the Word always remains unchanged, the way we *do* ministry should be constantly evaluated. There is no room for sacred cows. If the message isn't getting through because of dated methods, new ones should be prayerfully sought and adopted in order to effectively communicate the good news. However, we must adopt only those methods that are faithful to the unchanging Word. If a methodology compromises the Word, then it's not an option. And, we must never assume that methodologies can do what only relationships can.

Answer all the groans. Scripture says that all creation "groans" with longing for ultimate redemption (Rom 8:22). In Mark's account of the Great Commission, Jesus tells his disciples to "preach the good news to all *creation*" (Mk 16:15, emphasis added). Creation includes not only fallen humanity but institutions and systems. Yes, our ministries are primarily with people. But we must also care as Jesus cares for institutions and social systems marked by the fingerprint of the Fall. Dean Borgman says:

> To be concerned with a young person involves being concerned with the social systems that shape her life. Theology for those ministering to youth must address family issues, schools, the media, the community, peer groups, employment, and the kinds of society in which these youth are about to assume adult roles.[34]

A biblically balanced ministry that goes beyond getting people "saved" will command the attention of the young, showing them the

---

[34]Borgman, *When Kumbaya Is Not Enough*, p. 227.

relevancy of the gospel to *all* individuals and to *all* of life.

Use popular culture as a communication tool. Today's popular culture is filled with stories, video clips, lyrics and so forth that can help us to communicate the unchanging message in a relevant manner. Duane Elmer suggests that missionaries familiarize themselves "with the stories, parables, fables, legends and heroes of a culture in order to appropriately interpret their use in conflict situations."[35] Jesus consistently used word pictures, analogies and illustrations from his culture as tools for communicating unchanging truth. And Paul used Athenian idol inscriptions and poetry to build a case for the gospel (Acts 17). By using something familiar, we can lead them into an understanding of something new.

I've seen the fruit of this principle in my own efforts and in the ministries of others. On one occasion, a middle-aged pastor called me to ask, "Do you know of any lyrics from popular songs that reflect a sense of hopelessness?" He was having some difficulty connecting with the younger members of his congregation. I told him about Trent Reznor and the dark music of Nine Inch Nails, and faxed him some background information and lyrics. The next week he informed me that as soon as he mentioned Reznor's name in his sermon, the head of almost every usually bored teenager popped up to hear what he was saying. After the worship service, several commented enthusiastically about the relevance and timeliness of his sermon.

Understand your own cultural biases. When we cross geographical boundaries we expect that numerous differences between us and our audience will exist. Among other things we will see and hear obvious differences related to language, racial composition and dress. But crosscultural missions efforts across generational lines are prone to try our patience for the simple fact that we've been living in the same geographical world with our audience all of our lives. Since the differences are related more to values, attitudes and allegiances, the collision between worldviews that coexist in one place can be messy, loud and severely damaging to our ministry effectiveness. The reason? Our

---

[35]Elmer, *Cross-Cultural Conflict,* p. 181.

tendency is to spend a good amount of our "ministry time" convincing our audience that we are right and they are wrong. In other words, we must understand our own cultural biases and our inclination to see these biases as matters of right and wrong that we force on others as non-negotiables. Pete Ward warns that "the youth minister working across cultures and subcultures will need to develop an awareness of the way that his or her own understanding of the Christian faith has been shaped within a particular culture. This self-awareness is the first step in contextualizing the Gospel."[36] The reality is that our way of doing things is not the only way. God's world is wider and broader than what we've experienced. Duane Elmer notes that some of those things we define as right or wrong might actually fall into the category of normal differences we are sure to encounter when we engage another culture.

How you handle them determines your level of comfort, ability to function, level of satisfaction and degree to which God can use you. If I have a narrow category of differences, I will try to force nearly everything I see in the new culture into the categories of right and wrong. Furthermore, I usually make the decision of what belongs in which category by what looks like me or my culture—that would go in the category of right. What does not look like me would go in the category of wrong. I have established my culture and myself as the norm, the standard by which I judge others and their culture. People with a narrower category of differences have a greater tendency to do this, and this is a problem we must all guard against.[37]

Be intent on building relationships. The postmodern generation, like all generations, not only long for a connection with their Creator but also with their fellow humans. What sets them apart from prior generations is the deep level of brokenness they've experienced in their most basic relationship, the family. This leaves them intensely hungry for and open to relationships with others. Here's an opportunity for the church. But we must not be exploitative. Our interest in

---

[36]Pete Ward, *God at the Mall* (Peabody, Mass.: Hendrickson, 1999), p. 102.
[37]Duane Elmer, *Cross-Cultural Connections* (Downers Grove, Ill.: InterVarsity Press, 2002), p. 29.

them must be genuine and real; we must see them as people to be loved rather than projects to be completed or conquered.

Postmoderns put a premium on "subjective evidences for the validity of a religion."[38] In other words, they are not concerned with objective proofs and rational arguments supporting Christianity as a faith system. Instead, they simply want to know that it works. Seeing, not knowing, is believing.

Incarnational ministry is marked by relationships. Relationships open the ears, eyes and hearts of young people to the truths of God's Word. And through relationships we discover the real and felt needs of those we minister to. Duane Elmer notes that "in most cultures of the world, friendships and community are among the strongest forces for bringing people to faith in Christ. If we are not in good relationships, if we cannot create solidarity, from a human standpoint there is little that will attract people to the gospel."[39] Relationships are more often than not the doorway through which the emerging generations come to faith and learn what it means to live a fully integrated faith.

Love without condition or limits. One of the great crises in today's youth culture is the need to be and feel loved. In their hit song "Perfect," Canadian band Simple Plan sings the first-person hurt of those in the emerging generations whose fathers have ceased loving them:

I try not to think
About the pain I feel inside
Did you know you used to be my hero?
All the days you spent with me
Now seem so far away . . .
And nothing's alright

Henri Nouwen captures this reality: "Very few people know that they are loved without any conditions or limits. This unconditional and unlimited love is what the evangelist John calls God's first love. 'Let us

---

[38]Ajith Fernando, "The Uniqueness of Jesus Christ," in *Telling the Truth,* ed. D. A. Carson (Grand Rapids: Zondervan, 2000), p. 126.
[39]Elmer, *Cross-Cultural Conflict,* p. 53.

love,' he says, 'because God loved us first.' "[40] It is crucial that our initial contact with young people is filled with love. Yet they may be hesitant to return our "embrace" because we are from another generation and culture, or because of their deep relational brokenness. To help them overcome that fear, our love must be sincere and without condition or limit. Like Christ, we must simply love. Pete Ward says that when we first encounter a young person, we should accept them as they are simply because "we are visitors in their world" who need to learn how to relate.[41] As we build our relationships, we love them by serving them. In addition, we should elevate our love for other Christians—this will serve as a powerful testimony to the watching youth culture. They must see that the mark of the church is love.

Be willing to suffer "with." It is said that Bob Pierce, the founder of World Vision, was called to minister to the poor after praying a very dangerous prayer: "Let my heart be broken by the things that break the heart of God." It's dangerous because its answer can shake up our comfortable and self-centered priorities. When God answered Pierce's prayer, he felt a deep compassion for the hungry and poor that changed the course of his life and the world. For the church to effectively connect with and minister to the emerging generations, we must pray that same prayer. When God answers this prayer, we will fully realize the meaning of incarnational ministry to the young, and, like Jesus, our hearts will be broken by the depth of their spiritual and emotional pain. We will be driven to immerse ourselves in their world, their history and their humanity. In effect, we will have the "heart of God" for them. Nouwen says the heart of God "suffers immensely because it sees the magnitude of human pain and the great resistance to trusting the heart of God, who wants to offer consolation and hope."[42] To suffer "with" means that we will see, understand and respond to their hurt as God does.

Serve with vulnerable humility. Ultimately, humility flows from the recognition that any strength we possess is not our own. The source

---

[40]Nouwen, *In the Name of Jesus,* p. 25.
[41]Ward, *God at the Mall,* p. 58.
[42]Nouwen, *In the Name of Jesus,* p. 24.

of our strength (and achievement) is found in God alone. We are fully dependent on God's grace, and any ministry effectiveness we might experience is the result of that grace. As a result, we must realize that we are not "saviors." Rather, "we are sinful, broken, vulnerable people who need as much care as anyone we care for."[43] As Paul says to Titus, "show true humility toward all men" (Tit 3:2).

This type of humility should drive us to be vulnerable, a trait that builds relational bridges to the emerging generations. Young people value those who humbly share their own weaknesses. Postmoderns believe people who are transparent and honest, not those who put on false airs. If we are honest, we have doubts, fears, troubles and defeats. Faith does not eliminate our problems; it puts them in a new perspective. Perhaps one of the greatest favors we can do for those considering Christ is to ground them in realistic faith, not a "perfect" faith that is unattainable. Tell them the truth. If we are not realistic (e.g., "When you come to Christ all your problems, doubts and fears will disappear!"), we will set them up for failure and dissatisfaction with their Christian life. Eventually, they will throw up their hands in despair and walk away in defeat.

Provide a place and community. Loading our oldest daughter's possessions into a U-Haul trailer to move her to a new apartment in Pittsburgh was painful. While I knew it was time for Caitlin to be on her own, I felt that our family was losing a piece of itself. In one of our conversations prior to Caitlin's departure, she overheard her mother and me pondering whether we would move into a smaller house when we became empty-nesters. Caitlin quickly interjected: "Mom and Dad, please don't ever move from this house. This is where I grew up. This is where my family lives. When I have a family of my own, this is where I want to come to bring them 'home.' "

Those of us who have fond childhood memories can identify with Caitlin's feelings. We need the security of a place to live with and be loved by others: home. Today's emerging generations are no different. They long for a place to belong and to call home. For many, their

---

[43]Ibid., pp. 43-44.

yearning is amplified by the fact that broken family situations and the lack of healthy peer relationships have left them with a huge relational void. They want connections, relationships and community.

In order to fulfill its divinely ordained mission as the body of Christ *and* to effectively reach out crossculturally to the postmodern generations, the church must facilitate community in two ways. First, the larger body of Christ should include the emerging generations as it assembles for worship, mission, fellowship, education and service. In other words, we must stop our destructive practice of separating the body of Christ along generational lines. For example, we must ask ourselves why we are so quick to remove teenagers from the opportunity to worship with the older, wiser and spiritually gifted members of our congregation by starting a separate culturally relevant "youth worship." Doing so robs the body of Christ of its ability to function properly. Second, postmoderns are especially interested in the intimate community found in small groups. A small group serves as a place to be vulnerable and real while examining the claims of Christ or pursuing spiritual growth. Small groups are a place where the truth can be communicated, discussed and lived out in the context of community.

In his work with college students and young adults, Steve Garber has seen the valuable role Christian community plays in their spiritual awakenings, growth and nurture.

> From the most sophisticated cultural critiques to the street-level despair of the "dissed" generation, the evidence seems conclusive: for individuals to flourish they need to be part of a community of character, one which has a reason for being that can provide meaning and coherence between the personal and the public worlds. . . . Community is the context for the growth of convictions and character. What we believe about life and the world becomes plausible as we see it lived out all around us.[44]

Be a learning listener. The emerging generations have a twofold complaint about those of us who are older: we don't listen, and we

---

[44]Steven Garber, *The Fabric of Faithfulness*, (Downers Grove, Ill.: InterVarsity Press, 1996), p. 145.

don't understand. Understanding comes only through listening. Social researcher Judith Wallerstein has learned that listening is a key to connecting. She says, "I've discovered over many years of interviewing children and adults that people rise to lyrical heights when they feel that someone is finally listening."[45] By listening, we begin to learn about those we've been called to reach. Duane Elmer offers this advice:

> It takes time, conversations, questions, listening and the whole range of learning skills to form accurate perceptions about people who are different from me. I must suspend judgment, maintain an open mind and seek more information (especially from those people I am prone to judge) before drawing conclusions. If I am too quick to judge or draw a conclusion, my mind closes, learning stops, and the potential for building a relationship is lost.[46]

Our full attention and energy must be given to what the other person has to say.

Be a story-teller. "Please tell me a story" is the universal bedtime plea of children. The emerging generations love stories too. In fact, postmoderns place a higher value on subjective narrative than on objective fact. The avenue to the heart of young people is story. This is good news for those called to tell the biblical story of creation, Fall and redemption. James Sire says he knows "of no modern stories that are really comparable in relevance and power to those Jesus told."[47] Stories about Jesus' life and ministry have great ability to connect and bring truth to life for young people.

The emerging generations are especially curious about the relevance of the biblical story for today. We can help them realize that God is still redemptively active in the affairs of humankind by telling them our stories—how God has changed our lives.

A person of grace. A few years ago I researched the life story of Scott

---

[45]Judith Wallerstein, Julia Lewis and Sandra Blaskeslee, *The Unexpected Legacy of Divorce* (New York: Hyperion, 2000), p. xxxiii.
[46]Elmer, *Cross-Cultural Conflict,* pp. 16-17.
[47]James W. Sire, "On Being a Fool for Christ and an Idiot for Nobody," in *Christian Apologetics in the Postmodern World,* ed. Timothy R. Phillips and Dennis L. Okholm (Downers Grove, Ill.: InterVarsity Press, 1995), p. 123.

Stapp, a singer who was at the time fronting the popular band Creed. While completing the project I realized it was the story of a young man raised in a fundamentalist Christian home who was still longing for a relationship with his Creator. Like others, Stapp struggled because he never experienced grace, mercy and forgiveness in his relationship with his overly religious father. Gene Veith states that there is a time when people need to hear the law, especially when they are sinful, proud and self-righteous. But there is also a time for hearing grace. Today's post-modern youth culture, like Stapp, needs to hear God's grace proclaimed and see it demonstrated. "Those who are hurting," says Veith, "are plagued by guilt, hopelessness and despair, need to hear the Gospel."[48] This gospel of grace is best communicated as we enter into relationships while prayerfully seeking to live and share the grace of Christ. As we live in Christ's grace, we will help others hear Christ's voice calling them to come and experience it for themselves.

In the years since I first heard Scott Stapp's story, the singer has continued his search. While I don't know all the details of where his search led, Stapp has reported that he has embraced Christianity and experienced rebirth. We can be sure that along the way there were people of grace who pointed Stapp to what he was looking for.

Signposts on the Sidewalk

The Great Commission calls us to "get out of our offices and onto the sidewalk" of the emerging postmodern generations. We need to point them to the destination they so desperately seek. In *The Fight,* John White reminds us that we are signposts. "A signpost points to a destination," writes White. "It matters little whether the signpost is pretty or ugly, old or new. It helps if the lettering is bold and clear. But the essential features are that it must point in the right direction and be clear about what it is pointing to."[49] We aren't drawing attention to ourselves but to Jesus Christ, where redemption, new life and pur-

---

[48]Gene Edward Veith, *The Spirituality of the Cross* (St. Louis, Mo.: Concordia, 1999), pp. 27-28.
[49]John White, *The Fight* (Downers Grove, Ill.: InterVarsity Press, 1976), p. 61.

pose are found. The lettering is made "bold and clear" by entering into the postmodern world as motivated emissaries, serving our Sender by maintaining the necessary commitments and wearing the marks of a twenty-first-century missionary with joyful consistency. Doing anything less in our postmodern world jeopardizes our ability to effectively cross cultures into the world of young people.

9

PAUL'S MARS HILL MINISTRY FOR TODAY

WHEN CHRIS CARRABBA—a.k.a. "Dashboard Confessional"—straps on his acoustic guitar and steps on stage, an interesting phenomenon takes place. The crowds that gather to listen to his "emo-punk" hear him sing about his personal struggles to make sense out of life. But when Carrabba begins to sing, the crowd sings along—word for word—to music that is emotionally vulnerable. His music has connected with his audience at a deep level because his heart is their heart too. His struggles are their struggles, and like Carrabba, they long to make sense of life.

The last song on Dashboard Confessional's 2003 breakthrough album *A Mark, a Mission, a Brand, a Scar* captures the essence of the emerging generations' spiritual cry. "Pacific Sun, you should have warned us, it gets so cold here," Carrabba sings in "Several Ways to Die Trying," a song about the emptiness of life. He continues on, lamenting the fact that his generation's cries for help have gone unnoticed by those who know the secret to life:

And the night can freeze before you set it on fire.
And our flares go unnoticed.
Diminished, faded just as soon as they are fired.
We are, we are, intrigued. We are, we are, invisible.

Oh, how we've shouted, how we've screamed, take notice, take
interest, take me with you.
But all our fears fall on deaf ears.

If the contemporary church fails to open up to a crying and dying generation, the song's final lines might accurately describe the results:

Tonight, they're burning the roads they built to lead us to the
light.
And blinding our hearts with their shining lies, while closing our
caskets cold and tight. But I'm dying to live.

Postmodern youth are crying for redemption. Sadly, the church all too
often allows their cries to go unanswered because of ignorance, busy-
ness or even bigotry. After all, they look, think, talk and act in ways
that make us uncomfortable or that we just don't like.

Of course, our neglect leaves a bad taste in their mouths. In his riv-
eting novel, *Hey Nostradamus,* Douglas Coupland reveals that perspective through one of the book's main characters, a high school senior. She says:

It always seemed to me that people who'd discovered religion
had both lost and gained something. Outwardly, they'd gained
calmness, confidence, and a look of purpose, but what they'd
lost was a certain willingness to connect with unconverted souls.
Looking a convert in the eyes was like trying to make eye contact
with a horse. They'd be alive and breathing, but they wouldn't
be a hundred percent *there* anymore. They'd left the day-to-day
world and joined the realm of eternal time.[1]

Over fifty years ago French social critic Jacques Ellul addressed the
reality of the church's ineffectiveness as it played out in his contemporary situation, which was much like our own. He wrote, "The coun-
tries which are supposed to possess a Christian civilization are rapidly
becoming secularized, and people listen to the church less and less.
. . . The world as a whole no longer listens to the Gospel. The Word

---

[1]Douglas Coupland, *Hey Nostradamus* (New York: Bloomsbury, 2003), p. 27.

of God no longer penetrates into the reality of human life. Men seek other solutions, listen to other promises, to other Gospels."[2] Ellul knew that the problem isn't the gospel; it never ceases to speak to humanity's hunger and thirst for redemption. Rather, the problem is the messengers of the gospel and their method of communicating the good news.

In an effort to discover the solution that would remedy this problem, Ellul asked the questions we should ask ourselves: "Why are we in this condition, and what can we do about it?"[3] Ellul offers his answer:

> The Gospel no longer penetrates. We seem to be confronted by a blank wall. Now if we want to go further: either, we must find a door, or we must break down the wall! But first of all we must investigate this wall in order to find out whether there *is* a door: thus we need to explore this world in which we are now living. If there *is* no door (as seems to me to be the case) then we must find (or create) the instruments we need in order to make a breach in it.[4]

Our responsibility is to know the "wall" of the postmodern worldview so well that we either find or make a doorway for the gospel.

This book is about the need to listen to, understand and know the wall of postmodernity. This wall is marked by great need and great interest in spirituality, but little or no understanding of or regard for the Bible. But this isn't the first time such a world has existed. Christian missionaries past and present have engaged pagan cultures with no knowledge of the Bible. And in Acts we find a timely ministry model for responding to our postmodern culture. It is a model that we need to rediscover and implement in the church today if we hope to break through the wall.

---

[2]Jacques Ellul, *The Presence of the Kingdom* (Philadelphia: Westminster Press, 1951), pp. 138-39.
[3]Ibid., p. 139.
[4]Ibid.

Mars Hill Ministry Then

Today's church finds itself at a watershed moment. Unlike the last fifty years, people today are self-consciously seeking purpose and significance. They have consciously embarked on a search for spiritual fulfillment. As a result, it is critically important for the church to (1) listen to and fully obey the unchanging Word, and (2) listen to and understand postmodernity so the gospel might be advanced. The model that can help us seize this moment is found in Acts 17, where Paul engages the Athenians on Mars Hill.

In this chapter, we will examine Paul's encounter with the Athenians and attempt to understand his strategy for engaging them with the gospel. Then we will look at how we can apply it in our contemporary situation. The paradigm for Mars Hill ministry is found in Acts 17:16-34, as Paul engages the Pagan population of Athens in a variety of settings—including the Mars Hill Council—in a manner uniquely tailored to fit the contemporary worldview situation of the city's inhabitants.

The messenger: Paul. Born into a Jewish family that strictly observed the Old Testament Scriptures and traditions, Paul advanced "in Judaism beyond many Jews of [his] own age" (Gal 1:14). By virtue of his birth in the city of Tarsus, Paul was also a Roman citizen. Tarsus, an educational center and hub of learning, is where he was introduced to Greek literature, philosophy and culture. An opponent of Christianity and a persecutor of Christians, Paul was transformed by an encounter with the risen Christ on the road to Damascus. Christ called him to be his ambassador to the Gentiles (see Acts 26:17-18).

Paul's ministry is marked by *faithfulness* and *flexibility.* As a faithful servant of Christ, Paul resolved to never compromise the message of the gospel. He strived to be consistently faithful to Christ in word and lifestyle. His calling to crosscultural missions demanded a flexibility that he took very seriously. In his first letter to the Corinthians, Paul explains: "I have become all things to all men so that by all possible means I might save some. I do all this for the sake of the gospel, that I may share in its blessings" (1 Cor 9:22-23).

The place: Athens. After facing persecution in Berea, Athens served as a temporary stopping place for Paul as he waited for his missionary companions (Acts 17:14-15). Named for Athena, the Greek goddess of wisdom, Athens was a leading city of ancient Greece. The native city of Socrates and Plato, it was the adopted home of Aristotle and Epicurus. It set the economic, artistic, educational, religious and philosophical pace for the empire. By the time Paul arrived, the city's intellectual environment was multicultural and pluralistic. Its landscape was peppered with idols, an indicator of the population's interest in religion. While Athens in Paul's time was only a shadow of its former self, intellectuals carried on the traditions of discussing philosophy, religion and world events. It still was a leading center of intellectual inquiry, culture and religion.

The audience: Educated pagans. Paul's audience in Athens primarily comprised educated people preoccupied with discussing a spirituality that melded idolatry, superstition and philosophy in an endless number of combinations. The countless images, idols and monuments dotting the Athenian landscape witnessed to the "smorgasbord spirituality" of the city's population. The people of Athens were biblically illiterate. For this reason, the spiritual and intellectual mood in Athens bears a striking resemblance to postmodernity.

The method: Paul engages the pagan mind. The record of Paul's encounter with the Athenians in Acts 17 is a summary of what certainly was a much longer interaction. While a full account of Paul's words does not exist, the structure and flow of his encounter has been preserved. I will break down Paul's Mars Hill interaction to examine each of its elements in order to better understand the amazing similarities between Paul's ministry context and our own. In addition, I'll examine the method Paul used to present the truths of God's unchanging Word in and understandable and engaging manner to those steeped in the unique Athenian cultural reality and worldview.

As you read through Paul's encounter with the Athenians on Mars Hill, focus on how he uses his knowledge of their culture and worldview to shape the strategy, method and content of his message.

The Mars Hill Event

While Paul was waiting for them in Athens, he was greatly distressed to see that the city was full of idols. (v. 16)

With time on his hands, Paul embarks on a tour of this cultural center and immediately sees "a veritable forest of idols."[5] Pagan temples, statues, pillars and many phallic monuments were indicative of the city's immorality. His senses are bombarded with things of the world, the flesh and the devil.

Before examining how Paul responds to what he encounters, note what Paul *does not* do. First, there is no indication that his presence in this polytheistic culture compromises his holiness. Being in the presence of idols doesn't mean that he has worshiped them. It doesn't mean that he has adopted the philosophies and ideas of the Athenians. He is *in* but not *of* the Athenian culture. Paul knows this is where he belongs as Christ's ambassador to the Gentiles. He doesn't have a bunker mentality. Instead, his faith in Christ and his holiness demand his sustained presence in Athens.

Second, Paul isn't indifferent to the rampant idolatry he sees. Michael Green notes:

> At once we notice how different he is from us. We are surrounded by various forms of idolatry—worship of fame, sex, money, power, and it does not bother us. We have lost the ability to care. Our forefathers were moved to tears by the thought of people dying without Christ. This concern fuelled the worldwide missionary movement. But today in this pluralist society we do not feel it matters very much whether people become Christians or not.[6]

Luke tells us that Paul is "greatly distressed" by the idolatry he encounters. It's an uncontrollable reaction that flows out of his deep love for Christ and compassion for the lost. The verb used here, *paroxynō*,

---

[5]John R. W. Stott, *The Message of Acts,* The Bible Speaks Today (Downers Grove, Ill.: InterVarsity Press, 1990), p. 277.
[6]Michael Green, *Thirty Years That Changed the World* (Grand Rapids: Eerdmans, 2004), pp. 106-7.

indicates Paul is experiencing a paroxysm as he becomes deeply and emotionally concerned while feeling both anger and grief over the idolatry of the Athenians. This is the same verb used in the Greek Septuagint to describe God's response to idolatry. Paul feels the same grief God felt over Israel's idolatry. John Stott says that Paul's distress is due "to his abhorrence of idolatry, which aroused within him deep stirrings of jealousy for the Name of God, as he saw human beings so depraved as to be giving to idols the honor and glory which were due to the one, living and true God alone."[7] As a result, Paul *must* speak up.

So he reasoned in the synagogue with the Jews and the God-fearing Greeks, as well as in the marketplace day by day with those who happened to be there. (v. 17)

Instead of condemning the Athenians or retreating to a safe place, Paul goes right to where the people are. As is his usual practice when arriving in a new location, Paul stops first at the synagogue to meet with his fellow Jews and the "God-fearing Greeks." Paul probably "reasoned with them from the Scriptures, explaining and proving that the Christ had to suffer and rise from the dead," as he had done previously in Thessalonica (Acts 17:2-3). He doesn't just preach. In addition, he uses logic, dialogue and rhetoric. He interacts with his hearers, allowing them to respond to, question and interact with him about the gospel message he's proclaiming.

Paul also reasons in the marketplace. In Athens, the marketplace was known as the "Agora." Like a town square in early America, the Agora was the hub of civic activity, where the Athenian citizens gathered to meet their friends, hear the latest news, conduct business and chat about everyday life. The Agora was also the place where Socrates had sat years earlier to engage passersby in dialogue. Paul understands that the Agora has been a strategic central physical and intellectual location for a long time. It's not at all surprising that as he engages the Athenians he enlists the same method of dialogue—questions and answers—employed by Socrates when he sat in the very same place.

---

[7]Stott, *Message of Acts*, p. 279.

A group of Epicurean and Stoic philosophers began to dispute with him. Some of them asked, "What is this babbler trying to say?" Others remarked, "He seems to be advocating foreign gods." They said this because Paul was preaching the good news about Jesus and the resurrection. (v. 18)

While at the Agora, some philosophers in the audience begin to clash with Paul. In an interesting development, the philosophers are from two competing schools of philosophy dominating the intellectual scene in Athens, the Epicureans and the Stoics. Both however, espouse pagan philosophies and worldviews that are attempts to answer humanity's cry for meaning, purpose and redemption with no regard for the incarnate or written Word. Still, Paul does not write them off. His place is to be "in" but "not of" the world of their philosophies and worldviews.

In order to fully understand the Mars Hill ministry paradigm, it's important to understand the basic underlying beliefs of these two schools of philosophical thought. Each bears striking similarity to the way many contemporary postmoderns live and think today.

The Epicureans followed the teachings of Epicurus (341-270 B.C.), a philosopher who taught that the highest good and goal in life was pleasure—not in the sense of unbridled sensual hedonism but in terms of a life of peace and tranquillity free from the burden of worries, pain, fear and cares. The Epicureans were "feeling-oriented" people who believed that knowledge is a feeling that can be gained by pursuing pleasure (the good things in life) and avoiding pain (the bad things in life). Good and bad are determined by one's senses and feelings. The standards of judgment of each are subjectively rather than objectively determined. As far as God is concerned, they believed that gods existed but had no interest or involvement in human affairs. Consequently, they believed there would be no judgment or life after death. Since life on earth was all there was and it existed purely by the chance collision of physical matter, the pleasure of a worry-free earthly existence was to be sought and pursued as the source of all meaning in life. Their worldview and individualistic philosophy of life had no room for the resurrection. Death was the end as one's physical matter dispersed.

The Stoics followed the teachings of Zeno (340-265 B.C.) and took their name from the Stoa Poikile, the portico of the Agora where they met to listen to Zeno teach. In contrast to the Epicureans, the Stoics were the rationalists and thinkers in Athens and were the most popular of the two schools of thought at Paul's time. They believed that reason was to guide humanity and that the ultimate goal in life is to become self-sufficient, courageous and dutiful, while enduring life by working to live in harmony with nature. If one could no longer live a dignified life in harmony with the world, they believed it was proper to commit suicide. As pantheists, they believed that "god" was the world's soul, and that the world came into existence and continues on by chance. Divinity is the capacity for reason that lies within humanity. Humans therefore, can become "a god" in themselves. These beliefs worked themselves out in a practical life marked by tolerance and pluralism, as the existence of a world full of free souls is a world without distinction to nationality or class. Like the Epicureans, the Stoics had no room for the resurrection.

Because of their philosophic frame of reference, both the Epicureans and Stoics react against Paul and his teachings. Their worldviews are so antibiblical that what Paul is telling them is foreign, alien and ultimately revolting; it doesn't fit into any of their intellectual categories. This is what happens when the gospel is presented in a crosscultural situation to a pagan audience lacking knowledge and familiarity with the Word.

Paul's preaching about Jesus and the resurrection are so foreign to them that it draws two responses. First, some of them wonder out loud what "this babbler" is trying to say. The word *babbler* is used to describe a bird picking up scraps of seed and food in the gutter. Their use of this word indicates that it appears to them that Paul has only picked up "scraps" of plagiarized knowledge from a variety of sources combining in "a ragbag of other people's ideas and sayings."[8] And second, they accuse Paul of advocating foreign gods named "Jesus" and "Anastasis" (the Greek word for "resurrection");

---

[8]Ibid., p. 282.

many in the audience may have believed that when Paul spoke of the resurrection he was speaking of a person rather than a historical event. As odd as it may sound, even though Athens was home to multiple deities, it was an offense to introduce strange new gods as they might lead to rejection of the established deities and the disruption of the state religion.

Based on the reactions of the Athenians, one might assume that Paul would have been ignored or escorted quickly out of town. But the fact that he has come to them, met them on their own turf, and engaged them at the level of their interests and ideas sets the stage for something amazing to happen. The Athenians are so intrigued by what Paul has to say that they invite him to the Areopagus, or Mars Hill.

Then they took him and brought him to a meeting of the Areopagus, where they said to him, "May we know what this new teaching is that you are presenting? You are bringing some strange ideas to our ears, and we want to know what they mean." (All the Athenians and the foreigners who lived there spent their time doing nothing but talking about and listening to the latest ideas.) (vv. 19-21)

The Stoic and Epicurean philosophers—complex thinkers who were set in their ways—pay Paul a great compliment by inviting him to join them at the Areopagus, a judicial body named after the Hill of Ares— "Ares" being the Greek equivalent of "Mars," therefore also known as Mars Hill—where it met in early times.

The Areopagus is the main administrative body and chief court of Athens. This ancient court had a long and prestigious history and was responsible for the judicial, religious and moral well-being of the state. By the time Paul enters Athens, the Areopagus no longer functions as it once did, but it still serves an important role in Athenian culture as a judicial court dealing with matters related to homicide as well as general moral, educational and political issues and questions. The court was also given the power to examine, license, appoint and supervise public lecturers. Some suspect the Areopagus intended to put Paul through a type of preliminary interview to see if he was fit for such a position. This highly respected court is where Paul meets and engages the members of the Athenian "intelligentsia" who are the reigning intellectual movers and shakers in the culture.

Their invitation to speak is not necessarily an indicator that they are putting Paul on trial. Rather, they are asking him to give an account of his philosophy. What Paul was saying to them was strange and new. But so far, Paul's content and rhetorical method have engaged them enough to leave them curious and hungry to know more. For them, listening to Paul is one more opportunity to be intellectually stimulated, as they love gathering together to talk about new and novel philosophies and ideas. It appears from Luke's parenthetical remark that the Athenians are more concerned about pondering new ideas than they are about judging the potential truthfulness of what Paul is telling them. That said, what follows from Paul is not a legal defense, but a proclamation of the gospel.

So Paul begins to speak. The manner, shape and content of his argument provides us with guidance for how to engage the curious postmoderns with the gospel.

Paul then stood up in the meeting of the Areopagus and said: "Men of Athens! I see that in every way you are very religious. For as I walked around and looked carefully at your objects of worship, I even found an altar with this inscription: TO AN UNKNOWN GOD. *Now what you worship as something unknown I am going to proclaim to you."* (vv. 22-23)

Paul begins his proclamation by *commending* his idol-worshiping audience. This simple statement is the key to his ability to connect with the Athenians. He affirms them for being "very religious," a positive note as well as a characteristic he shares with them. Paul respects and affirms their religious endeavors even though the Athenian's allegiances are misdirected.

Note that Paul doesn't begin by reciting Old Testament Scripture. It would be counterproductive for him to appeal to texts the Athenians don't know. Michael Green says, "Sometimes [Paul] has been rebuked for not quoting the Old Testament. But of course he does not do that here, as he would in a synagogue, because the Athenians did not know the scriptures nor recognize them as an authority. In apologetics you can exercise no leverage unless you use an authority your opponents recognize."[9] Paul's crosscultural approach adapts the unchanging Word without compromise so it can be heard in the Athenian context.

Paul has done his homework. He "walked around and looked carefully," studying Athenian life and idols not only because he wants to understand their religion, worldview and allegiances, but to find a point of contact from which to launch his proclamation of the gospel. He knows that to fully proclaim the gospel in this Greek context, he will have to speak about ideas contrary to the Athenian philosophies, including a personal God, the resurrection and judgment by the one true God. That point of contact is found in the altar "to an unknown God." F. F. Bruce suggests that this inscription actually becomes Paul's "text."[10] Paul then states his intent to answer the question, "Who is God?" In doing so, Paul is making a smooth transition from commendation of the Athenians religiosity, to a confrontation of their misdirected idolatry and pantheism.

As Paul stands before the gathering of the Areopagus, his opening comments indicate clearly that he not only knows what the Athenians believe, but he also knows their manner and format for discussing their ideas. In our contemporary postmodern situation it is our responsibility as crosscultural missionaries to enter into a discussion of *their* ideas, in *their* world, in *their* manner, but only after we've taken the time to be informed and educated on *their* philosophy, worldview, allegiances and other cultural nuances. Paul addresses their ignorance by telling them about the true God who can be known.

"The God who made the world and everything in it is the Lord of heaven and earth and does not live in temples built by hands. And he is not served by human hands, as if he needed anything, because he himself gives all men life and breath and everything else." (vv. 24-25)

Paul begins his proclamation with the one true God and his visible creation, contrasting this God with the idols of the Athenian culture. His statements are a direct challenge to the Stoic's pantheism, the Ep-

---

[9]Green, *Thirty Years That Changed the World,* p. 108.
[10]F. F. Bruce, *The Book of the Acts,* New International Commentary on the New Testament (Grand Rapids: Eerdmans, 1983), p. 356.

icurean's deism and the rampant polytheism of Athens. In other words, Paul directly challenges their theological errors. He explains that the unknown God is the Creator, the sovereign Lord over all things, who does not need humans and is independent of his created order, which is wholly dependent on him.

In a masterful way Paul finds common ground between the truth about the one true God and Epicurean and Stoic philosophy. He corrects their errors by using their own teachings that resonate with biblical truth. He affirms the Epicurean doctrine that God needs nothing from humans. He affirms the Stoic belief that God is the source of all life and that he can't be contained in a temple built by human hands. In effect, he uses their doctrines—where those doctrines are in line with biblical truth—as his texts. Michael Green states that Paul uses "their clothes to present his (biblical) message."[11] Paul couldn't have done this if he hadn't studied their worldviews.

Having identified the one true God, Paul then proclaims our need to be in a relationship with God.

"From one man he made every nation of men, that they should inhabit the whole earth; and he determined the times set for them and the exact places where they should live. God did this so that men would seek him and perhaps reach out for him and find him, though he is not far from each one of us." (vv. 26-27)

Paul goes back to the creation account without making overt references to the Old Testament Scriptures. He begins with the "one man" (Adam), which appeals to and affirms the Stoic belief in the connection between all humanity. Paul then explains how the sovereign God cares enough about his creation to order all its affairs—a challenge to the deists and polytheists of Athens. The fall of humankind into sin and the resulting separation from God are addressed in a manner that would resonate with those longing to worship and know "the unknown god" of the Athenian altar. The consequence of the Fall is separation from God and the resulting sense among humanity that something has gone wrong in the world. Because God is not aloof from his

---

[11]Green, *Thirty Years That Changed the World*, p. 108.

creation, he wants humanity to seek (or more accurately "grope") after him. Paul makes it clear that God is not "in" the creation (as in
pantheism) or disinterested in it (as in deism). Yet God is directly involved with creation (immanent), which appeals to the Stoics. Then
Paul recognizes the earnest spiritual search of the Athenians individually ("God did this so that men would seek him") as they long to have
the God-shaped holes in their souls filled, which also marks our postmodern world.

Paul's next move is key to the Mars Hill ministry paradigm.

*"'For in him we live and move and have our being.' As some of your
own poets have said, 'We are his offspring.'"* (v. 28)

Before entering Athens, Paul had been a student of Greek culture
and had developed a working knowledge of their worldview, its philosophical sources and its popular expressions. When he enters Athens,
Paul takes the time to listen to and understand the Athenians by engaging his senses and mind in a tour of the city. In verse 28 he taps
into the database of knowledge he's accumulated as a result of diligently doing his crosscultural homework, to illustrate and drive home
his message to the Athenians. Specifically, he uses the popular culture
of the Athenian philosophers as expressed in their poetry to illustrate
the truth about the one true God and his relationship to those he's created. Paul quotes directly from two Greek poets who are familiar to
and revered by his Mars Hill audience.

First, he quotes from Epimenides, the one who it is believed may
have instructed the Athenians to erect altars to unknown deities. In its
original poetical context, the phrase "For in him we live and move and
have our being" was used in reference to Zeus as spoken by his son,
Minos. Paul uses the quote to affirm the one true God as the source
of life who is active and involved in the affairs of his creatures. Paul is
challenging the Stoic belief in pantheism.

Second, he quotes a line penned by two different Stoic poets and
philosophers, Aratus and Cleanthes. In its use by Cleanthes, the
phrase "we are his offspring" is also a reference to Zeus. Paul uses
these words to explain that God is the source and Creator of all humanity, a humanity he has formed in his own image.

William J. Larkin notes the obvious parallels between Paul's message to the first-century Athenians and our contemporary situation:

For first-century Epicureans and twentieth-century moderns, the fact that God is the Father of humankind is challenging good news. No longer need we settle for the reductionistic explanation of humankind and its activity. We are not simply a complex interplay of electrical impulses, chemical processes, subatomic DNA and environment. And for Stoics and postmoderns, this good news makes us both less and more than they understand us to be. Pantheism or the "God within" is revealed as false, but in its place is the person made in God's image, living in conscious dependence on God.[12]

While Paul does not agree with the philosophical beliefs and worldviews of these poets, he sees nothing wrong with gleaning indisputable truth about God from their words. In effect Paul uses the popular culture of the Athenians to proclaim the gospel. He uses familiar and authoritative texts to establish the authority of the one true God. John Stott says, "His precedent gives us warrant to do the same, and indicates that glimmerings of truth, insights from general revelation, may be found in non-Christian authors."[13] In our present day situation, we too must utilize "texts" from the postmodern "philosophers" and "poets" of film, music and literature.

Next, Paul presents the core of his message.

"Therefore, since we are God's offspring, we should not think that the divine being is like gold or silver or stone—an image made by man's design and skill. In the past God overlooked such ignorance, but now he commands all people everywhere to repent. For he has set a day when he will judge the world with justice by the man he has appointed. He has given proof of this to all men by raising him from the dead." (vv. 29-31)

Paul tells the Athenians that because they are children of a living,

---

[12]William J. Larkin Jr., *Acts*, IVP New Testament Commentary (Downers Grove, Ill.: InterVarsity Press, 1995), p. 259.
[13]Stott, *Message of Acts*, p. 286.

personal and sovereign God, they err when worshiping a lifeless object. Idolatry is wrong. They have attempted to create God in their own image.

Paul calls them to turn away from their idols to the one true God, who will no longer overlook their sin. Then Paul discusses the coming judgment, the work of Christ and his resurrection—all radical and new ideas to the gathered philosophers. He informs them of the urgent need to be rescued from their sin. Jesus Christ, approved by God in his resurrection, is God's appointed judge. As Paul brings his proclamation to the Areopagus to a close, he concludes with the very topic—the resurrection—which had caused so much confusion in the first place. Paul's movement from the familiar philosophical categories of his audience to clear biblical truth is a masterful crosscultural paradigm for us. When his appeal is complete, the Athenians know with certainty that Paul is calling them to a radical reordering of their priorities and an equally radical shift in worldviews.

When they heard about the resurrection of the dead, some of them sneered, but others said, "We want to hear you again on this subject." At that, Paul left the Council. A few men became followers of Paul and believed. Among them was Dionysius, a member of the Areopagus, also a woman named Damaris, and a number of others. (vv. 32-34)

There were three basic responses to Paul's proclamation. First, most of the Epicureans, because of their belief in annihilationism, and the Stoics, because of their belief in the immortality of the soul and in reincarnation, "sneered" at the resurrection of the dead. In addition, his mention of the need to repent, the reality of an impending judgment and the return of Christ would have been too much for them to handle. But some were curious and wanted to hear more. (Whether Paul actually addressed them again is unknown.) Finally, a few "became followers of Paul and believed."

Paul's message provides a powerful example of how to engage the emerging postmodern generations with a crosscultural apologetic. N. T. Wright says:

Let me say three words about that remarkable address. First, Paul

affirmed what could be affirmed within the Athenian culture.
. . . At the same time, Paul confronted rank idolatry. . . . Third, he
outflanked their thinking. . . . Affirmation, confrontation, and
outflanking opposition: If you want to interact with and transform your culture, study the Areopagus speech and see how Paul
went about his task, then go and do likewise—if you dare. Affirm
what can and should be affirmed, confront what can and must
be confronted, and outflank that which is looking in the right direction but which then turns back and settles for second best.[14]

Did Paul Abandon His Mars Hill Paradigm?

Because some Athenians "sneer" and only "a few" believe, some
Christians teach that Paul's Mars Hill ministry was a miserable failure.
They contend that after Paul left Athens he renounced this approach
to proclaiming the gospel. Still others believe that Paul was unfaithful
in his message, preaching something other than the gospel. In other
words, he focuses so much on using intellectual and philosophical arguments that he minimizes the message of the cross. Then, recognizing his error, Paul resolves in Corinth to preach nothing but Christ and
the cross.

> For Christ did not send me to baptize, but to preach the gospel
> —not with words of human wisdom, lest the cross of Christ be
> emptied of its power. . . . Where is the wise man? Where is the
> philosopher of this age? Has not God made foolish the wisdom
> of the world? For since in the wisdom of God the world through
> its wisdom did not know him, God was pleased through the fool-
> ishness of what was preached to save those who believe. . . .
> When I came to you, brothers, I did not come with eloquence or
> superior wisdom as I proclaimed to you the testimony about
> God. For I resolved to know nothing while I was with you except
> Jesus Christ and him crucified. (1 Cor 1:17, 20-21; 2:1-2)

---

[14]N. T. Wright, "Transforming the Culture," *Latimer Fellowship* <http://latimer.godzone.net.nz/comment.asp#culture>.

Is it possible that Paul abandoned his crosscultural approach to ministry, telling us it's a paradigm to avoid?

There is no evidence to suggest that Paul sees his ministry in Athens as a failure due to the limited response to the gospel. Neither Luke nor Paul mention the limited response in negative terms, nor do they cite it as a reason to see Paul's Mars Hill message as a failure. If numbers are the measure of success, then with Jerram Barrs we must ask, "When we are not told of conversions in the Gospels after Jesus ministered to a group of people, are we to conclude that Jesus was a failure and that His ministry was inadequate or His approach was mistaken in some way?"[15]

To condemn Paul's effort as a failure is to criticize the Holy Spirit for not moving in a greater number of Athenian hearts and lives. Who are we to level such a criticism? Even if Paul had only planted spiritual "seeds" in Athens, his mission would have been a success. Yet the Holy Spirit obviously was at work bringing some in this difficult pagan audience to faith.

People too often misread Paul's opening words to the Corinthians. He is not saying, "I used my intellect in my preaching in Athens, and it was wrong." If that were the case, why did he later reason in the synagogue in an attempt to "persuade Jews and Greeks" (Acts 18:4), "argue persuasively" in the Ephesian synagogue and have "discussions daily in the lecture hall of Tyrannus" (Acts 19:8-9), or answer the challenge of Festus with the claim that the Gospel is "true and reasonable" (Acts 26:25)?

Nor is Paul admitting that he spent too much time discussing philosophy at the expense of preaching the cross of Christ. One must remember that Luke's record is merely a short outline of what is a much longer and detailed sermon. Speeches made before the Areopagus were typically long and involved. Because we know that Paul spoke to the Athenians about the resurrection of Christ, we can ask with John Stott, "For how could he proclaim the resurrection without mentioning the death which preceded it? And how could he call for repen-

---

[15]Jerram Barrs, *The Heart of Evangelism* (Wheaton, Ill.: Crossway, 2001), p. 253.

tance without mentioning the faith in Christ which always accompanies it?"[16] Throughout his ministry both before and after his visit to Athens, Paul's primary concern is to preach Christ and the cross. However, he always adapts his message and methodology to the audience and their culture in an effort to effectively connect, lead them to faith, and correct the errors in their understanding.

From all the evidence, we must assume that Luke included the record in Acts to give us a historical account of how to engage intellectuals who are not familiar with the Scriptures or the Christian worldview.

But there's no escaping the fact that Paul is renouncing something as he speaks to the Corinthians. What Paul renounces in Corinth has everything to do with the situation in Corinth, and nothing to do with seeing his approach in Athens as wrong or failed. In Corinth the church is full of intellectual pride. These are people who trust themselves and worship their own wisdom rather than trusting and worshiping God. In 1 Corinthians 1—2 Paul is denouncing their misplaced faith in wisdom and rhetorical skills. "If we compare Paul's argument in Acts 17 in the Areopagus with his words in 1 Corinthians 1 and 2 . . . we will discover that in each of these passages . . . Paul's message is the same. People in their rebellion against God think they are being wise; but the truth is that it is their thinking that is foolish and God's Word that is wise."[17]

Paul does not reject his Mars Hill method. Acts 17 offers a valuable paradigm for ministry, which we are wise to embrace.

Mars Hill Ministry Now

The parallels between first-century Athens and our postmodern culture are striking. The ancient Mars Hill ministry model is unquestionably suited for our times. It offers the church an approach for infiltrating, understanding and transforming culture with good news. But

---

[16]Stott, *The Message Of Acts*, p. 289.
[17]Barrs, *The Heart of Evangelism*, p. 259.

before describing how we can follow Paul's lead in our culture, there are several basic tenets that we must understand.

First, the Mars Hill ministry paradigm is not a step-by-step evangelism method that dictates presentation and content. Rather, it's a framework that guides how we live in, listen to and understand culture so that our response will be thoughtfully and sensitively constructed.

Second, the Mars Hill ministry paradigm is not a recipe for success. While it does deepen our understanding of and increases our effectiveness in our mission field, the advance of the kingdom is entirely dependent on God's Spirit. The Mars Hill ministry approach does not "save" people. Nor does it guarantee that many will come to faith. We can even expect some to sneer at us. The paradigm's value lies in its ability to help us more effectively communicate the good news in an understandable, relevant and timely manner.

Third, to effectively use the Mars Hill ministry paradigm we must prayerfully enter into our postmodern culture with the conviction that today's emerging generations are desperate for redemption. They do not lie outside the scope of God's redemptive plan, nor are they hopelessly lost.

The Mars Hill ministry paradigm is not a method but a model for living. It is a model for living that is both timely for our postmodern world and timeless in its ability to be used in any particular place and time. As a model for living, the steps should be taken and retaken with each person, each setting, each situation, each minute and each ministry opportunity God sends our way. It's not a "once and done" endeavor. Instead, it's a lifestyle that ensures our minds are constantly and consciously engaging the culture with an eye toward effective crosscultural ministry.

Initially, it will take some effort. Eventually it will become for us—as it was for Paul—second nature. Parents will find it helpful as a tool to generate a deepened understanding of their children, the issues they face, and what issues to address as they fulfill their responsibility to nurture their children in the Lord. The paradigm is indispensable to youth workers in their quest to understand, connect with and minister with relevance to their students. Pastors will discover that living the Mars Hill ministry paradigm can bring their preaching to life in a way that facilitates deep connections with their postmodern audience. Consciously walking through the Athens of the emerging generations will yield an overflow of knowledge including sermon illustrations and applications that will bring the Word to life for young people in the pews. Educators should live the paradigm as a way to increase their ability to understand their students and shape them for the kingdom. The list goes on and on.

The following steps will help you minister as Paul did in Athens.[18]

Step 1: Prepare to walk through Athens. Your "Athens" is found on the streets, in movies, where youth hang out and wherever their ideas are trumpeted or discussed. You'll want to examine Athens on three levels. First, you'll "walk through" their collective culture, that is, all that's common to the globalized youth culture (see chapters two to three). Because culture is fluid, the walk will never end.

You'll also walk through the local culture of the young people you minister to. While they certainly are a part of the globalized youth culture, they also live in an particular localized culture that shapes who they are. For example, high school seniors living in inner-city Los Angeles, the suburbs of Boston or the rural plains of Nebraska are observably different. At this level, it is helpful to focus on schools, neighborhoods and communities. We must examine the elements that are particular to students living in our particular time and in our particular ministry setting.

Finally, you'll walk through the individualized culture that a teen lives in every day. You want to know his or her individual tastes, likes, dislikes, interests, hobbies, gifts, abilities, family situations, values, attitudes, behaviors and allegiances.

For those of us who work with student athletes, we might want to walk through the ingredient of the local high school football team. If

---

[18]The Center for Parent/Youth Understanding website (www.cpyu.org) offers updated information on culture that will help put meat on the bones of this paradigm. The site includes daily analysis of the youth culture. It's updated daily. Sign up to receive a biweekly e-mail update that includes the most recent research, lyrics, quotes, etc.

we work with a student who hangs out at the local café, that café becomes an ingredient we want to examine. If your students are spending time each week immersed in watching the MTV reality show *The Real World*, you'll want to go there. Wherever you walk, you must engage in the ongoing disciplines of consistent prayer and Bible study. Your crosscultural missions venture will be met by spiritual opposition and challenge. You'll need to pray for God's promised protection. Bible study will keep you sharp and free from error as you put on "the full armor of God" (Eph 6:10-18). Proper spiritual preparation will (1) ensure that you know your own limits, (2) protect you from harm, (3) give you discernment and (4) cause you to be spiritually "distressed" by that which is immoral and idolatrous.

Step 2: Close your mouth. Open your ears and eyes. Walk around. Appalled by what you first see, you may be tempted to denounce what you find so offensive. But remember Paul's model. Even though he grew distressed over the spiritual condition of the Athenians, he continued to observe their culture, wanting to learn as much as he could about their way of life.

As you enter your Athens, heed the advice of Solomon: "Answering before listening is both stupid and rude" (Prov 18:13 *The Message*). Thus take your crosscultural trek through their world with your ears and eyes fully open and your mouth shut. As you walk, ask the following questions about the members of the emerging generations:

- What is their race?
- What is their ethnicity?
- What is their socioeconomic status?
- What is their geographic location? Where do they live, work, play, go to school?
- What is their gender?
- Are there any unique physical characteristics or disabilities?
- What are their religious heritage, practices and preferences?
- What's peculiar about their language and slang?

- Do they have any unique mannerisms and gestures? What about facial expressions, posture and body language? Are there other noticeable habits or behaviors?
- What is their clothing style? Do they have any piercings, tattoos or body markings?
- Who are their peers? What are their characteristics? What is their social organization and hierarchy?
- What is their family situation and context?
- What kind of music are they listening to, and what does it say? Do they listen to the radio? What stations? What are those stations playing?
- What movies and television shows are they watching? What is communicated in those shows?
- What books and magazines are they reading, and what do these promote?
- What kind of art do they view or create?
- What kind of vehicles do they own?
- What are their hobbies and interests?
- Are they involved in any extracurricular activities?
- Who are their heroes and role models?
- What kinds of jobs do they have?
- Do they frequent particular websites? Have they created any websites?
- What foods do they prefer?
- Do they have favorite places to hang out?
- What do they spend their money on?

When you speak, it should be to ask questions about what you encounter or to solicit more information. Francis Schaeffer said, "We must realize that we are facing a rapidly changing historical situation, and if we are going to talk to people about the gospel we need to know what is the present ebb and flow of thought-forms. Unless we do this, the unchangeable principles of Christianity will fall on deaf ears."[19]

I take regular walks in the music world. Youth are typically drawn to music that expresses what they are feeling, sometimes better than they can express it themselves. I observe the collective culture's music on MTV. I also stay in touch with the music of the local youth culture by listening to the radio or by asking students what their peers have in their CD players or iPods.[20] When I encounter a student who loves a particular artist or group, I get to know that music. In those cases it is particularly helpful to ask a student about his or her favorite video or song and then focus on the lyrical and visual content of that one particular piece. The same is true for film, television, video games, websites, local hangouts, shopping malls, school events or any other place where youth gather.

As we walk, we should seek like Paul to see what they see, touch what they touch, hear what they hear, taste what they taste, and feel what they feel. Our second step, simply stated, is to listen to them and their world so that we might begin to understand them and what makes them tick.

Step 3: Look for cultural characteristics and distinctives, including values, attitudes, beliefs, behaviors and problems. While observation is a necessary first step, you can't stop there. Like Paul, you must "get under the skin" of the visible, objective culture of postmodern kids. Your goal in this third step is to understand how observable behavior reflects subjective realities.

In this step you'll continue the process of "cultural exegesis." Your walk through Athens focuses not only on the authors' meaning of the "texts" important to the emerging generations but also on what those texts mean to those who have embraced them. For example, if I discover that a student loves Dashboard Confessional's "Several Ways to Die Trying," cultural exegesis first requires that I understand songwriter Chris Carrabba's intended meaning for the song. This will deepen my

---

[19]Francis A. Schaeffer, *Escape from Reason,* in *The Complete Works of Francis Schaeffer,* 2nd ed. (Wheaton, Ill.: Crossway Books, 1985), p. 269.
[20]To access and download a helpful and extensive music and media survey to administer to students, visit the Center for Parent/Youth Understanding website at www.cpyu.org.

understanding of the song. But in a postmodern world where the emphasis is placed not so much on the author's intent but on what it "means to me," I have to discover what it means to the student.

Misattribution is one of the fastest ways to destroy lines of communication with the emerging generations (see p. 116). Misattribution is the blunder we make when we assume or attribute *our* meaning to someone's beliefs or behaviors based on our own opinion, cultural categories, worldview or personal preferences.[21] Responsible cultural exegesis is the antidote. With your mouth shut and your eyes and ears open, carefully and prayerfully begin to probe the depths of the subjective culture of the youth you know and love.

The list of questions in step two help us observe the objective culture of postmodern youth, but to discern the underlying meaning, more penetrating questions must be asked. The following are sample questions to ask of the subcultural "texts" that you view while walking through Athens[22]:

- How has their race influenced and shaped their values, attitudes and behaviors?

- How has their ethnicity influenced and shaped their values, attitudes and behaviors?

- How has their socioeconomic status influenced and shaped their values, attitudes and behaviors?

- How has the geographic location of where they live, work, play or go to school influenced and shaped their values, attitudes and behaviors?

- How have their gender and their understanding of their gender role influenced and shaped their values, attitudes and behaviors?

- How have their unique physical characteristics or disabilities shaped their values, attitudes and behaviors?

---

[21]Patty Lane, *A Beginner's Guide to Crossing Cultures* (Downers Grove, Ill.: InterVarsity Press, 2002), p. 27.

[22]The Center for Parent/Youth Understanding website (www.cpyu.org) is designed to help you as you take this third step. Updated daily, we post information on the emerging objective postmodern culture along with analysis regarding the subjective culture that lies beneath.

- How have their religious heritage, practices and preferences influenced and shaped their values, attitudes and behaviors?

- Why do they use their language and slang as they do, and what does it mean to them?

- What is behind their dress and clothing styles, and why have they chosen to dress this way?

- What is the meaning of their unique mannerisms and gestures? What do their unique facial expressions, posture and body language tell me about who they are and what they feel? Where do their noticeable habits and behaviors come from, and what do they mean?

- What does their peer group tell me about who they are? What is the meaning of their social organization and hierarchy, particularly where each one falls on the pecking order?

- How have their family situation and context shaped who they are?

- What is the meaning of their music (for both the creator and the consumer), and what does their music tell us about them? What does allegiance to the radio stations they listen to tell us about them?

- What is the meaning of their movies, and why are they drawn to them? Is there significance in their choice of TV programs? What do those movies and TV shows tell us about them?

- What is the meaning of the books they read, and why are they drawn to those books? What lessons are their magazines teaching? What do those books and magazines tell us about what they value and what brings meaning and purpose in life?

- Does the art they view and create tell us anything about them? What?

- How does what they drive serve as an extension of who they are and what they value?

- Do their hobbies and interests offer any insight into their values, attitudes, allegiances and behaviors?

- How has their school shaped who they are? What do their extra-curricular activities tell us about them?
- Do their heroes and role models reveal any significant clues about their hopes, dreams and desires?
- Does where, when and how much they work reveal who they are and what they value in life?
- Do their online habits offer clues into their lives?
- Do their food preferences and eating habits offer any insight into their lives?
- What is the significance of their favorite places to hang out?
- What can their spending habits tell us about what they value in life?
- Are there any themes that emerge over and over again? And if so, what significance do they have?
- What does all of this tell me about the circumstances, cares and concerns of the emerging generations?

In addition, the following questions will help you dig deeply into each specific text.

- What is the main topic or theme?
- What's the mood of the text?
- Does the text manipulate viewer emotions in any way?
- Does the text make any overt or covert suggestions on how to think, talk or act?
- What does the text say about the way the world is?
- What does the text say about the way the world ought to be?
- Is there right and wrong? If so, what? And how are they determined?
- Are there heroes and villains? If so, what do they stand for?
- What values and beliefs are portrayed as positive? Negative?
- Who or what is the source of authority? What is the attitude toward authority?

- Who or what is God? How is God portrayed?
- How are humans portrayed? Where is human worth found?
- How is beauty established, portrayed and defined?
- How should we treat others?
- What is the source of happiness and satisfaction in life?
- What makes a person successful?
- What's the solution to life's problems?
- Who or what is glorified?
- What does it say about peace and hope? Where are they found?
- What character traits are portrayed as positive? Negative?

Step 4: Look for evidence of a spiritual quest. Because all humans have been created for a relationship with their Creator, the unredeemed long to fill the God-shaped hole in their soul. Consequently, their lives will always be marked by "spiritual hunger pains" of some type. G. K. Chesterton said that even "the man who knocks at the door of the brothel is looking for God."[23] Paul knew this was the case with the Athenians. During his walk through their city, he went to great lengths to look for evidence of their desire to know the one true God.

The good news is that in our postmodern culture we don't have to look far to see evidence of this spiritual quest. Popular culture is filled with examples of music, movies, television and books that overtly address the postmodern spiritual hunger. We must look for signs of spiritual longing similar to the inscription to "the unknown God." *Everything* we see should be viewed against the backdrop of the yearning for restored fellowship with the Creator.

One classic and regularly quoted expression of postmodern spiritual hunger is found in Douglas Coupland's novel *Life After God*. The book's young-adult narrator speaks openly about the ups and downs of a broken life. His lament comes to a close with this transparent confession:

---

[23]G. K. Chesterton, quoted in Richard J. Mouw, *Distorted Truth* (Pasadena, Calif.: Fuller Seminary Press, 1999), p. 1.

Now—here is my secret: I tell it to you with an openness of heart that I doubt I shall ever achieve again, so I pray that you are in a quiet room as you hear these words. My secret is that I need God—that I am sick and can no longer make it alone. I need God to help me give, because I no longer seem to be capable of giving; to help me be kind, as I no longer seem capable of kindness; to help me love, as I seem beyond being able to love.[24]

David Wells believes that the proliferation of overt spirituality indicates "that the Church finds itself once again in the Areopagus. . . . This spiritual yearning and the inability of human nature to live comfortably in a world evacuated of meaning is the best 'point of contact' with postmodern culture."[25] Wells says that our role as the people of God is to look for signals of transcendence, "indicators that life is more than its natural processes, that human beings are anchored in a moral world to which they always have conscious connections."[26] He believes that finding and citing these signals will help people experience the restoration of who they really are.

This is the strategy Paul used and the strategy we must employ in our present-day Athens.

Step 5: Identify doorways of opportunity for connection, conversation, evangelism and discipleship. As Paul walked through Athens he surveyed its culture for things he could use as doorways to dialogue (*after* he has carefully listened). Athenian idols and philosophy became Paul's touch points. Even though Paul's message was strange to Greek ears, those listening didn't turn a deaf ear to him. Instead, they invited him to tell them more. Paul did his homework.

As you walk through Athens, constantly ask yourself, "How can I use this to open the doors of communication with my audience?" Specifically, you want to open four consecutive doorways.

First comes the doorway of *connection*. Find something that offers a point of entry that allows you to make a connection across cultures.

---

[24]Douglas Coupland, *Life After God* (New York: Pocket Books, 1994), p. 359.
[25]David F. Wells, *Losing Our Virtue* (Grand Rapids: Eerdmans, 1998), p. 194.
[26]Ibid., p. 148.

With genuine interest, ask about something in the youth culture you don't understand. For example, "Tell me about your tattoo. Is there a story behind that?" Or you might ask someone to explain the lyrics of a favorite song. Doing so says: "You are important to me."

The doorway to connection leads quickly to the doorway of *conversation*, a necessary ingredient in healthy dialogue. Because of their deep spiritual need and hunger for relationships, today's youth are usually open to conversing with people who are genuinely interested in them. By discussing what's important to them, you keep these lines of communication open.

Next comes the doorway of *evangelism*. Here you'll use postmodern expressions of spiritual hunger to proclaim the gospel. Paul does this magnificently in Athens. Because he is speaking to pagans, he avoids anything that might be irrelevant or confusing. Instead of appealing to the Old Testament, Paul employs truths from their culture as doorways for evangelism. Find a line from a film, a song or even a popular commercial that can serve as a bridge to presenting the gospel. Scan the landscape of their culture for expressions of need that only Christ can meet.[27]

The last doorway is *discipleship*. Once they've accepted Christ, what you've found in the culture can spark discussion regarding how to grow in faith and the need to integrate that faith into all of life.

Step 6: Discern cultural elements that can be celebrated and embraced, and those that must be challenged and opposed. Paul doesn't fall into the error of accommodation by thoughtlessly accepting every element of the Athenian culture. Neither does he retreat into a bunker and issue a wholesale condemnation of Athens. Instead, Paul understands that Athens—like every other human culture—is marked by the fingerprint of the Creator *and* by the Fall. Thus

---

[27]Again, one source for discovering these touchpoints is the Center for Parent/Youth Understanding's website (www.cpyu.org). There you will find a growing catalog of quotes, lyrics, news, trends, information and analysis that will save you valuable time as you take your walk through Athens. In addition, we monitor and post information on the latest elements in the cultural soup that are "mapping" the lives and worldviews of the emerging generations. Because the contemporary postmodern culture is changing so rapidly, this information is updated on a daily basis.

Paul affirms the good and denounces the bad. Jerram Barrs notes:

> There will always be elements of truth in any unbelievers' think-
> ing because they have to live in God's world. There will always be
> signs that individuals still bear God's image in their deepest be-
> ing, for God has not abandoned humanity. People have not be-
> come demons, so there is always something to commend in their
> way of life.[28]

You should applaud virtuous and commendable behavior, and celebrate elements of the youth culture that are good, true, noble and
honorable. On the other hand, to see the culture renewed and transformed, speak against cultural elements that are clearly unbiblical or
ungodly. When you have listened and understood, the postmodern
generations will be more open to hearing your message and considering your challenge.

Step 7: Apply what you have learned to your particular ministry
with your particular audience. Use popular culture to draw postmoderns' attention, but then point them to God—in terms that they
can understand. In what ways can we use what we find in our particular ministry setting? At times, our use of our audience's culture will
be simply personal as what we see and hear informs and shapes our
ministry approach. For example, we may discover that this culture is
prone to respond more positively to our ministry efforts if we employ
a particular methodology. In today's postmodern world, one of the
methods our culture tells us we must employ is the use of story. At
other times, what we discover on our walk might raise a particular issue that our proclamation or ministry must address.

Finally, there will be times when we can incorporate the culture of
our audience into our message and content. This is what Paul does as
he quotes their culture. Some of what he learns finds its way into his
verbal proclamation of the gospel. Specifically, he uses their poetry,
philosophy and inscriptions to affirm their thinking where it is right,
and to challenge their thinking where it is wrong. He carefully takes

---

[28]Barrs, *Heart of Evangelism*, p. 206.

their culture and adapts it for his purposes. In effect, Paul quotes the film, music, books, television and other cultural vehicles of his day in his communication with the Athenians.

His approach was rooted not in manipulation but in empathy. Richard Mouw states, "In this encounter the apostle genuinely engages those to whom he speaks. He probes in an intelligent way the agenda of their hopes and fears."[29] Mouw says that Paul's "empathetic probing" should be part of our evangelistic efforts. "As we speak to others about the claims of the gospel we must allow their spiritual quests to enlarge our own hearts and minds. Doing so can help us testify more effectively to the power of God."[30] When we know the specific shape their spiritual longings take, it is then easier to help them see what their longings are ultimately for.

In our present day situation we must use the popular culture to not only inform us of the worldview pulsing through the veins of the emerging generations, but we must use it to reveal to the lost the truth about who and what they are ultimately longing for. We can use their culture to draw attention to the questions they ask. We can use their culture to point them to the answers God gives in terms that they can understand. Asking ourselves the following questions as we walk through Athens can help us shape our use of what we've encountered in our ministry efforts: What have I encountered that

- can inform and shape the manner and method of how I do ministry?
- raised particular issues or situations that I must address as I do ministry?
- I can employ to help the emerging generations see their spiritual need?
- I can employ to affirm where they are correct in their thinking?
- I can employ to challenge where they are incorrect in their thinking?
- I can employ to illustrate the truths of the gospel?

---

[29]Mouw, *Distorted Truth*, p. 28.
[30]Ibid.

- I can employ to apply biblical truth to their lives?
- can be used as a "redemptive analogy"?[31]
- I can use to challenge and equip individuals to live an integrated faith?

Following in Paul's footsteps through Athens will assure that our method for sharing the gospel will advance rather than impede the life-changing message the emerging generations so desperately need.

---

[31] "Redemptive analogy" was first introduced by missionary Don Richardson in *Eternity in Their Hearts* (Ventura, Calif.: Regal Books, 1981). The concept teaches that in every culture God has placed something that can be used to illustrate the gospel and thereby bring people to faith. In our present situation, the world of popular media—particularly music, television and film—is especially rich in redemptive analogies to use with the emerging generations.

WILL WE LISTEN?

THIS BOOK HAS TAKEN YOU on a journey into the world of the emerging generations. They are growing up in a confusing and difficult culture. They are being shaped by a postmodern worldview that has little or no regard for Christ. Yet they hunger and thirst for a restored relationship with their Creator. For a variety of reasons the church has failed to connect with them. Consequently, we've forfeited our influence and in many ways impeded the advance of the gospel. In obedience to the One who has commissioned us to go into their world, we are responsible to overcome the obstacles to communicating the gospel without compromise and with relevance. This book is a call to listen and to understand so that the good news can be meaningfully shared with postmodern youth. I believe that Paul's Mars Hill ministry paradigm is a valuable and timely model for doing ministry. As our world continues to change, this paradigm will continue to serve as an effective strategy for whatever shape our world will take. Our task is to first listen and understand. Then and only then can we engage our rapidly changing mission field with the good news.

Over the years, I've been personally challenged to consider the great needs of the emerging generations and the responsibility of the church to respond. One incident that hit me particularly hard occurred when Caitlin was fifteen years old. She was having a horrible day, and my wife could see it on her face as soon as Caitlin climbed into the car after soccer practice. Through her tears Caitlin explained that a student at her school had ended his life the night before.

Caitlin didn't know Dan personally, but she knew who he was. As we listened to Caitlin recount what little she knew about his life, it became increasingly obvious why a young man like Dan might find self-inflicted death more attractive than a hopeless life. Dan lived in a postmodern world where hope, support systems and the resiliency that comes with each are all largely absent. Dan struggled with academics. His family was shattered by divorce. He was overweight. Kids picked on him. Caitlin commented that she often saw him walking down the hall between classes, and his head always hung low. In the cafeteria she would see him eating alone. Kids say that the day he died, he had been picked on particularly hard. He ended his life at the end of a rope.

While Caitlin and her friends had never picked on Dan, they were all thinking about what they might do differently if they could somehow rewind the clock back a week or two. Maybe they would have talked to Dan in the hall. Perhaps they would have sat with him at lunch. But the ugly reality is that the cries of kids like Dan go unheard—until after they've stopped. By then, it's too late.

Why do we fail to hear the cries of the hopeless and hurting outcasts coming from so many corners of today's youth culture? Why have we ignored the cries of an emerging generation that longs for redemption? Are we too busy? Don't we care? Would getting involved require more of ourselves than we're willing to give? Or are we scared that going to them would take us to places we don't want to visit?

A religious man who saw himself as wholeheartedly devoted to God once tested Jesus with this question: "What do I need to do to get eternal life?" Jesus responded with a question: "What's written in God's law? How do you interpret it?" The man answered, "That you love the Lord your God with all your passion and prayer and muscle and intelligence—and that you love your neighbor as well as you do yourself." Jesus affirmed this answer: "Do it—*keep on* doing it—and you'll live."

Backed into a corner, the inquisitor knew he had not loved in this way. Looking for a way out, he asked Jesus to define *neighbor,* hoping to prove that not all people (especially those he does not like or have time for) qualify as neighbors.

Jesus told a story that most of us have heard many times. It's about a Jewish man who is beaten, robbed and left for dead on the side of the road. A religious man (a priest) comes by, and rather than stopping to help, he passes by on the other side. Another religious man (a Levite) comes along, sees the hurting traveler and passes by as well. A third man walks by. He's a Samaritan—the least likely of the three to reach out and help a Jew. Yet this Samaritan *hears* the cries, *takes pity* on the dying man and *meets his needs.*

Jesus ended the story by asking, "What do you think? Which of the three became a neighbor to the man attacked by robbers?" The religious man answered, "The one who took pity and treated him kindly."

Jesus then looked at his questioner and said, "Go and do—go and *keep on* doing—the same." We are called to exhibit the divine compassion of Christ at the sight of deep human need.

The roadside of today's youth culture is littered with bruised and battered kids—outcasts crying for help. Too many people claiming to be followers of Christ never stop to help. Perhaps we should pray Bob Pierce's prayer: "Let my heart be broken by the things that break the heart of God." If our prayer is sincere, I believe it will yield in us Christ's compassion for the lost in today's emerging generations. It is a compassion and pity rooted in our innermost beings.

Late on the night of March 13, 1964, a twenty-eight-year-old New Yorker named Kitty Genovese was walking home from work when she was attacked. She screamed for help as she was beaten, assaulted, stabbed and raped. Her attacker left her for dead. A few minutes later he came back and attacked her again. She screamed for help, and he left. He came back and assaulted her a third time. Genovese screamed again. Then he walked away. It wasn't long before Kitty Genovese died on the New York City street.

What makes this story particularly appalling is that as Kitty Genovese screamed, numerous people got out of bed and watched from their windows. Yet no one helped her; no one called for help. When Kitty Genovese's cries stopped, they turned out the lights and went back to sleep.

Eventually, police identified and captured her attacker, Vincent Mosely. Their search for witnesses led to the grim discovery that thirty-eight people had watched and done nothing. During the trial the witnesses were asked why they did nothing to help Miss Genovese. Their collective answer—"We didn't want to get involved." When Mosely took the stand, he was asked why he kept coming back to attack Genovese when he could see people watching from their windows. He responded, "I knew they wouldn't do anything—they never do."

Could the same be said of the church today?

In her best-selling book *Traveling Mercies,* Anne Lamott chronicles her unusual journey to faith. I was in the middle of reading Lamott's book on the day Dan was found dangling from a rope. Lamott's confusing life echoes the little bit I've heard about Dan. There was one big difference: when Lamott (a self-described outcast) lay hopeless and dying on the side of the road, a small group of people from a church stopped to help. She writes: "When I was at the end of my rope, the people at St. Andrews tied a knot in it for me and helped me hold on. The church became my home in the old meaning of *home*—that it's where, when you show up, they have to let you in. They let me in. They even said, 'You come back now.'"[1]

And Jesus says, "Go and keep on doing the same."

---

[1] Anne Lamott, *Traveling Mercies* (New York: Pantheon Books, 1999), p. 100.

BIBLIOGRAPHY

Barna, George. *Real Teens: A Contemporary Snapshot of Youth Culture.* Ventura, Calif.: Regal Books, 2001.

Barrs, Jerram. *The Heart of Evangelism.* Wheaton, Ill.: Crossway, 2001.

Beaudoin, Thomas. *Virtual Faith: The Irreverent Spiritual Quest of Generation X.* San Francisco, Calif.: Jossey-Bass, 1998.

Blamires, Harry. *The Post-Christian Mind.* Ann Arbor, Mich.: Vine Books, 1999.

Borgman, Dean. *Hear My Story: Understanding the Cries of Troubled Youth.* Peabody, Mass.: Hendrickson, 2003.

———. *When Kumbaya Is Not Enough: A Practical Theology for Youth Ministry.* Peabody, Mass.: Hendrickson, 1997.

Carson, D. A., gen. ed. *Telling The Truth: Evangelizing Postmoderns.* Grand Rapids: Zondervan, 2000.

Chapell, Bryan. *The Wonder of It All: Rediscovering the Treasures of Your Faith.* Wheaton, Ill.: Crossway, 1999.

Christenson, Peter G., and Donald F. Roberts. *It's Not Only Rock & Roll: Popular Music in the Lives of Adolescents.* Cresskill, N.J.: Hampton Press, 1988.

Colson, Charles. *How Now Shall We Live?* Wheaton, Ill.: Tyndale House, 1999.

Coupland, Douglas. *Hey Nostradamus.* New York: Bloomsbury, 2003.

———. *Life After God.* New York: Pocket Books, 1994.

Danesi, Marcel. *Cool: The Signs and Meanings of Adolescence.* Toronto: University of Toronto Press, 1994.

Dawn, Marva J. *Is It a Lost Cause? Having the Heart of God for the Church's Children.* Grand Rapids: Eerdmans, 1997.

Del Vecchio, Gene. *Creating Ever-Cool: A Marketer's Guide to a Kid's Heart.* Gretna, La.: Pelican, 1997.

Detwiler, Craig and Barry Taylor. *A Matrix of Meanings: Finding God in Pop Culture.* Grand Rapids: Baker, 2003.

Dockery, David S., ed. *The Challenge of Postmodernism: An Evangelical Engagement.* Grand Rapids: Baker, 1995.

Elkind, David. *All Grown Up and No Place to Go: Teenagers in Crisis.* Reading, Mass.: Addison-Wesley, 1984.

Ellul, Jacques. *The Presence of the Kingdom.* Philadelphia: Westminster Press, 1951.

Elmer, Duane. *Cross-Cultural Conflict: Building Relationships for Effective Ministry.* Downers Grove, Ill.: InterVarsity Press, 1993.

———. *Cross-Cultural Connections: Stepping Out and Fitting In Around the World.* Downers Grove, Ill.: InterVarsity Press, 2002.

Erickson, Millard J. *Postmodernizing the Faith: Evangelical Responses to the Challenge of Postmodernism.* Grand Rapids: Baker, 1998.

Fischer, John. *Fearless Faith: Living Beyond the Walls of "Safe" Christianity.* Eugene, Ore.: Harvest House, 2002.

———. *Finding God Where You Least Expect Him.* Eugene, Ore.: Harvest House, 2003.

Ford, Kevin Graham. *Jesus for a New Generation: Putting the Gospel in the Language of Xers.* Downers Grove, Ill.: InterVarsity Press, 1995.

Gaines, Donna. *A Misfit's Manifesto: The Spiritual Journey of a Rock & Roll Heart.* New York: Villard, 2003.

Garber, Steven. *The Fabric of Faithfulness: Weaving Together Belief and Behavior During the University Years.* Downers Grove, Ill.: InterVarsity Press, 1996.

Green, Michael. *Evangelism in the Early Church*, rev. ed. Grand Rapids: Eerdmans, 2003.

Grenz, Stanley. *A Primer on Postmodernism.* Grand Rapids: Eerdmans, 1996.

Groothuis, Douglas. *Truth Decay: Defending Christianity Against the Challenges of Postmodernism.* Downers Grove, Ill.: InterVarsity Press, 2000.

Guder, Darrell L. *Missional Church: A Vision for the Sending of the Church in North America.* Grand Rapids: Eerdmans, 1998.

Guinness, Os. *Prophetic Untimeliness: A Challenge to the Idol of Relevance.* Grand Rapids: Baker, 2003.

Henry, Carl F. H. *Twilight of a Great Civilization: The Drift Toward Neo-Paganism.* Westchester, Ill.: Crossway, 1988.

Hesslegrave, David J. *Communicating Christ Cross-Culturally: An Introduction to Missionary Communication.* 2nd ed. Grand Rapids: Zondervan, 1991.

Horton, Michael S. *Where in the World Is the Church? A Christian View of Culture and Your Role in It.* Phillipsburg, N.J.: P & R Publishing, 2002.

Howard, David. *The Great Commission for Today.* Downers Grove, Ill.: InterVarsity Press, 1976.

Howe, Neil, and William Strauss. *Millennials Rising: The Next Great Generation.* New York: Vintage, 2000.

———. *The Fourth Turning: What the Cycles of History Tell Us About America's Next Rendezvous with Destiny.* New York: Broadway Books, 1997.

Kelly, Gerard. *Retrofuture: Rediscovering Our Roots, Recharting Our Routes.* Downers Grove, Ill.: InterVarsity Press, 1999.

Kuyper, Abraham. *Christianity: A Total World and Life System.* Marlborough, N.H.: The Plymouth Rock Foundation, 1996.

Lane, Patty. *A Beginner's Guide to Crossing Cultures: Making Friends in a Multicultural*

World. Downers Grove, Ill.: InterVarsity Press, 2002.

Lickona, Thomas. *Educating for Character: How Our Schools Can Teach Respect and Responsibility.* New York: Bantam, 1991.

Lingenfelter, Sherwood G., and Marvin K. Mayers. *Ministering Cross-Culturally: An Incarnational Model of Personal Relationships,* 2nd ed. Grand Rapids: Baker, 2003.

Long, Jimmy. *Generating Hope: A Strategy of Reaching the Postmodern Generation.* Downers Grove, Ill.: InterVarsity Press, 1997.

Mahedy, William, and Janet Bernardi. *A Generation Alone: Xers Making a Place in the World.* Downers Grove, Ill.: InterVarsity Press, 1994.

Mayers, Marvin K. *Christianity Confronts Culture: A Strategy for Cross-Cultural Evangelism.* Grand Rapids: Zondervan, 1974.

McCallum, Dennis. *The Death of Truth: Responding to Multiculturalism, the Rejection of Reason, and the New Postmodernity.* Minneapolis: Bethany House, 1996.

McGrath, Alister. *A Passion for Truth: The Intellectual Coherence of Evangelicalism.* Downers Grove, Ill.: InterVarsity Press, 1996.

———. *The Unknown God: Searching for Spiritual Fulfillment.* Grand Rapids: Eerdmans, 1999.

Middleton, J. Richard, and Brian J. Walsh. *Truth Is Stranger Than It Used to Be: Biblical Faith in a Postmodern World.* Downers Grove, Ill.: InterVarsity Press, 1995.

Mouw, Richard J. *Called to Holy Worldliness.* Philadelphia: Fortress, 1980.

———. *Distorted Truth: What Every Christian Needs to Know About the Battle for the Mind.* New York: Harper & Row, 1989.

———. *He Shines in All That's Fair: Culture and Common Grace.* Grand Rapids: Eerdmans, 2001.

———. *When the Kings Come Marching In: Isaiah and the New Jerusalem.* Grand Rapids: Eerdmans, 2002.

Mueller, Walt. *Understanding Today's Youth Culture.* Wheaton, Ill.: Tyndale House, 1999.

Naugle, David K. *Worldview: The History of a Concept.* Grand Rapids: Eerdmans, 2002.

Netland, Harold. *Encountering Religious Pluralism: The Challenge to Christian Faith and Mission.* Downers Grove, Ill.: InterVarsity Press, 2001.

Niebuhr, H. Richard. *Christ and Culture.* New York: Harper & Row, 1951.

Overholt, L. David, and James Penner. *Soul Searching the Millennial Generation: Strategies for Youth Workers.* Toronto: Stoddart, 2002.

Phillips, Timothy R., and Dennis L. Okholm, eds. *Christian Apologetics in the Postmodern World.* Downers Grove, Ill.: InterVarsity Press, 1995.

Plantinga, Cornelius, Jr. *Engaging God's World: A Christian Vision of Faith, Learning, and Living.* Grand Rapids: Eerdmans, 2002.

Richardson, Don. *Eternity in Their Hearts.* Ventura, Calif.: Regal Books, 1981.

Romanowski, William D. *Eyes Wide Open: Looking for God in Popular Culture.* Grand Rapids: Brazos, 2001.

Rookmaaker, H. R. *Modern Art and the Death of a Culture.* Wheaton, Ill.: Crossway, 1994.

Roxburgh, Alan J. *Reaching a New Generation: Strategies for Tommorrow's Church.*

Vancouver, B.C.: Regent College Publishing, 1998.

Schaeffer, Francis A. *The Complete Works of Francis Schaeffer: A Christian Worldview,* 2nd ed. Wheaton, Ill.: Crossway, 1985.

Schultze, Quentin J, Roy M. Anker, James D. Bratt, William D. Romanowski, John W. Worst, and Lambert Zuidervaart. *Dancing in the Dark: Youth, Popular Culture, and the Electronic Media.* Grand Rapids: Eerdmans, 1991.

Sire, James W. *The Universe Next Door: A Basic Worldview Catalog,* 4th ed. Downers Grove, Ill.: InterVarsity Press, 2004.

Staub, Dick. *Too Christian—Too Pagan: How to Love the World Without Falling for It.* Grand Rapids: Zondervan, 2000.

Stott, John R. W. *Authentic Christianity: From the Writings of John Stott.* Edited by Timothy Dudley-Smith. Downers Grove, Ill.: InterVarsity Press, 1995.

———. *Christ the Controversialist.* Downers Grove, Ill.: InterVarsity Press, 1970.

———. *Christian Mission in the Modern World.* Downers Grove, Ill.: InterVarsity Press, 1975.

———.*The Contemporary Christian: Applying God's Word to Today's World.* Downers Grove, Ill.: InterVarsity Press, 1992.

———. *Evangelical Truth: A Personal Plea for Unity, Integrity and Faithfulness.* Downers Grove, Ill.: InterVarsity Press, 1999.

Sweet, Leonard. *Postmodern Pilgrims: First Century Passion for the 21st Century World.* Nashville: Broadman & Holman, 2000.

Tripp, Paul David. *Age of Opportunity: A Biblical Guide to Parenting Teens.* Phillipsburg, N.J.: Presbyterian & Reformed, 1997.

Triton, A. N. *Whose World?* London: Inter-Varsity Press, 1970.

Veith, Gene Edward. *Postmodern Times: A Christian Guide to Contemporary Thought and Culture.* Wheaton, Ill.: Crossway, 1994.

Wallerstein, Judith, Julia Lewis, and Sandra Blaskeslee. *The Unexpected Legacy of Divorce.* New York: Hyperion, 2000.

Walsh, Brian J. *Who Turned Out the Lights? The Light of the Gospel in a Post-Enlightenment Culture.* Toronto: ICS, Spring 1989.

Walsh, Brian J., and J. Richard Middleton. *The Transforming Vision: Shaping a Christian World View.* Downers Grove, Ill.: InterVarsity Press, 1984.

Ward, Pete. *God at the Mall: Youth Ministry That Meets Kids Where They're At.* Peabody, Mass.: Hendrickson, 1999.

Wells, David. *God in the Wasteland: The Reality of Truth in a World of Fading Dreams.* Grand Rapids: Eerdmans, 1994.

———. *Losing Our Virtue: Why the Church Must Recover Its Moral Vision.* Grand Rapids: Eerdmans, 1998.

———. *No Place for Truth: Or Whatever Happened to Evangelical Theology?* Grand Rapids: Eerdmans, 1993.

Wolters, Albert M. *Creation Regained: Biblical Basics for Reformational Worldview.* Grand Rapids: Eerdmans, 1985.

Zollo, Peter. *Wise Up to Teens: Insights into Marketing and Advertising to Teenagers.* Ithaca, N.Y.: New Strategist Publications, 1999.

Names Index

Be sure to visit the companion website for *Engaging the Soul of Youth Culture* at the Center for Parent/Youth Understanding website:

www.cpyu.org

Click on the book cover to access a categorized and growing library of articles and practical information that will help you bridge teen worldviews and Christian truth.

The Center for Parent/Youth Understanding provides cutting-edge information and analysis on today's youth culture from a biblical perspective. The mission of CPYU is to work with churches, schools, and community organizations to build stronger relationships between young people and those charged with helping them grow into healthy adulthood. This mission is accomplished by

- helping parents understand and respond to the complex world of their children and teens from a distinctively Christian point of view
- equipping teenagers to deal with the challenges of adolescence
- equipping parents and teens to respond to these challenges through a distinctively Christian world and life view
- raising the youth culture awareness of youthworkers, pastors and educators, thereby helping them increase their effectiveness with teens, children and parents

For more information contact

Walt Mueller
Center for Parent/Youth Understanding
PO Box 414
Elizabethtown, PA 17022
cpyu@cpyu.org
www.cpyu.org